Spiritual Restoration

Reclaiming The Foundations of God's World

Volume 3

By Skip Moen, D. Phil.

Copyright 2012

Reclaiming God's World

This is the third volume of collected daily explorations of the vocabulary, culture and idioms found in biblical texts. Like the previous volumes, this book guides the reader into the Hebraic worldview by examining individual words and phrases within the context of the culture, history and language of the first audiences. Obviously, much more needs to be added to fill in the full implications of understanding the texts in their own framework, but I hope the reader will find this a gentle beginning.

In the first volume, we looked at the significant differences between our Greek-based, Western understanding of the world and the biblical ancient near-Eastern, Semitic view of the world. Those two paradigms represent radical changes in perspective when it comes to social structures, education, relationships, public and private mores and government. These differences play a major role in the exegesis of biblical texts. We discovered that far too often our understanding of Scripture is really determined by our contemporary worldview rather than by the ancient worldview of the authors.

The second volume explored the areas of idolatry in both ancient and contemporary cultures, discipline and discipleship, leadership, and the unity of work and worship. Examining these topics brought us closer to an appreciation of the biblical framework surrounding ordinary living. We learned that God's view of human activity is not compartmentalized. From a biblical perspective, human life is a unity of activity, a unity that includes worshipping the one true God, expressing His character and purposes in the world, acting as His regents over His creation and demonstrating a life-long commitment to knowing Him.

This third volume of the collection of *Today's Word* editions brings together material about the biblical description of the worshiping community. It covers the topics of the Church, prayer, evangelism and the perennial misunderstanding of the relationship between Law and grace. I hope you will find these explorations enlightening and challenging as you seek to read the Scriptures in their own context.

Skip Moen

Montverde, 2012

Table of Contents

The Church

What is the church? Most believers readily admit it isn't the building on the corner or the headquarters in some distant town or the representative "holy" city in Rome. Believers will proclaim that the real church is the people. Exactly *which* people seems to depend on who happens to agree with the official theology, but at least most believers don't see the church in terms of its physical assets. Unfortunately, even this definition doesn't fit the "church" that we find in Scripture.

Readers of the Book of Acts are often dismayed when they discover the vibrancy, community interdependency, demonstration of God's activity and spiritual strength in the stories of the early Messianic believers. They are dismayed because they see so little of this evidence in our mega-religious environment today. As one pastor from Africa said after visiting the largest churches in Orlando, "I had no idea you could do so much without God."

This discomfort has forced many believers to take a much harder look at the environment, culture and teaching of the early believing communities reported in the New Testament. What we find is shocking. The first thing we notice is that the "church" doesn't begin at Pentecost. Translations that suggest otherwise are simply inaccurate. Translation manipulation has created this false historical perception based on a theological presupposition rather than the text. In most English Bibles, the well-known word *ekklesia* is not translated as "church" when the references indicate Old Testament communities.   But when we maintain translation uniformity, we discover that the "church" is the equivalent of the Kingdom, the assembly of citizens at

Sinai. Of course, this means that Israel is the church and Gentiles are grafted into that body (as Paul clearly says), but since this flies in the face of a theology that claims the Church has replaced Israel, translators conveniently substitute "congregation" where the word *ekklesia* refers to Israel rather than use the word "church." We need to rethink the relationship between the "church" and Israel.

We also discover that the synagogue plays a much larger role in the early Messianic communities of Scripture. Our theological bias based on the idea that the Church replaced Israel prevents us from realizing that the Jewish synagogue is the center of the Messianic community. Perhaps even more importantly, we find that these early believers did not abandon the practice of the Torah. In fact, evidence now suggests that Torah observance was a vibrant part of the Messianic community into the *fourth* century. These believers honored the Sabbath (not Sunday), maintained the dietary regulations and followed the Jewish festival calendar. All of this evidence causes us to re-evaluate our current idea of church and church practices. We need to rethink what it means to be a believer in the church.

But it doesn't stop here. When we acknowledge that every author of Scripture was either Jewish or a proselyte, when we realize that the word "conversion" is never used of Jews but only of pagan Gentiles, we begin to understand that God's view of His people hasn't changed since the beginning. That means we are called to think about His plan and His purposes from a different perspective. We need to rethink the cultural influences and the Hebraic orientation of God's community.

That's what this chapter is all about.

1.

*This is what everyone **who is numbered** shall give: half a shekel according to the shekel of the sanctuary . . . half a shekel as a contribution to the LORD.* Exodus 30:13

A Question of the Tithe

Who Is Numbered – Very few Christians tithe. I don't suppose that surprises you. Something less than 6 percent of evangelicals and less than 1 percent of Catholics actually tithe at all. For many, tithing has no significant importance in religious practice (After all, God does not need our money. He has plenty of His own).

There are many suggested reasons for the noticeable decline in tithing over the last decade. Perhaps they are valid. But I wonder if we haven't replaced the intention and motivation of the original idea behind the tithe with something needed to support an institutionalized church and all of its trappings. A brief glance toward Moses reveals something extraordinary.

Who paid the half-shekel into God's tabernacle treasury? Those who are numbered. That turns out to be every male over the age of twenty. In other words, everyone in the census – essentially the number of households. Moses then adds something quite significant. "The rich shall not pay more and the poor shall not pay less." Everyone owed exactly the same amount. Why? Because everyone had exactly the same need – atonement. There is no gradation in the need for grace, nor is there any gradation in the expression of thanksgiving for grace received. At least, not when it comes to financial obligation.

Some important results follow from this equality. First, everyone has the same stake in the game. This "tithe" brings communal unity. No one has more or less status than another – and more importantly, no one can claim any special honor or rights based on giving. Secondly, the operational budget of the tabernacle is limited to a single, annual contribution from each household. The organization of religion cannot spin out of control, demanding more and more funds to grow larger and larger. The ceiling is fixed. Live with it! Finally, since the ceiling is fixed, the vast majority of religious activity must be carried out in the household, not the tabernacle-temple. Church cannot replace worship at home. Sunday school cannot usurp godly, parental education. There is no money to support the human temptation to take control of religious activity.

Moses' stipulation seems entirely reasonable. So what happened? How did we become a religion fixated on places, programs, professionals and procedures? When did we push worship from the home to the "house" of God? And why do we go on sinking billions of dollars every year into all this infrastructure, not a single brick of which will be present in eternity?

When did we forget that God is the God of the kitchen, the living room and the bedroom? When did we decide to put Him in the old folks' home and only visit Him on Sunday?

2.

*And He said to them, "It is written, 'My house shall be called a house of prayer;' but you are making it a **robbers**' den."*
Matthew 21:13

Selling St. Peter's

Robbers' – The Vatican is perhaps the most overwhelming monument in the world to the power of Christianity. Just standing in the square in front of St. Peter's basilica leaves you breathless. To enter that marbled, gilded, towering structure, filled with relics and reminders, is almost more than the mind can absorb. But then you remember the words of Yeshua, the One that all of this is supposed to honor. "It is written, 'My house shall be called . . .'"

On the day I stood in awe of the human edifice, I saw something that made me weep. Crouched on the stonework of the square was an old woman, begging for coins. Many walked by, avoiding or ignoring her. They came to see the spectacle, not be obedient to the King in the least of these. What was the woman doing here, anyway? Didn't she know she was in the way? Maybe she was a scam artist. The crowd pushed toward the vendors selling replicas of the saints, cold drinks, Vatican banners and other useless mementos. "You see, we've been to the Vatican. We saw its marvels. We were blessed." I stooped to touch the old woman. "Can I pray for you?" This is, after all, God's house. She smiled.

The Greek New Testament uses the word *leston*. It means those who take the property of another in the open and by violence. Does it fit all those who conducted their business in the square? Yes, I think so. Certainly they were not hiding the commercialization of this monument to God. They were using the place to their advantage. Tragically, no one objected, not even the church. The Vatican collects millions of dollars every day from all those tourists wishing to observe these treasures once dedicated to God. Violence? Yes, violence, for in the

midst of all that marketing, God is defiled. His name is
dragged through banker's mud. His honor is sold to
everyone who can afford to pay. What about the beggars
in the square? Well, just step aside. They don't belong in
this place. They have no money to spend.

Watchman Nee once said that men have the innate ability
to take something of the Spirit and convert it into a self-
sustaining enterprise where God is no longer needed or
desired. What do you suppose would happen if Yeshua
visited the Vatican? Do you think we would welcome
Him as He cried out for reverence and prayer? Or would
we point to our balance sheets, our artifacts and prestige
and say, "We have written, 'My house shall be a house of
profit.'"

3.

*and greet the **church** at their house, and my beloved
Epenetus* Romans 16:5

The Event of Church (1)
Church – Something's missing. That seems to be the
general consensus of a large number of those who attend
church regularly. We're not quite sure what it is, but we
know that our expectations are often greater than the
actual delivery. We want that mysterious something –
desperately – and so we travel from congregation to
congregation, searching, hoping, waiting for the final
spiritual enlightenment that will tell us, "You're home."
What is most discouraging in this quest is the picture
painted of the early church in the book of Acts. It seems
more vibrant, more filled with the Spirit, more apostolic.
Miracles accompany its proclamation. Power and deep
humility attend its leaders. "Why can't we have that?"
"What's wrong with us?"

When people don't know what to do, they do what they know. Like good Christians, we go back to the planning table and come up with another program, another series of sermons or another revival meeting. We see change, but it doesn't last. And back we go again. Maybe there is another way.

We could start by noticing some important connections in the words (where else? ☺). First, the Greek word here is *ekklesia*. You undoubtedly know that. But did you know that the word *ekklesia* is never used in the gospels (except in Matthew 16:18 and 18:17). You might think that this only means that Yeshua and the disciples used the word "synagogue," but you would wrong. The only place where the early Christians used the word *synagoge* (which is also a Greek term) is in James 2:2. Now, this should make us pause. If Yeshua doesn't use the word *ekklesia*, and the disciples do not use the word *synagoge*, then how are we supposed to understand what the church is?

Let's add two more crucial facts. The Old Testament uses two different words for the religious gathering of God. They are almost interchangeable – almost, but not quite. The first is *qahal*. This word means "assembly" and is used for nearly any kind of gathering, even gatherings in rebellion against God.   However, in connection with Israel, it is especially the *assembly for religious purposes* such as the giving of the Law (see Deuteronomy 9:10). There is another Hebrew word, *'edah*, that also generally means "assembly" and is often translated "congregation." But, while the noun *qahal* can be translated by both Greek words, *ekklesia* and *synagoge*, *'edah* is never translated as *ekklesia*. Only *synagoge* translates both *qahal* and *'edah*. That means that *ekklesia* can be an assembly, but it can never be a congregation (in Hebrew).

Only a *synagoge* can be both an assembly *and* a congregation. I know that this seems confusing, but hang in there. Something's happening, and you don't want to miss it. There is a clue here that the modern church lost along the way.

Hebrew culture used *qahal* for a very important concept: *gathering to accept the covenant.* *Qahal* is a word that carries the idea of calling by appointment to a particular purpose of God. This is an *event*, not a place! It is focused on God's purpose, not our participation. However, when it comes to "congregation," the word is almost always *'edah*. 123 times this word is found in the Torah. It is related to the verb "to appoint." It is all about the *unity* of those appointed, not about the individuals gathered. It is not bound to a special place or time. It is always about a special people *appointed as one unified whole* before God.

Isn't it interesting that *ekklesia*, the word that we usually take to mean "the church" is *never* connected to this Hebrew idea of perfect unity in appointment and purpose? Something's happening. Can you feel it?

4.

and greet the **church** *at their house, and my beloved Epenetus* Romans 16:5

The Event of Church (2)

Church – Yesterday we discovered that the two Hebrew words for "assembly" are not quite the same. *Qahal* (and *qehillah*) focuses on the *event* of experience with God. *'Edah* focuses on the *unity* of the whole people God appoints. We found that *ekklesia*, the Greek word translated "church" is never *'edah*, only *qahal*. But *synagoge* can be both *qehillah* and *'edah*.

9

What can we conclude? Please remember that the doctrine of the church is not going to be concluded in just a short look at the words. We can only *point* the direction since there is so much more to consider, but we can say at least this much. It appears as though the Hebrew idea behind *ekklesia* is about a "happening", an *event*, not a place. A church is a gathering event called by God for *His* purposes. It doesn't appear to be a routine meeting in a particular place with a set agenda. Remember that *qahal* is first found in the idea of a gathering of soldiers for war. It is the *purpose* that precipitates the gathering, not the other way around. Church, from a Hebrew perspective, is all about *why* we come together, not about *where* we come together.

Recently I read a comment by a man who was distraught because he didn't seem able to *plant* a new church in his community. You can see how his thinking has been affected by the idea that church is a place. Maybe we should *have church* rather than *go to church*. How much more might we accomplish for the Kingdom if we began to think of church as an event rather than a building?

But there is more. When we point in this direction, we realize that there is an element in the Hebrew idea that is *not present* in the Greek word *ekklesia*. *'Edah* – the *unity* of the gathered assembly – is never picked up by the word *ekklesia*. The *event* of church does not mean *unity*. The event is focused on the reason for the event, namely, the call of God. We gather because God calls us to gather, and we gather because He has something to tell us and something for us to do. But that is not the same as being in unity. It is the word *synagoge* that enables us to communicate the idea of a single, unified whole. If we are going to experience *'edah*, our gathering cannot focus on the individuals in the group. It must focus on the whole group all together. Does this give you a clue about Paul's comments on sharing the single mind of Christ or Yeshua' comments on unity?

The "church" is a unity, a single body (remember Paul's language) where every individual fades into the whole, integrated unit, where no single member is any more valuable than any other and where every member is vital to the functioning of the whole. *'Edah* is a body without hierarchy, without "professionals", without status-seekers and without individual glorification. It is the *one* assembly, doing what God commands.

What directions begin to emerge? Perhaps we need to re-think "church." If the Bible's view of church is an *event* called for a purpose of a *single, completely unified* body, a lot of things will have to change. Now, what will you do about it?

5.

and greet the **church** *at their house, and my beloved Epenetus* Romans 16:5

The Event of Church (3)

Church – One more pointer, and then I promise to let this go. L. Coenen says, "If one compares the two Hebrew words, it becomes clear . . . that *'edah* is the unambiguous and permanent term for the covenant community as a whole. On the other hand, *qahal* is the ceremonial expression for the assembly that results from the covenant."

Only one of these ideas is captured in the word *ekklesia*,

that is, the ceremonial expression of the assembly. If that is true, then "church" is not only *event* oriented, it is also a formal occasion built on ritual. So, God calls His people. They gather (the event) under certain, prescribed ordinances (the ritual) for a particular purpose (the reason for the gathering). This is *qahal*.

But there is also *'edah*. In order for the church to also be *'edah*, it must *belong*, not as individuals, but as a whole unit, to God's permanent, covenant family. Let this sink in a bit. The conclusion is shocking. The covenant is not about individuals. I do not have a personal covenant relationship with God. My covenant relationship with God is based in the *community as a whole*. Furthermore, church as *'edah* is **not** for the non-believer. If you are not part of the covenant family, you are not part of this assembly – and you shouldn't be there!

This is a dagger in the heart of the "seeker-friendly" idea of church. The seeker-friendly church is not a church from the Bible's point of view. It is a *meeting* of mixed minds and motives. It is equivalent to the crowd who heard Peter preach on the day of Pentecost. He had only one message – Repent! All of the rest of the teaching, training and equipping is for the *family* of the covenant community, not for the outsiders.

Now we might realize why our churches are so bland and anemic. We have the wrong audience. When we mix family and strangers, what kind of signals are we sending? How can you gather at God's call for His purposes when half your crowd doesn't even know Him? How can you be of single-minded unity when your audience is filled with rebels? What made you think that God even called those idol-worshippers to His event? In our efforts to make the "church" relevant, we have destroyed it. We no longer gather at His request to receive His purposes and act as a single body in the world. We gather in a meeting, filled with all kinds of agendas, rebellious enemies standing side-by-side with devoted followers. And we hope to encounter God!? How crazy is that?

Clean house! That's what Peter says. Start on the inside! Our churches are filled with the great unwashed, and, as a result, our focus is anything but pure. Of course, we must reach to the lost, but separate *church* from *meetings* and you just might discover that the body is nourished.

End of the pointing. Beginning of the enabling. Are you staggering out of sanctuary?

6.

*And Moses assembled all the **congregation** of the sons of Israel and said to them, "These are the words which the Lord has commanded, to do them."* Exodus 35:1

50% Church

Congregation – It's quite common for us to refer to the church as the *ekklesia*. That's Greek for "called out ones." That is an apt description. The church is called out. But unless we understand the *Hebrew* background behind this Greek word, we will only be a half-church. You see, there are two words in Hebrew that describe the assembly of the children of God, and *ekklesia* is only one of them.

We have examined the two words *qahal* (Hebrew for

"assembly") and *'edah* (Hebrew for "congregation"). *Qahal* is translated *ekklesia* because this word focuses on the two aspects of *assembly*. First, it focuses on the fact that someone *calls* the individuals together. Secondly, it focuses on the *purpose* of that call. In other words, an *ekklesia* is an assembly called by someone for a purpose. That's precisely why the church is an *ekklesia*. God calls it for the purpose of accomplishing His will on earth. That's pretty clear.

But there is another aspect to the Hebrew idea of the church. That word is *'edah*. It is the word for congregation. It focuses on the singularity of the group. It emphasizes that fact that the assembly of the children of God is not a collection of *individuals* but rather a single unit, undifferentiated before God. Here's the critical point: *'edah* is **never** translated *ekklesia*. If the church is only an *ekklesia*, then it is only half of what God intended. If the church is only about its called-out purpose, then it is only a fifty percent operation.

Think of it like this: The outward function of the church is to complete the mission of the Lord on earth. We are called to that task. That's what the *ekklesia* is all about. If your chosen assembly of worship is not fulfilling the mission of the Lord, then you are not an *ekklesia*. But, there is another part. There is something more than just proclaiming the good news. There is *'edah*, a word that describes the *homogenization* of the church, the undifferentiated unity of all the pieces. Paul does have a word for this in Greek. That word is "body". A church is not just the called-out ones with a purpose. A church is also the unity of all the individuals in a single body.

Paul's thought is very much like the new clothes of the new man. The clothing is the outside purpose-driven view. The "body" is the inside unity of every member that gives shape to the clothes. If you (plural) are an assembly, an *ekklesia*, without a body, an *'edah*, then you have only half of God's design in place. You will know that it is only half the story because you will know that there is something missing in spite of the purpose-driven activity. You will know that the inside is empty. There is no body under the clothing.

This is the biggest problem in the Western church. The body has shriveled and died. The clothes are draped on a mannequin. There is no unified, singular, Spirit-filled manifestation of God underneath the activity. It's just outward, glorious emptiness.

7.

remember that you were at one time separate from Christ, excluded from the **commonwealth** *of Israel, and strangers to the covenants of promise, having no hope and without God in the world,* Ephesians 2:12

God's Politics

Commonwealth – God has a government. He rules in a particular way. His authority is unquestionable, His legislation perfect. If we want to live, we must be included in His kingdom. Fortunately, by faith, we are. The question is *what that means.*

We have to do a good deal of detective work with this one. Of course, when we see a word like "commonwealth," we naturally think of a nation or state. But when we look at the New Testament itself, this word is used only one other place, in Acts 22:28, where it is translated "citizenship." What's worse is that the only places where it is used in the LXX is in Maccabees. We will have to dig deeper.

The root of this word is *polis*. You will certainly recognize that this is the basis of our English word "politics," but what you might not realize is that the word in Greek is about a city, not a nation. This word points to the Greek city-state, a time when individual cities like Athens and Sparta were separate ruling bodies. The *politeia* (the word in this verse) is a citizen (a city member). A citizen is one who lives in good conduct according to the laws and customs of the governing body. In Greece, not everyone who occupied a city was a citizen. Membership had requirements. Correct behavior was one of those requirements. Citizenship simply by being born someplace is a modern invention. In Paul's day, citizenship was hard to come by. So, citizens took their responsibilities very seriously.

What can we learn from Paul's deliberate use of this rare word? Perhaps we need to re-think our idea of the heavenly government. We tend to imagine that God runs His government like our earthly nations, but, of course, that isn't the case. First, God is building a city, not a country. Abraham looked for a *city* whose builder and maker was God. The new Jerusalem is a *city*, not a nation. What this means is that God's idea of governance is far more intimate than our present national concepts. In God's city, everyone knows who you are. There are no strangers living in distant places. All the citizens are within the protective walls of the city of Zion.

Furthermore, becoming part of the "commonwealth" of Israel is really the equivalent of being adopted into city membership. Did you every wonder why God chose to bring His message of salvation to the world through such a small and insignificant nation as Israel? Actually, God chose one man, Abraham, and built from one man a tribe and then a people and finally a nation. In this tiny nation, everyone is *related* to everyone else. This is a nation where membership means bloodline *and* obedience. God seems to enjoy these humanly unreasonable and inefficient methods. Instead of choosing mighty Assyria or prestigious Babylon, God made Himself a city-state from one nomadic family.

We need to re-think heavenly citizenship. It's a privilege granted to us, a place of intimate, family government where heritage matters. It's our city of brotherly love. Live accordingly.

Evangelism

In a Greek-based model of education and information, evangelism becomes the process of transferring information about correct doctrines from one person to another. This Greek model is interested in making sure that the other person has the right "beliefs." This does not require a *direct and immediate* change in behavior, although of course, that is supposed to follow. In the Greek worldview, evangelism shifts from discipleship – the modeling of behavioral change – to communication, the adoption of correct beliefs. In the Greek model, discipleship *follows* conversion. A convert must *first* acknowledge the right beliefs and then he can learn how to live by them. That means our view of evangelism slides toward communicating the "saving knowledge" of Yeshua in the most efficient way possible. We think of evangelism in terms of campaigns, mass meetings, radio and television preaching, tracts and a host of other communication devices and techniques that efficiently "spread the word."

The rise of the "seeker-friendly" movement is a reaction to this communication goal. A century ago, sermons were exegetical eloquence of rational enlightenment. Today they are attempts to elicit feelings. When the whole world pushes us toward greater rational compartmentalization, we seek retreat in emotions, whether these mood alteration mechanisms are drugs, dance or spiritual discoveries.

The contemporary church attempts to become relevant to a population that is information saturated. In the "seeker friendly" world, the emphasis is often on the "experience." This gives rise to the harmonic monotony of typical praise songs; a sort of substitute group chanting directly connected to mood alteration. Music, once completely absent from worship, is now front and center. We can hardly imagine having any experience with God that is not prefaced with a dozen refrains of the latest mind-numbing spiritual melody. Our contemporary view of evangelism is based either on rational convincing or emotional comforting. There is almost *no* emphasis on actually changing behavior. It's head verses heart. Hands and feet have nothing to do with it.

The Hebrew way is very different. Since it is fundamentally about what I do, the focus is on behavior. In the Hebrew model, I must change my behavior before I can rightly be called a believer. This does not happen by willpower alone. In the Hebrew worldview. Man is ultimately frustrated by the enemy within. Assuming that it is simply a matter of personal resolve is disastrous. God must intervene, and He does. The Hebrew version of evangelism begins with discipleship, mentoring, accountability and transparency. It does not at about the most efficient means of communicating the right doctrine or the quickest way to make me feel better. Its goal is *effective transformation*. The road is long. The way is difficult. And few there are who find it.

Once you understand this shift, a lot of things change. Your *life* becomes the tool for reaching others. Your work becomes a vehicle for worship. Your actions speak louder than any words (but we knew that already, didn't we?). Evangelism is no longer "soul-winning." It is living in harmony with God and crossing paths with others. Saint Francis understood it quite well: "Preach the gospel at all times, and when necessary use words."

This chapter collects studies about the difference between our Western view of evangelism efficiency and the Hebrew view of discipleship effectiveness.

1.

*"You are my **witnesses**," declares the Lord, "and My servant whom I have chosen, so that you may know and believe Me and understand that I am He. Before Me there was no God formed, and there will be none after Me."*
Isaiah 43:10

Subpoenaed

Witnesses – When Yeshua gave us the Great Commission, He did not offer a new directive. The Father developed the strategy Yeshua mentions hundreds of years before Yeshua arrived. Once we see the Great Commission of the Old Testament, we will understand more about the Great Commission of the New Testament.

God elaborates His commission through the prophet Isaiah. It begins with the purpose of election. The first declaration is that all of God's people, including those who are grafted into the Kindom, are *witnesses*. The Hebrew is *edai*. Although the word comes from legal language, our role as witnesses is more than just faithfully recounting the facts. In this case, we are witnesses only because we have been chosen by the court. This court does not ask for volunteers. It issues a subpoena. You are required to comply. You have been called to testify. Implied in that divine subpoena is the fact that your testimony has been accepted as true. What you say and do really matters, not only to the court, but to all the world observing this grand legal proceeding.

Notice that you *cannot be a witness* unless you are chosen. God does not use just anyone. He uses only those whom He chooses, those to whom He has revealed certain, special things. Now that you are included on His witness list, you will have your turn on the stand and He will accept your testimony as true. All of those who claim to speak for God, but are not chosen by Him, have neither a true testimony nor are their claims accepted. In this courtroom, the Judge determines who will appear on the witness stand and who will be heard.

Finally, the Hebrew verse shows us that the word *witnesses* is plural but the word *servant* is singular. The verse does not say, "You will be my witnesses and my *servants.*" It says, "You will be my witnesses and my *servant.*" Did Isaiah make a grammatical mistake? Not at all! We are witnesses (plural) but our role is characterized as *one* servant. Isaiah's passage looks forward to the time when a single Servant will fulfill completely the role of the many witnesses. Our testimony is never divorced from the function of the true Servant. We are a community of one voice, fulfilling a destiny that is summarized in one man, standing before the Judge as one person acceptable to Him. Without the Son, there is no point in being a witness. God's plan for the rescue of men comes in only one way. We are witnesses because there is one Servant. Our multiple testimonies are based on the actions of *one* Servant.

The contemporary Christian church puts a lot of emphasis on witnessing. Of course, glad-handing people in the name of Yeshua is not what God has in mind when it comes to giving testimony in His court. Perhaps we would all be refreshed and renewed if we realized that our calling to be witnesses is not *our* choice. It is God's. He has equipped each of us to deliver acceptable testimony because we have a direct relationship with the Servant. Speaking up for God is really declaring the truth of the Servant's handiwork in my life. You might say that our multiple witness to the one Servant is the heart of the plan.

2.

*"You are my witnesses," declares the Lord, "and My servant whom I have chosen, so that you may **know** and **believe** Me*
*and **understand** that I am He. Before Me there was no God formed, and there will be none after Me." Isaiah 43:10*

Three Transformations

Know, Believe, Understand – Consider this part of the verse very carefully. Did you notice that God's choosing comes *before* you know, believe and understand? In other words, the call to be in intimate relationship with God as His witnesses is *prior* to the revelation of Who He is. Furthermore, your knowing, believing and understanding is not going to happen because you go out and search the universe for the "divine essence." Until and unless God decides to choose you, you just don't have a clue.

If you let the truth of this declaration sink in, you will find enormous relief for your soul. The delivery of the vital information and the essential relationship between God and men is *not up to us*! Election precedes information. Relax a bit. God is working to accomplish His purposes in and through those He has chosen. The weight of the universe does not rest on your shoulders – and, by the way, neither does the conversion of that lost soul over there.

The three verbs here really cover all we need to be fruitful witnesses. *Yada* (to know) includes the relational and experiential aspects of knowing another person. *Aman* (to believe) is really about providing stability, confidence and support. It is the basis of faithfulness and trustworthiness ("believe" is not about creeds or confessions, is it?). And *biyn* (to understand) is a verb about discernment, perception and due diligence. God has empowered *all* He has chosen so that they can be intimately acquainted in real-time ways with Him, have confidence in Him and discern His handiwork. What more would you need to be a witness?

God chooses you in order that He might provide for you all three aspects of being a witness. You should expect, and look for, *yada*, *aman* and *biyn* in your walk with Him. You should find a deeper and deeper personal relationship, a growing confidence and an improving discernment. That's been the strategy for a long time. God has decided that all He chooses will experience a transformation that shows up in these three verbs. And all of that was determined long before you came on the scene.

Isn't it reassuring to know that God is working all this out in our lives? So many times we start to think that somehow God has forgotten us. The bills pile up. The job doesn't go too well. Someone is sick. The weather doesn't cooperate. Our focus is so easily diverted to what is happening now. That's when we need to think about Isaiah's verse. God has already called you as a witness. Now He is merely equipping you for something that has eternal consequences. Shift your vision to the horizon. Can you see Him over there, beckoning you to keep moving? Knowing, believing and understanding are guaranteed to all who follow.

3.

*"You are my witnesses," declares the Lord, "and My servant whom I have chosen, so that you may know and believe Me and understand that **I am He**. Before Me there was no God*

formed, and there will be none after Me." Isaiah 43:10

The Divine Summation

I am He – So, you're a witness. A witness to what?
Everyone called to be a witness has truthful declarations
to make about the *verdict* in the case. You are not called
to simply say what's on your mind. God's court is not
interested in hearsay. You are subpoenaed because you
have reliable evidence that pertains to the outcome. You
are a witness to only one critically important thing: that
God is!

You are a witness to the verdict, "I am He" (in Hebrew *ki
anihu*). What could be more important than this! God is
– He is the One and only God. The court declares the
verdict. Imagine what this means? No more striving to
come to some understanding of what the world is all
about – and why you are here. God is – and He knows.
No more entertaining hope in one version after another
of "fate control". God is – and He is in charge. No more
despair over the monotony of life and the inevitability of
death. God is – and He redeems. God not only provides
the courtroom; He provides the witnesses to His very
existence. The summary of the argument is this: God is.
What that implies touches every aspect of life, whether
you like it or not.

Sure, you can carry the Four Spiritual Laws in your back
pocket. That helps. But the witness of your life is a
witness, not to God's wonderful plan, but to the very fact
that God is the only God. If there is but one God, and this
God decides to reveal Himself to Mankind, then *no man*
can afford not to seek such a God, especially since this
God willingly offers what men need to know.

Do you want to be a witness? Well, actually, you don't

have a choice in the matter (remember, God chooses). Once you are conscripted into the witness declaration program, you will be equipped to give faithful testimony to who God is. Supported by the Spirit, endorsed by the Son, guaranteed by the Father, that testimony is enough for anyone to realize that God has a claim on life itself.

Oh yes, by the way, Yeshua understood the power of this phrase and all that it implies. It's only unfortunate that we can't see it in our translation of Matthew 14:27 (where the Greek reads, "I AM," not "It is I") and in the numerous occurrences in John ("I am he," "I am the truth," "I am the bread of life," "I am the resurrection.") We are called by the God Who is. What difference does that make to you today?

4.

*For God so loved the **world** that He gave*   John 3:16

A Wonderful Plan

World – When Bill Bright introduced the now-famous phrase, "God loves you and has a wonderful plan for your life," he captured the spiritual desperation of the time. In that day, life seemed purposeless. At the end of the industrial revolution, we all felt like cogs in the vast, corporate machine. We needed to know that God cared about each of us – and that He had *individually important* roles for us to play. If we mattered to God, then we really mattered.

But theology must be done in each generation. Today, Bill's famous phrase faces a problem. Watchman Nee recognized the problem years. Bill Bright articulated the vision. Every development touched by human beings can always be turned into a self-sustaining endeavor. We are more than capable of shifting our dependence from the Spirit to the system. It appears that we took the idea of a wonderful plan and converted it to a personal goal. Instead of seeing God's purposes surrounding our lives, we started looking for our purposes assisted by God's care. We made God the *means* to our *ends*. We forgot that the verse does not say, "For God so loved *me*." It says, "For God so loved the *cosmos* (the Greek word)," a concept that reaches well beyond me, my generation and my desires. We need to retrace our steps and pay attention to the real words, not the ones we see at football games.

Cosmos does not primarily mean "the world." The primary meaning of the word is *order*. It is a term for the regulation and disposition of a deliberate arrangement. God loves *His order*. He loves the way that He planned things to be. He loves the work of His creative effort. God is a God of order and He longs to bring the entire created order back to its original design, freed from the chaotic disruption of sin. When we translate this word as "world," we move the focus from God's *entire, ordered creation* to the realm of our human occupation. We reduce the grand plan of redemption from a *cosmic* scale to a *human* scale. Suddenly, it appears as if God's grand plan revolves around *me!* From there, it is an easy step to think that God is really my personal genie, ready and willing to help me achieve the wonderful plan for my life. We need a much bigger perspective.

God loves you and *His wonderful plan includes your life*. On the plane of humanity, God's plan is to bring about ordered community, under His sovereign rule. We are invited to become members of that community. God wants to *include us* in what *He* is doing. Today, in a step away from the individualism of a previous age, we are challenged to move toward the organic whole of redeemed creation. The critical issue of our age is not individual importance. We have had fifty years of individuality therapy. What we need now is a *body* concept rather than a view of the parts. We know how to be individuals. But we don't know how to *belong* to something bigger than ourselves. God loves the *cosmos*, the divine order of things – something so carefully fit together that every part belongs to every other part – something so big that only God can see its full design. Wouldn't you rather be included in that than go on living your neat little isolated life?

5.

*And this is eternal life, that they may **know** You, the only true God, and Yeshua Christ whom You have sent.* John 17:3

Return on Relationship

Know – Yeshua defines eternal life solely in terms of relationships. Is that the way you define it? There is not a single mention of heaven, salvation, forgiveness, blessings, victory, power, purpose or possession. The entire summation of eternal life is found in *knowing* God, not knowing about Him, not being assisted by Him, not claiming acquaintance with Him. Eternal life is found exclusively and entirely in relationship with Him – and not just any kind of relationship, but the kind that requires the Greek verb *ginosko*, in the present, active, subjunctive tense.

So, first *ginosko*. The Greek verb covers the ground from "to come to know," "to perceive, to learn, to gain knowledge" to "to have knowledge in a completed sense,"

29

"to acquire a complete understanding of." Yeshua's definition puts all this in the present tense. It is an on-going, immediate experience of full relationship. It is *active*. I am thoroughly engaged and involved in the process, not merely the recipient of disseminated information. It is *vital* to me. And finally, it is *subjunctive*. This is a description of the mood of the verb. For us it means that this verb pushes us toward *continuous action*. There is also a kind of tentativeness about the subjunctive. We might suggest that this kind of knowing is quite special, requiring active participation, not found in every situation.

But never forget that Yeshua spoke Hebrew, not Greek. The Greek phrase is an attempt to capture what He said in Hebrew. So, that means we must look at Hebrew roots to understand the full impact of this definition. We would not be surprised to find that the word *yada*, in all of its range of meanings, comes into play. To *know* God is to fully embrace Him as intimate companion, dearest friend, lover of my soul, sage of my life, provider and protector. It is a lot more than conversation and a lot more than acknowledgment of His title.

When I have this kind of penetrating, personal relationship with God, I am experiencing eternal life. Think about that. Eternal life is not *some thing* that I am given, as though I can wrap it up and store it away for a rainy day. It is not an entry pass. It has no *substance*, anymore than my love for my wife has physical substance. It is found only in the interaction and relationship between persons. As I share in that relationship, I experience eternal life as a present reality. It manifests itself in all kinds of tangible ways, but none of those tangible by-products are what it really is.

Try this little exercise. Make a list of those tangible by-products of your relationship with God that you might at one time have labeled "eternal life." Then, one-by-one, remove them from the list by asking yourself the question, "If this were not part of my definition of eternal life, would I still enjoy the present reality of a full relationship with God?" You might be surprised at what you have added to the definition.

6.

*Now as He drew near, He saw the city and **wept** over it*
Luke 19:41

Tears of Heaven

Wept – There are two Greek words for "wept" in the New Testament. If you don't know which one you're reading, you will miss the whole point. In this verse, the word is *klaio*. It means to lament, wail, weep with deep emotion. These are tears shed from a ruptured heart, in agony over unrequited grief. The other word is found in John 11:35 (a great favorite for memorization), "Yeshua wept." That word is *dakruo*. It should be translated "shed a tear," not "wept," because weeping in first century Israel was an expression of intense grief whereas *dakruo* shows only the slightest sadness. Yeshua never cried over death. He simply shed a tear. But He wept with agony over the lost.

We serve the broken-hearted God, a God Who, at great expense, attempts to redeem His children from certain, eternal torment. No wonder He staggers with agonizing shudders of sorrow when He confronts the self-destructive choices of His children. The tears of heaven drove Yeshua to the cross. Every teardrop mixed blood and water. If you really want to see what it means for God to cry, look at His Son hanging on the tree.

31

So, I ask you, "Do you weep over the lost?" Are you so in tune with the heart of the Father that you stagger and stammer under the burden for these suicidal children? It's not popular in a culture of "tolerance" to agonize over the inevitable fate of non-believers. It's much easier to think (falsely) that somehow God will work it all out without my involvement. After all, most people are pretty good, so why should I press them about faith in Yeshua? The combination of tolerance and privacy in religion will leave the world wide open to the mouth of the pit.

When was the last time (if ever) you were so gripped by the fate of those who still reject Him that you fell to your knees in wailing lament? When did you last find yourself so tortured by the fate of your friend, your relative or your child that the tears just wouldn't stop as you raised their pitiful condition before the King of glory? When have you echoed Paul, wishing you could be extinguished from living if it would only rescue this other one?

We are much more likely to celebrate half the God of heaven. We want the half of power, joy, peace and blessing. But when we look deeply into the heart of God, we find a disquieting unrest, a frightening torment over the ones who have not experienced His sacrifice. If you want a God of blessing, you must also have a God with a broken heart. And if you are to be conformed to the image of His Son, you will have to know the difference between *klaio* and *dakruo*.

7.

*Whether it is good, or whether it is evil, we will obey the voice of Jehovah **our God**, to whom we send you; so that it may be well with us when we obey the voice of Jehovah **our God**.* Jeremiah 42:6

Proper Pronouns

Our God – A strange thing happens when you move from verse 5 to this verse. In verse 5, the people refer to Jeremiah's God as *"your* God." They say that they are ready to obey all that "your God" will tell them. But, when they repeat the idea in verse 6, the pronoun changes. Once obedience enters the picture, "your God" becomes "our God" (*eloheikha* becomes *eloheinu*). This tiny shift is worth contemplating. Until I obey, I cannot call God *my* God. He is simply the God of someone else. But when obedience becomes the basis of my relationship with Him, then He becomes *my* God.

Dallas Willard brings home this point in his book, *The Great Omission*. Christianity has forgotten that obedience – discipleship – is not optional. It is not something that I add to forgiveness. Forgiveness is not earned. It is given. My *only* proper response is obedience. And only when God is the Lord of my life do I experience the truth about forgiveness. God does not forgive so that I can get a pass on sin. He forgives so that I can obey. He forgives so that I can make a deliberate choice to become His slave for life – and the life of a slave is one of constant obedience. Real Christianity requires the proper application of the possessive pronoun. God is not mine until I serve Him.

Of course, if we lived in the culture of the ancient near-East, we would not have to go through this explanation. In those days, the land was ruled by kings. I had no protection, no rights and no status unless I lived under the rule of a king. To be a "free" man was a terrible thing for it meant that I lived without royal protection of a sovereign. My life depended on alliance with a ruling lord.

Unfortunately, our spiritual views have shifted with our political ones. Now we think that all men desire freedom. We think that God should run a democracy. We view God as a presidential advisor rather than an absolute dictator. What a mess such thinking causes!

We no longer see that slavery is the only real freedom and that obedience is the only real protection. We act as though we can go it alone. The only one in the Bible who had such a twisted view of reality was Cain, and even he pleaded for God's protection.

Reconsider your personal application of the possessive pronoun. Is God really *your* God? Are you committed to absolute obedience to Him, whether it seems good or evil to you? Are you ready to follow His instructions, no matter what the cost? Forgiveness is *not* the end of the story. It isn't even the purpose of redemption. It is simply the starting point. Right?

8.

*He who **mocks** the poor taunts his Maker; he who rejoices at calamity will not go unpunished.* Proverbs 17:5

Arrogant Affluence

Mocks – Who would dare do such a thing? Who would ridicule, deride, insult or scorn the poor? Actually, most of us. Let me tell you why.

First, the word for "poor" here is the Hebrew word *rush* (with a long *u*). These are the ones in society without status and possessions. They are the destitute, surviving, if at all, by a daily dose of begging. These are not the politically oppressed, not the ones who lack life's basic needs, not the ones who are part of unrecognized masses. These are the ones without an advocate, without resources, without the ability to care for themselves. They are the bottom rung of the socio-economic ladder. If you want to meet some of them, come with me to an orphanage in Zambia. The children are there because *all* of their parents have died from AIDS. They have *nothing*.

I am quite certain that as you read this you will feel a throb of compassion. You may have to hold back tears if you have ever been in close contact with these children of a lesser god. So, how is it possible that you might *mock* them?

The verb is *la'ag*. It is a strong, vile, offensive verb. Proverbs tells us that the one who *despises* the poor taunts his Maker. Here comes the blow to our hearts. Do you think that God gave you all that you have so you could ignore, avoid or minimize the destitute among us? How much more insulting to the Creator can it be than to take His gifts and refuse to use them on His behalf. God gives – abundantly – without regret or recompense. But most of us *take*! Can you imagine the enormity of our insult to the Father of all good gifts when we say, "It's not my problem?" Of course it's your problem – and mine. We are here as children of salt and light. We are vice-regents of the image of God, called to be stewards of His treasury. If God gives until He bleeds, do we think we can do any less?

I'm sure you've heard all of this before. Executives at World Vision once told me that they knew exactly how many photos of sick children they had to run on television to raise money. But garnering donations isn't the point. The point is that God places obligations on those who have *simply because they have*.

God is the author of all good things. Not me. Not you. If He elects to give me more than I need, that extra comes with a cosmic responsibility. And when I act as though what I have is *mine*, I mock His sovereignty. I insult His decision to put in my hands a measure of His possessions. I display arrogant affluence, an attitude that says, "What's mine is mine. I earned it. If you can't take care of yourself, that your own fault."

This is not social redistribution by government edict. This is the heart of God, displayed in my attitude toward others. I have a choice. I can take what God gives and use it without regard to the cosmic agenda, or I can align my heart with His, and discover the joy of being salt and light. God holds me accountable for that choice. There is no avoiding it.

9.

*He who mocks the poor **taunts** his Maker; he who rejoices at calamity will not go unpunished.* Proverbs 17:5

Living As If

Taunts – Ninety-seven percent of people in America say that they believe there is a god. So what? For the vast majority of these people, the belief that there is a god has absolutely no impact on their lives. They don't tremble at the thought of God's cosmic agenda. They don't base decisions on His moral government. They just do what they want and live as if there were no god at all. For all intents and purposes, they are worse than atheists. They *taunt* God's rightful authority over their lives by claiming He exists and then paying no attention to His will.

We have seen what this looks like in the form of affluent arrogance. It means adopting an attitude of accumulation and despising all those who don't meet the wealth standard. But taunting God comes in more flavors than just economic vanilla. Any deliberate decision to do it my way regardless of God's direction taunts the Maker. It doesn't matter if it is direct disobedience or, as in this verse, an indirect rejection of a heart attitude. The result is the same. God is dishonored – and what dishonors God will not go unpunished.

The verb here is *haraph*. You can think of it as a cattle prod. It is a verb about inciting someone by mocking, belittling, cursing, dishonoring or reproaching. This is the sharp stick of abuse. It brings with it disgrace. Imagine how God will react to those who treat Him in this way. Actually, you don't have to imagine it. All you have to do is read Jeremiah. God pours out His wrath on those who refuse to honor Him. By the time He is finished, the dead are piled so high there are is no more space in the graveyards.

Taunting God is a very serious offense. He will not let it pass. Proverbs tells us that maintaining an attitude of arrogance over the destitute is a sharp stick poked at God Himself. But there are other ways to taunt God. Any action on your part which endorses the question, "Where is God now?" is likely to lead to taunting. The semantic range of *haraph* shows us the wider picture. Speaking against God, blaspheming (basically using God's name and reputation for my own purposes), bringing shame upon Him, defaming His character, cursing Him, diminishing His worth and significance and treating Him as unimportant all fall within the category of taunting God. It does not matter if God is the direct object of these actions or if the direct object is His creation or His community. Whatever offends God's glory is the sharp stick of abuse of the Holy of holies.

I wonder if our lackadaisical attitudes toward worship, obedience, study and spiritual challenge are not really forms of abuse. Do you suppose that we have more to confess than cheating, stealing or coveting? Do you suppose that deep within us is a unmitigated desire to tell God off, to claim that we have the right to our own choices? Maybe repentance needs to unearth the root of *haraph* that grows in the dark, musty soil under our skin.

10.

*"I do not ask Thee to **take them out** of the world, but to keep them from the evil one."* John 17:15

No Vacation Plans

Take Them Out – Yeshua wants us to stay. Believe me, there are plenty of days when I would like to leave. I need a permanent vacation from this world. I get tired of fighting with sin. I hurt all over. I want to sit on the beach near The Crystal Sea and converse with angels.

But Yeshua asks the Father *not* to snatch me away. It's the same word we saw in the parable of the sower – when Satan comes and *takes away* the word of the Lord before it can produce fruit. Here the Greek is about us – *ares autos ek*. Yeshua is **not** preparing our vacation travel documents. He is asking the Father to leave us right here, in the midst of the battle.

Why would He do that? Why is it that I have to stay here after I accept His redemption? Why can't I be snatched away when I am most ready – at the moment my sins are forgiven?

The answer is so simple – and so humbling. God's plan is not about my vacation. God is restoring the entire universe. I don't join in order to retire to a comfortable room in the heavenly hotel. I join because there is a lot to do, especially in me! Quite frankly, I am not yet ready for heaven. God has a lot of pounding and shaping and smelting and casting to do in my life before I will be truly fit for eternal service. And all of that work has to be done in combat because, first, I need the transformation and second, I need to understand that God is a God of community, not my personal travel agent.

But there are still days that I would like to leave.

I stay because Yeshua wants me to. I stay because I want to serve Him, please Him, live for Him and get ready for the long run. I am His voluntary slave. That means I go where the Master sends me, and for the moment, He sends me here. My perspective is not focused on the escape route to heaven. It is focused on the redemption of the world from hell. If you thought that forgiveness was about a one-way ticket out of here, you have the wrong boarding pass. If the Master says, "Stay," we stay. That's what it means to be an alien resident in a world that hates who we are. We are here to do His bidding, and it is here that we will become the people He desires.

Yeshua prays, "Don't snatch them away." But then He offers me all that I need in order to stay the course. "Keep them from the evil one." If I am going to stay here, I will need protection. The entire world, all of its systems, purposes and plots, are under the influence and power of the evil one. I need a shield, a helmet and a sword to survive. I don't need a nice, insulated cocoon. I don't need a beach bag. I need *battle* instruments. There are no vacation plans in my army backpack.

11.

*"Enter by the **narrow gate**, for the gate is wide and the way is broad that leads to destruction, and many are those who enter by it."* Matthew 7:13

Unscathed Salvation

Narrow Gate – Yeshua had been there before - at the narrow path; the place where there is unseen danger; where the blind have no idea what lies ahead. Ah, but if you didn't know that *narrow path (gate)* is the Hebrew word *mish'ol*, then you would never realize that this word is found in the Torah only once, in the story of Balaam's donkey. The Angel of the Lord (a title used in the Old Testament often considered as the pre-incarnation theophany of the Messiah) once stood in the narrow space. With a sword in hand, He opened the eyes of Balaam's donkey to see the danger. But, not Balaam's. Oblivious of the flaming sword, the fool beat his donkey for turning aside – until at last, he too saw the Angel of the Lord. If you are going to pass through the narrow gate, you better have your eyes wide open.

No one goes through unless they see the danger and obey the command. You can read it yourself in Numbers 22. Now Yeshua instructs his followers. Did he point at the royal gate into the city? The Greek words, *stenes pules*, indicate that Yeshua identifies a large, recognizable door, like the door to the city or to the temple. In Greek, this kind of gate is distinguished from a common entrance (*thura*). But ask yourself, "Does this make sense?" Why would Yeshua tell His followers to enter by a clearly marked, formal gate when He has just indicated that this way in is *not* wide, broad and easy? If we look at the Greek, even when we restrict it to a *narrow pules*, we are still in the wrong world. We are in the Greek world, with its careful distinctions between the *kinds of gates*. But Yeshua is in the Hebrew world, a world where *narrow gate* has only a single occurrence in all of the Scriptures, an occurrence where Yeshua Himself guards the entrance to prevent the spiritually blind from entering. Now what do you think He was talking about?

No one passes through the narrow gate without seeing and obeying the sovereign Angel of the Lord. No one comes to the narrow gate unscathed. There is mortal danger here; danger to all those who blindly think that they can push their way forward toward some human goal. Oh, it is certainly true that many will walk the wide road to destruction. They are spiritually asleep, dead to their sinful state. Just like Balaam, they are beating their possession in order to achieve something for themselves. What they don't know is that they stand in the presence of destruction.

But if you thought entering the narrow gate was simply a matter of saying the Sinner's Prayer or feeling sorry for your mistakes, you are worse than the donkey. At least the donkey knew that this is a matter of life and death. You aren't getting past the flaming sword without being singed. Is that what you thought about the narrow gate? Or were you congratulating yourself that you entered into heaven so efficiently and easily?

Oh, yes, and just in case you didn't catch His drift, *few* actually pass through.

12.

*I have **not hidden** Your righteousness within my heart; I have spoken of Your faithfulness and Your salvation; I have not concealed Your lovingkindness and Your truth from the great congregation.* Psalm 40:10

Clothes Make The Man

Not Hidden – You are what you wear. Isn't that the idea behind "clothes make the man?" The point of fashion, besides ego-enhancement, is to provide an external portrayal of some inner quality. Of course, the world is full of posers; people who wear the fashion but don't have the quality. Just think of all those sports jerseys, celebrity look-alikes and designer copies, all pretending to be what they aren't.

David knew something about fashion. In the 10th Century BC, he used the word *kasah* to express what he wore. It means, "to clothe, to cover, to conceal." It's used of all kinds of covering, from articles of clothing to spreading dirt over blood, from the sea covering the Egyptians to the cloud covering God on the mountain.

Of course, it is also used metaphorically – covering sin or concealing motives. What David says is this: "I didn't hide Your righteousness under my vest, Lord. I wore obedience on my sleeve." When David puts on the shirt embroidered, "God is good," he means it. He is no poser. He knows God's goodness in affliction and in victory.

This word is particularly important in an age when religion is seen as a matter of the heart. Today, it's alright to believe whatever you want, provided you keep it private. God-fearers are expected to hide their zealous commitment, so that they don't "offend" those who hold different beliefs. David would have gagged. *King* David was ready and willing to let the whole congregation know that he served the God of righteousness. He proudly proclaims that he has *not hidden* (*lo-khisiti*) the things of God in his heart. He is right up front about his faith. He serves God in public and in private.

Yes, it's appropriate to keep the mysteries of God in our hearts. Yes, it's right to retain His wonderful compassion toward us. Yes, He whispers secrets to our souls. But God never intended that His glory be kept under covers. He is not a hidden God, nor are His people to be hidden under a bowl (or a bushel). The light has come. The night cannot swallow it up. Throw off the restraint of a culture that loves the darkness and let God's righteousness illuminate the world through you. A lot of rats might scurry for the corners, but that's what happens when the lights come on.

Stand with David today, and say, "I have *not hidden* Your righteousness in my heart." You have something of immense value to share with a dark world. Uncover it.

13.

*I have not hidden Your righteousness within my heart; I have spoken of Your faithfulness and Your salvation; I have **not concealed** Your lovingkindness and Your truth from the great congregation.* Psalm 40:10

Eraser

Not Concealed – Have you concealed God's covenant

commitment and truth from the great assembly? It's easy to do so. All it takes is a little change in words and deeds. Let me give you an example.

At my last job interview for a position with a commercial company, the employer asked me what I offered that made me different than the other candidates.. I could have told him about my background and past successes. But God gave me a nudge. I said, "If you employ me, your business will be blessed, because I will act like Joseph in the Old Testament, and God will bless you through me." That's about as up-front as you can get. I had no idea if this man was a believer. In fact, I am pretty sure that he was not, but it didn't matter, because what I told him was the truth. I am not like any other candidate. I am a servant of the King.

And so are you!

How much easier it would be to just give the usual explanation. No controversy. No confrontation. But that would conceal God's covenant commitment with me, and since I believe that God is sovereign over all life's circumstances, including job interviews, I knew that listening to His gentle suggestion would serve Him, even if it meant that I did not get the job (and, by the way, I didn't). I want to stand with David and say *lo-khikhadti* (I have not concealed). The verb, *kakhad*, has other nuances that expand the thought. It is used to describe destroying or making something disappear. In Zechariah, it is used to describe effacing and scattering. *Kakhad* is more than simply covering up something. It is about *erasing* something.

Once we realize that the idea behind *kakhad* is to erase or eliminate, then we see that concealing God's goodness can be accomplished in many different ways. It's not just

44

choosing words that leave God out of the picture. It's also *acting* in ways that ignore or deny His sovereignty. When the leaders of a nation exhibit behavior that ignores or denies God's sovereignty, grace and truth, all the people suffer. Sometimes the suffering goes on for centuries (to see just how deep this goes, take a look at what happened in the translation of the King James Bible at this web site: *http://inthebeginning.com/books/ecc.htm*). We can participate in erasing God's truth without ever knowing it. I am quite sure that God forgives such transgressions before we ask. But there are others that are not overlooked. Endorsing a lifestyle of indulgence, ignoring the cries of the weak, overlooking the needs of the desperate, acting as if life is about possession and accumulation, denying responsibility to the community – all of these and more *erase* the image of God in the world.

David was an eraser more than once. You and I have done our share of removing God from His rightful place. It's time to change all that. Make God's mark on your life indelible. Say it and show it in front of the great assembly.

14.

*You shall not **bow** yourself to them nor **serve** them, for I, Jehovah your God, am a jealous God* Deuteronomy 5:9

Idolatry in Action

Bow – Serve – Idolatry comes in two related flavors. The first is *shachah*, to bow down in submission or reverence or worship. Hollywood has exploited this flavor of idolatry with its scenes of pagan rituals. Of course, that external obeisance is only a small taste of the real heart commitment to another god. Isaiah 2:12-17 uses this word to show us that all who are proud and arrogant are licking the *shachah* flavor – and they will all be judged because of this. You don't have to flop before a statue in order to retain pride and arrogance in your heart, do you? In fact, if we think about those actions and attitudes that elevate us above others or contribute to our disdain of others, we might just discover that the *shachah* tendency runs deeper than we thought.

But that isn't the end of the story. God tells us that there is another flavor mixed into this lethal brew. It is *avad*, a very important word in Hebrew thought. *Avad* is the umbrella word for labor. It includes both work and service, and in the context of this commandment, that means that work can also be seen as worship.

When work is dedicated to the Lord's purposes, it becomes worship. When it is not dedicated to the Lord's purposes, *avad* is service to false gods. The commandment prohibits providing economic leverage to those idols that oppose God's plans. The attitude of arrogance and pride will find its expression in opposition to God, even if the false gods are telling you just how "good" the work is. Work and worship are intimately connected.

What does this mean for the daily grind? First, it implies that a follower of the Way sees all daily activity in a spiritual context. I don't go to work just to fill my time so that I can get money to fill my desires. If I am a follower of the Way, work is the place God puts me to experience His engineering of my life. I come with contentment because I know that He orders my day. I serve with gladness because I am where He wants me to be, whether at the register in Target or at the gas pump or at the boardroom table. If I am not there because God wants

46

me there, then my *avad* probably serves another god.

The same can be said for my purposes. No matter where God places me, I still serve (work for) Him. Isn't this exactly what Paul suggested? But if I find that what occupies my effort is directed toward desires not in line with the will of the Father, then my *avad* is passive rebellion, denying God's authority and ownership of all my endeavors.

David said that all the earth will worship (fall down and serve) the Lord. If the sun, moon and stars sing His praises, and if every hill and valley, ocean and stream shout out the magnificence of the Holy One of Israel, can we do any less and claim that we are obedient to this second commandment?

Today, you may walk humbly before your God. You may serve Him with contentment and joy. Or, you can look to others gods in your *attitude and actions*. It's really up to you, isn't it?

15.

*I brought you out of the land of Egypt, saying, "You **only** have I known of all the families of the earth."* Amos 3:2

Broken Vessels

Only – Why did God choose you and me? He did, you know. He started this plan of redemption and restoration by choosing Abraham. He continues the plan by grafting the Gentiles into the family of Abraham. Now you and I are part of His family. So, the words of Amos apply to us. God brought us out of Egypt. We look back and see His handiwork and glory. We are part of it all. We have always been part of it all (from God's perspective). But why? Why choose me? Or you?

The Hebrew word here is *raq*. It is our badge of exclusivity. Memorize it! You would notice in the Hebrew Bible that this is the *first* word in the sentence – the place of emphasis. *"ONLY you have I known,"* is the better translation. God picked Abraham, David, John, Paul and you and me for this task. He is going to restore His creation *through us*. What an awesome responsibility and privilege we have been given.

But there are plenty of days when I just don't feel up to this. There are days like today when I can't understand why God would choose me. I am broken. I am disobedient. I am a failure in holiness. Frankly, I'm a mess. I'm what you call a *hopeful hypocrite*, that is, I know how I should act and I speak about how I should act, but the truth is that I don't always act that way. I *hope* that some day my words will be matched by my behavior. I expect that God will keep prodding me toward that day. I know that I will have plenty of pain before I get there; the pain I suffer as God removes my fear-based alternatives and replaces them with trust. But when I look at my life, I just can't imagine why God would use someone so flawed. Surely there are others more qualified than I. I can even point to a few. So, why me?

And, guess what? God does *not* provide an answer. God doesn't tell me why He chose me, or why He chose you. He just did. That is the reality of my life. God placed an obligation on me when He grafted me into His family. That obligation was to abide by His covenant *in order that* all the world might see His righteousness and return to Him. The purpose of living the covenant life is not to make my experience better. Oh, it does that too, but that is the by-product of the way God designed the plan. The purpose of living the covenant life is so that others (who were not given this elected obligation) may see His glory and turn to Him. And the only way they can see this is in the messed-up, broken vessel that I am.

The hardest part of studying God's words is that you and I become accountable for them. Each new word reveals a deeper degree of obligation – a tighter connection with the covenant. Of course, that is also the great joy of God's words. They bring comfort right along with conviction. Apparently, you can't have one without the other.

So, how are you doing? Are you experiencing your brokenness in God? Is He pushing you along the road to righteousness?

16.

*"Whoever then annuls one of the least of these commandments, and teaches others the same, shall be called least in the kingdom of heaven; but whoever **keeps and teaches** them, he shall be called great in the kingdom of heaven."* Matthew 5:19

Both And

Keeps and Teaches – Apparently Yeshua did not view the Law as an "either/or" option. He says quite clearly that we are to *keep* and *teach* these commandments. That is the practical equivalent of discipleship. It's not possible to be a disciple and simply keep in alignment with the Father. There is another condition. The point of discipleship is to *reach out to others*, not to store up a good life for yourself. But if you were Hebrew, you would have intuitively known this to be true. In the Hebrew culture, what helps one helps all and what harms one harms all. The sense of community comes before any consideration of individual well-being. Maybe that's why there are only two great commandments: love God first and love your neighbor second (and, by the way, don't get trapped in the current psychobabble about loving yourself in order to love your neighbor).

The Greek text uses the two words *poieo* and *didasko*. The meanings are pretty much what the translation says, but notice the *order* of these words. The priority of *keeping* (the Greek verb means "to do") before *teaching* (the Greek means "to instruct verbally, to admonish and to influence the understanding") is Yeshua' way of addressing hypocrisy. Oh, the sting of these words! You cannot effectively communicate what you do not practice. If you want someone else to see the light, you must be walking in the light. It is simply spiritually impossible for darkness to bring about light.

Yeshua pushes us right into the heart of the commandments. They are not just good to know. Nothing important happens in your life by collecting valuable information about God's word. In fact, God has designed His universe so that *you cannot learn unless you put it to use*. In God's reality school, no one ever receives a social pass. You can stay in Kindergarten all of your life if you choose not to obey, and God will keep you there until you do obey because *information can't save you*. Only obedience lifts your life out of the ditch.

We probably find this particularly difficult and uncomfortable. We have been taught all of our lives that gathering information is the first step toward effective decision-making. Get the facts, then the solution will present itself; but not in God's world. God does not run Wikipedia. The Bible is not a storehouse of information. It is a *recovery* book and God is running a military campaign. He sends orders to the troops so that they can follow *His* plan of action. He does not need to give me all the information in order for me to know what to do next. Some things God knows are for *His eyes only.* So, in a world where I tend to withhold commitment until I see where things are going, Yeshua reminds me that *doing* comes before teaching. If I am going to fulfill the great commission by making disciples, I must first be a doer of the word – no exceptions. Take a look at the order of your priorities. Are you Hebrew or Greek?

17.

*And you shall become a **kingdom of priests** for Me, a holy nation.* Exodus 19:6

Tactics, Not Strategy

Kingdom of Priests – God chose Israel before He gave them the commandments. He elected Abram *before* he became Abraham and *before* he knew anything about God's plan. He picked Isaac, not Ishmael. He blessed Jacob, not Esau. God chooses whomever He wishes to choose. We have no say in the matter. After all, it's *His* plan. We don't get to decide the strategy, but we have a lot to do with the tactics.

God's strategy has never changed. He has always chosen to reach *all* through *some* in the same way He chose to redeem *all* through *one.* He often chooses those who seem ill-equipped or completely rebellious. He seems to prefer *reluctant leaders*, not campaigning politicians. If you're anxious to have the job, you're probably not the right person. God's jobs require humility, self-abasement, sacrifice and, usually, lack of recognition. No one (except Yeshua) volunteers for this kind of duty.

But that doesn't mean that everyone chosen has no part to play. God determines the strategy and assigns us the tactics. This verse tells us the part we play. All those chosen by Him (whether as original vine or grafted branches) are to live as priests *so that the rest of the world* may see His glory. While the class of priests developed later in Israel's history, God's call comes before the Levites are designated, in fact, before the Law is given. Merely fifty days after delivery from Egypt, God announces His grand strategy. His chosen will be a *kingdom* of priests. That means that every citizen has a priestly function. Every citizen under God's reign and rule carries a special mission.

This has a very important meaning for the children of Israel. In Egypt the term for priest (*w'b*) basically meant "a pure man" and there was *no professional clergy*. Every able-bodied man was a priest in his own home. Imagine the impact of God's announcement. The Hebrews just spent the last 200 years under Egyptian rule and influence. They knew quite well that Egyptian gods were served by every man in every home. But they were slaves. No god battled for them – until Yahweh arrived and showed Himself superior to every Egyptian god. Then Yahweh tells His people, "All of you will be my priests. You will become what Egypt attempted – holy servants of mine, not to serve yourselves but to serve Me by bringing the world back to My glory."

How will God's children accomplish this grand strategy? Simple - by keeping the commandments! In other words, God's strategy is fulfilled when God's people live in accordance with God's way of life. God guarantees it. Our mission, should we chose to accept it, is to live as pure men and women so that the entire world will marvel at the acts of God through us. Whenever we fail to live as pure men and women, we fail to accomplish God's mission. The strategy does not change. We simply fail to participate in the greatest mission ever conceived. But when we put these tactics in play, God promises to do wonderful things through us so that the world will come to Him. What kinds of wonderful things? Well, that's another story.

18.

*Hear, O Israel! The LORD is our God, the LORD is **one**!* Deuteronomy 6:4

Inside the Text

Witness – When God's children observe His commandments, He enables them to be a witness to Him. That's the point of being Torah-observant. Yes, of course, living according to God's Word brings joy and peace and well-being (God promises that). But that's not the end of the story. All of God's actions are set within the redemptive purpose of reclaiming His creation.

Did you get that? God's plan is not to rescue you. It is to rescue the world through you by delivering you. God's plan doesn't stop with your best life now. Your best life now isn't the end of the story; and it is certainly not the end of what God wants to do with you and through you. In fact, your best life now might just be a life of living on the edge of survival because *that serves God's ultimate intention* – to redeem the world. If you are serving God in order to meet your goals and objectives, no matter how ethical and noble they are, you have missed the point. It's not about you! (Where have we heard that before?). Did you think that Paul said that all things work together for *your* good? Think again. All things that God does work together for *the* good, namely, His good purposes – and your good is to fit into that framework.

If we read Hebrew, we would be reminded of this perspective every time we saw the great call here is Deuteronomy 6:4. In the Torah scrolls, the last letter of the word "hear" (*shema*) and the last letter of the word "one" (*'ehad*) are written larger than the rest of the text. Why? Because the two letters together form the Hebrew word *'ed* which means "witness." One rabbi says it this way, "The enlarged letters allude to the thought that every Jew, by pronouncing the *Shema*, bears witness to [God's] unity and declares it to all the world." In other words, every time you repeat God's call, the central purpose becomes top of mind. To declare God as Lord is to witness to the world.

How does this intricate and esoteric textual insight become practical reality? The answer is also bound to the call. When do I declare God as my Lord? When things are going great? Certainly. But what about when things are going terribly wrong? What about when I am abused, persecuted, rejected or ignored? Isn't God still my Lord? What about those times when I just can't see what God is doing, or when He is silent? He's still my Lord, right? Whether I sit on the throne or stand in the welfare line, God is still my Lord. And when I declare His sovereignty over me, no matter what my circumstances, I proclaim Him to the world that watches. In fact, my guess is that more people come to Him when I declare His Lordship in my pain and suffering than when I mention His name from my comfortable castle. Are we attracted to Yeshua because He was on the cover of Forbes or voted Man of the Year? I don't think so.

Are you keeping the commandments of your Lord with His purpose in mind?

19.

*and you shall **remember** that you were a servant in the land of Egypt and the Lord your God brought you out from there with a strong hand and with an outstretched arm; therefore the Lord your God commanded you to keep the Sabbath day.* Deuteronomy 5:15

Personal and Practical

Remember – Most Christians think that God instituted the Sabbath as a memorial to His rest after creation. Of course, that's the reason given in the declaration of the Ten Commandments in Exodus 20:11. But that's not the only reason. Here, Moses reveals another connection between Israel's past slavery and honoring the day of rest. Why is it important for Israel to keep the Sabbath as a day set apart from work? Because Israel was a slave under a cruel yoke until God brought them out with a mighty hand. On the Sabbath, Israel is to remember (*zakar*) not only the eternal and cosmic application of the Sabbath (creation) but also the temporal and practical demonstration (freedom). The first might be theologically glorious, but the second is the very reason for Israel's existence.

Maybe you thought that honoring the Sabbath was only about creation theology. That's lofty and inspiring, but it won't do much good for the man or woman who is enslaved to the work world. There's not much relief in the gristmill just because there are stars in the sky. So, God brings us out. He frees us from the crushing yoke of slavery. We don't have to be Jewish to appreciate how important this is. All we have to do is be human. Everyone feels the sting of the tyrant's whip and the ache of the load of bricks as we trudge through life in the fallen realm. We know what it's like to carry sin's weight. It's killing us. We know what it means to toil in sorrow. It's crushing us.

God is not deaf to our cries. He is compassionate by nature. He rescues by choice. If you've spent your life on the grinding wheel, then you have a very practical reason to keep the Sabbath. It is your personal reminder of life after relief. So, while you're fishing or enjoying the sunrise or hearing the rustle in the leaves, remember. Remember what life was like when there was only tomorrow's work. Remember what it felt like to carry the weight alone. Remember how bitter were the mornings when the only purpose for living was to survive the day. Remember the bite of the accusations, the lash of guilt, the hopelessness of hell on earth. And then you will know why God commands rest. The Sabbath is the living memorial to your redemption. When you keep it, you deliberately recall the days in Egypt, when God seemed as distant as those ancient patriarchs. You meditate on the agony of going to bed tired and waking up even more tired. And then you feel the strain lifted. The Sabbath was made for man, so that man could feel the freedom of God.

Perhaps that's a good test of your Sabbath-keeping attitude. When you set aside the day for delight, do you feel God's wave of freedom? Are you gloriously grateful for the relief He provides? Is the day a *celebration* for living out from under the wheel?

20.

and you shall remember that you were a servant in the land of Egypt and the Lord your God brought you out from there with a strong hand and with an outstretched arm; therefore the Lord your God commanded you to keep the **Sabbath** *day.* Deuteronomy 5:15

A Creative Act

Sabbath – God's command concerning the Sabbath has some entirely unique features. We find them buried in the very word itself. The Hebrew word is *shabbath*. The first thing we notice is the doubled middle consonant (*bb*). When a consonant is doubled like this, it's like putting an exclamation point in the middle of the word. It's like saying, "Pay attention. This is important." There is something special about this word – and what it means.

The second thing we notice is that this is the *only* day with a name. If you look at the Genesis creation story, you see that all the rest of the days are simply numbered. Day 1, day 2, day 3 and so forth, until we come to *shabbath*. Once again, something important!

Then we notice that *shabbath* comes from a root word

shavath, a verb that means, " to rest, to get rid of, to still and to put away." Remember that Hebrew is an *action* language, deriving its nouns from the verbs. The very idea of a day of rest is about *activity*, not sitting around doing nothing. Maybe this helps us understand that odd phrase in Hebrews 4:11 about working to enter into rest.

Finally, we need a little cultural linguistics. No other ancient Semitic culture or language has a designation for a Sabbath day. In fact, none of these ancient cultures even have time calculated in terms of a week (a seven-day cycle). When God established the seventh day, He created something entirely unique. The way that He viewed the relationship between work and rest was exclusively His.

These facts offer another deep insight into the theology of the Sabbath. First, it belongs entirely to God. He created it. He named it. He exclaimed it. Second, since it belongs entirely to God, our participation in it underlines our *dependence* on Him. It is God's day, but He asks us to enter into it. It is His gift to us, a continual reminder of our need for Him. Finally, it is restful action. This is not a day of lethargy. It is a day of celebration, and parties are active events. It is a shift away from the days of working out stewardship over creation. It is a day of lifting up the glory of the God Who made all of it, redeems all of it and enjoys all of it.

Is it any wonder that the Sabbath is held in such high regard? Makes you question why we don't worship on the Sabbath, doesn't it? (By the way, church on Sunday has nothing to do with the resurrection. Thank you, Emperor Constantine.)

21.

Going, *then, disciple all nations, baptizing them into the name of the Father and the Son and the Holy Spirit,* Matthew 28:19

Osmosis Evangelism

Going – The Evangelical world has enshrined this verse as Yeshua' Great Commission. Over and over, we hear these words as a *command* to spread the good news. So, we mount our campaigns, run our revivals and make sure that there is an altar call at the end of every service, just in case someone in the audience hasn't yet proclaimed faith. From D. L. Moody to Billy Graham, we have become so accustomed to evangelism by appeal that we no longer read this verse the way it was written. Let's stop a moment and see what Yeshua really says.

First, of course, we have to enter the Hebrew mind. Hebrew "evangelism" is much more about transformation of life than it is about correcting statements of belief. Greek might be about my mental assent to the truth, but Hebrew is about the way I walk along life's dusty roads. So, Yeshua starts where any good rabbi would start – with walking. The Greek is the verb *poreuomai*, which comes from a noun meaning "to pierce or run through." You can think of it like the word "porous". Things just run right through it. This verb takes on the sense of passing from one place to another - in other words, moving on down the road. That is precisely what the Hebrew metaphor would be for walking with God. Over and over, the Old Testament uses the verb *halak* to describe a continual and habitual relationship with God as life moves from one day to the next. It's all about walking.

While it is usually translated as a command (Go!), that really isn't the sense of it. The command in this verse is to disciple others. The sense is "as you are going along, be deliberate about discipling." Of course, that's very much a Hebrew thought where there is no difference between the secular and the sacred in life. All life is work/worship to God. So, as you are going about in your work/worship, disciple others.

This is osmosis evangelism. Is it deliberate? Of course it is! But that is not the same as handing out tracts or giving invitations. This kind of evangelism comes from close proximity – living life together is such a way that *who you are and what you do* glorifies God and others are compelled to ask, "How can you be the kind of person you are?" If you're going to pour yourself out for the Lord, make sure your life is full of holes. Let Him pass right through you as you pass right through life.

Oh, yes, and by the way, perhaps the greatest evangelism occurs when life *isn't working*. Anyone can glorify God when things are good, the bank is full and we are living happily ever after. But only those who know how to walk this way with God are able to offer praise and glory in the midst of real crisis and turmoil. And that's when osmosis evangelism is at its best.

22.

*Going, then, **disciple** all nations, baptizing them into the name of the Father and the Son and the Holy Spirit,* Matthew 28:19

Choosing An Apprentice

Disciple – What's the difference between making a disciple and teaching? Not much, if you subscribe to the usual patterns of religion these days. We tend to think that making disciples is just a matter of transferring the right information to another person so that person *believes* the same thing we believe. As long as the doctrine is correct, we've done the job. Nothing could be further from the truth, even in the Greek world.

The Greek word here is *matheteuo*. It means to become *attached* to a teacher and become a follower of the teacher's conduct of life. Yes, the disciple does get verbal and written instruction, but that is not sufficient. A disciple is not the same as a pupil. To be a disciple, I must become an apprentice of the Master, attending to and *copying* His actions, thoughts and decisions until I act, think and decide just like the Master. Greek makes this quite clear because it uses a different word (*matheo*) for learning without becoming an apprentice. I can go to school (or to a members' class) for *matheo*, but it will not make me a disciple. To be a disciple, I have to live life with the teacher.

Yeshua is adamant here. As you go down the road of life, gather to yourself someone to apprentice. *Show them* the kingdom of heaven in thought, word and deed so that your apprentice's life is transformed into a perfect reflection of your life. In other words, walk with them until they get it. Then send them out to do the same thing.

The church today has thousands of pupils, most of whom are still in the elementary grades. To overcome this, we send our experts to special schools, until they come back ready to give us more instruction in belief systems. But we don't make disciples. We make head-filled spectators. They come for the stage show – the great music, inspiring settings and a charismatic orator behind a glass pulpit. I simply can't imagine Yeshua anywhere near such spectacles of religiosity. I see Yeshua walking along the road, serving those in need, gathering to himself a small group of chosen apprentices. I see Him spending His time *living in community* with those He disciples, until they are ready to do the same. Information is not transformation, and it can't be communicated in the way that I deliver content in an e mail (I'm sorry to say this, but it's true. All we can do in *Today's Word* is *start* the process of apprenticeship). If you want to "make" an apprentice (disciple), you will have to rub elbows together, walk together, eat together, play and experience pain and joy together. No man or woman can disciple someone *occasionally*. You can't become a carpenter by using a hammer once a month. You need to go on the job with a journeyman carpenter for a few years.

It's time to stop recruiting spectators for membership. It's time to choose an apprentice and get to work – together.

23.

*Going, then, **disciple** all nations, baptizing them into the name of the Father and the Son and the Holy Spirit,* Matthew 28:19

Selling the Gospel

Disciple – So, we clarified a few things. First, evangelism *happens*. It is the by-product of walking the life with God, of "going" down the road. Secondly, Yeshua calls us to *disciple* others, not recruit them. There is a big difference between pushing information into someone's hand or head and living life together in holy community. Now let's pay attention to one other important part of this "great" commission. No one can disciple the masses! Discipleship requires personal life involvement. It is a one-on-one long encounter. I can deliver loads of information to thousands in just a few minutes, but discipleship takes time and a lot of life together. Yeshua did not call us to spread the good news in the most efficient way possible. He called us to enter into the lives of others with the deliberate intention of demonstrating the will of the Father. Not once, but continuously . . . and not anonymously. Can you imagine how ridiculous it is to think of choosing an apprentice anonymously? I can't be an apprentice unless I *know* the one I am copying. You can't be a disciple-maker unless you *choose* someone to follow you.

Did you get that? Yeshua *chose* twelve. They did not volunteer or vie for the positions or stand in line or send in resumes. Yeshua picked them for His own reasons. In fact, the New Testament doesn't tell us *why* He picked them. It only tells us that the Father was instrumental in drawing each one to Yeshua. The teacher picks the learner because it is not about passing tests and memorizing facts. It is about *living as one*.

What this implies is that real evangelism is never anonymous. I can't disciple someone that I don't know. I must confidently travel my pathway with God, allowing Him to bring into my life those whom I might choose. Then, with prayerful consideration, I invite some to join forces with me. I commit my ways to them. I embrace them in a day-to-day experience that takes us to the cutting edge of God's kingdom. And away we go, following the same road together until the Lord brings us to a parting fork. Evangelism is not efficient, but it is incredibly effective. It doesn't happen quickly, but it lasts. It might start with a sense of deep conviction and repentance, but it will not proceed without copying life transformation.

Contemporary Christianity has been trying to sell the gospel for more than a century. We have packaged it so that we can deliver the goods in three points and twenty minutes. We have condensed it to the minimally necessary truths required to communicate information about Yeshua. But we don't disciple anymore. We're too busy with our own lives to even think about day-to-day meshing with someone else's life. It's just easier to invite a friend to watch a man in a suit parade across the stage. Don't you think Yeshua will ask you whom you chose as an apprentice when you stand before Him? Then what will you say?

24.

*Going, then, **disciple** all nations, baptizing them into the name of the Father and the Son and the Holy Spirit,* Matthew 28:19

Nouns and Verbs

Disciple – You probably know the translation of this verse as "make disciples of all nations." But have you thought about the implications of adding "make" to the Greek verb *matheteuo* and changing the form to a noun? The addition moves the action from the subject (you) to the object (disciples). With the addition, the command appears to call you to produce a disciple. In other words, it implies that you have to do something that *results* in a disciple. The focus is on the result, not the process.

Now, get ready for a shock. The Greek text is not about the disciple at all. It is about the *process* that you undertake to disciple another. In other words, the command is about *you*, not the result. Yeshua does not command us to go out and produce anything or anyone.

He commands us to go about discipling. What matters is your obedience. The result is up to God.

This is such a fundamental shift in our thinking that it may take quite awhile to sink in. We have been trained to believe that we are to produce spiritual results – to save souls. But Yeshua is Hebrew, not Greek. Hebrew derives nouns from verbs. The fundamental perspective of the language is on the *action*, not the person, place or thing. Greek, on the other hand, derives verbs from nouns. The emphasis is on the resulting person, place or thing. If we want to understand Yeshua here, we must enter the Hebrew mind. We must see that the Great Commission is not about the results; it is about the process.

Yeshua does not command you to get out there and make things happen. He does not order you to knock on doors, pass out tracts, invite pagans to church or run crusades. All of those activities are useful ways to reach the lost, but they do not fulfill the Great Commission. The Great Commission is about your commitment to discipling someone else. The focus is not *outward*. It is *inward* – looking inside to see if you are discipling. And what does discipling look like?

Well, it starts with a choice. You choose someone. Then you embrace that person with the heart of God. You demonstrate compassion, mercy and grace. You instruct (*yasar* - discipline) and encourage. You enter into the life of another in thought, word and deed. You are present in the pain and the joy. You walk the road with the same dust on your feet. You do life together. You can't disciple by proxy, any more than you can raise your child with a surrogate parent. If you want to disciple, you have to get into the life of the other person.

Very few contemporary visions of the Great Commission are about discipleship. Most are about marketing the gospel. But that is not Yeshua' way. Yeshua is Hebrew. That means He focuses on personal obedience and corporate community. Yeshua builds deep relationships. That's what transforms life. Are you discipling?

25.

*And they said, "Believe in the Lord Yeshua, and you shall be saved, you and your **household**."* Acts 16:31

Rescuing One

Household – In an age that emphasizes *personal* salvation and *individual* belief, we have a hard time understanding Paul's statement. We re-read this as if it meant that each one of the people in the jailer's house had to come to a personal saving faith in Yeshua Christ. We are so conditioned by the Greek mindset of the individual that we forget that Paul is a Hebrew, and that the Hebrew point of view is about community. It would be perfectly natural for Paul, as a Hebrew, to speak to the jailer and the "house of you" (*oikos sou*) as a single community. Salvation – *yasha* (rescue) – visited them all at once. What the head of the household accepts alters the identity of the entire household.

Before you throw up your hands and groan, remember how long we have been taught to think as separate individuals. Did you know that the current stress on *personal* relationship with Christ came into existence with D. L. Moody and Billy Graham? Yes, we find personal relationship language throughout the Scriptures, but it is almost always set in the context of community. I am not an island in the Hebrew world. My sins affect everyone in the community. My faith affects everyone in the community. We function together, intimately woven into a fabric of God's own making. I do not exist apart from you, able to carry on my own agendas without interaction and intervention. The *house of God* is a single entity, not a collection of multiple individuals. So, Paul simply speaks as a Hebrew, telling the jailer that his actions affect all under his authority. We would do well to give some serious consideration to this point of view.

If there is anything that the church needs today, it is the living reality of community. Our lives are full of fragmented existence; a piece for work, a piece for family, another piece for our friends, our church and our social commitments. By the time we try to balance it all, we're overwhelmed and exhausted. This is the *direct* result of living as independent individuals. But it doesn't work. The truth is that we are fighting the design of the universe in our attempts to remove dependencies. Everything in creation depends on everything else – and we are no different. Until *dependence* reigns supreme in the church, it will never be a living community of the Spirit. It will only be a conglomeration of individuals. It's time to think in terms of the household. What happens to one happens to all. That's the Hebrew way.

My guess is that underneath all the separateness of our lives, we actually long for true community. We know that independence doesn't work, but the systems of this world all seem to push us toward this destructive end. We want to belong, to be known, to be loved, but everywhere we go we find more separateness. How can the true church, the *ekklesia*, have anything to offer a fragmented world if it continues on its path toward *individualism*? That's just what the world preaches (and much more effectively). How can I really know and love hundreds or thousands of people in a Sunday service? It's self-defeating. God is the God of the household. Until we understand what that really means, we will be nothing more than islands in the stream.

26.

*"Come to Me, all who are weary and heavy laden, and I **will give** you **rest**."* Matthew 11:29

Rest From The Rabbi

Will Give Rest – Yeshua gives rest like no other. Why? Because He knows exactly how you were designed and what purpose you are to serve. No one, not even you, knows more precisely what you need to be satisfied. But wait! This kind of rest isn't swinging in a hammock. It's not the cessation of activity. It is *work* that refreshes. You see, God's plan has always been that Man should work in ways that refresh. That's the kind of rest Yeshua offers. Let's take a closer look.

Yeshua elaborates the Father's perfect plan for Man. In that plan, the Potter designed each of us for a particular use. We fulfill our essential purpose only when we are used as we were designed. Yes, you can carry water in a hat, but a hat was designed for something else. Here's a test of your personal design. Are you refreshed in your work? Are you perfectly comfortable with your service and purpose, discovering that it energizes you? Or are you exhausted from trying to carry water in a hat?

The Greek here actually helps us see the nuance. *Anapauso* comes from *ana* (again) and *pauo* (to rest, cease). It means "Relax!" That's not the same as "Stop!" The idea is to find that place of comfortable purpose where activity satisfies. When Yeshua offers us rest, He does not mean that we quit doing things. He means that He, and only He, can arrange the universe so that we become who we are. We rest because we are doing exactly what we were meant to do. It is the *second* wind in our effort, when we are suddenly in the groove and things just come easily.

There is a first rest. God made all that there is – and rested. He ceased His creative activities in that phase of existence. The Sabbath honors God's first rest because the Sabbath honors God's sovereign creative power. But there is a second rest – a rest that comes from fulfilling the purpose of creation. God rested when He completed all that was necessary for His purposes to be fulfilled. Now Yeshua offers us the second rest, the state of being where our *activity* fulfills God's purposes, glorifying Him and satisfying us.

Maybe that's why the author of Hebrews tells us to *work* in order to enter into that *rest*. Maybe that's why Yeshua tells us to *come* (an action) to Him in order to find that *rest*. We are weary of the road. We have tried so long to find the real reason for our lives – and we have failed. We are not capable of discovering that reason without the hand of the Potter shaping us for His use. We are heavy laden. We carry a load of mistakes, guilt, shattered dreams, disappointments and obligations. Most of them are the direct or indirect result of not being used for the Potter's purposes. We have tried again and again to carry water in hats, but the cistern is not full. We know exactly how much emptiness remains in our lives, and we know that unless we find the use that we are meant to fulfill, the emptiness will never leave us.

"Come to Me." Yeshua promises to give us exactly the usefulness that we are missing – the *rest* of our lives.

27.

"Take My **yoke** *upon you, and learn from Me, for I am gentle and humble in heart, and* YOU SHALL FIND REST FOR YOUR SOULS*"* Matthew 11:29

Rest Under Restraint

Yoke – How can we enter into the second rest that Yeshua promises? Well, not by sitting under a tree! Yeshua says that *rest* comes when we are *bound* to Him. Just think about that picture for a minute. Most of us would never consider being yoked to someone else as a means of finding rest. The picture looks more like pulling in tandem. That's the picture of the Greek word, *zugos* – something that binds together. It still sounds like work, doesn't it? Of course, now we know that Yeshua' point of view is Hebraic. Rest is not ceasing from activity. It is relaxing under restraint. Being bound to Yeshua means that He does exactly what His name implies. He rescues us in the middle of our burdens. That's the Hebraic view of *yasha*, remember? Rescue comes to me where I am. It's not an escape valve. It's not an "Easy Button." It's sharing the load.

There are two great worldviews when it comes to responsibilities and obligations. The first is the world of the individual. I am responsible for my own destiny. I carry the load. I shoulder my own consequences. I make choices based on what's good for me. This view dominates the world system. In one form or another, it has been around since the day after Adam and Eve left the garden.

The second great worldview is God's perspective. This worldview is *shared* responsibility and *shared* obligation. I am who I am because I belong to a community. That community may be called the family of God, the elect, the house of Israel, the church or the bride of Christ. The names are interchangeable, but the concept remains the same. I am intimately and inextricably linked to all my brothers and sisters in the family. I do *not* stand alone. What happens to me, happens to you and vise versa. Community comes *before* individuality. I become who I am in relationship with others.

Yeshua invites me to join Him in this community of the rescued. The yoke that I take is bound to Him – and bound to every other sibling in the kingdom of heaven. The rest that I discover is *shared* life, not isolated individualism. My second wind comes when I am bound to others. So, here's a hint. Whenever I am inclined to pursue those activities that separate me from community, I am moving away from *rest*. I will never find my deepest sense of purpose and my greatest enjoyment in work in isolation because I was designed to be in relationship with God and with others. When I take the yoke that Yeshua offers, He puts me into community with all other burden bearers who belong to Him. That's when I am able to discover what I was made to do because my doing it will be of benefit to all those other people who lift me up.

There is no rest without restraint. Rest is not achieving the dream of independence. It is exactly the opposite: dependent on Yeshua and connected to family.

28.

*"Take My yoke upon you, and learn **from** Me, for I am gentle and humble in heart, and* YOU SHALL FIND REST FOR YOUR SOULS" Matthew 11:29

Prepositional Power

From – Don't read this too quickly! You might see the King James Version instead. That version says "learn *of* me." The implication is that the more we know *about* Yeshua, the more we will find rest. But that's not what the Greek text says. The preposition is *apo.* In Greek, this preposition usually means movement *from the edge* of something as opposed to movement *within* something. So, if I went from Jerusalem to Samaria, I would use *apo*, but if I went from inside the house to outside the house, I would use *ek*. Now, let's apply this and see what Yeshua really means.

To learn *from* Yeshua is simply to see what Yeshua does and copy it. It is to observe the movement of Yeshua (His actions and words), not to examine His inner motivation or intention. That makes perfect sense. I really *can't see* someone's intentions or motivations, can I? But I can certainly see how someone behaves. So Yeshua says, "Watch Me, and do as I do." In other words, I don't have to have Yeshua' theological expertise or mental acumen. All I have to do is *copy* the Master.

Isn't that easier? Imagine how difficult it would be if the only way that I could enter into rest was to have all the same mental, emotional and intentional capacity of Yeshua. It would be hopeless. I can never be exactly like Him. But, if entering into rest simply means copying

What He does, then I have a chance. I can do what Yeshua does because He is human, just like me. I can minister to the sick, pray to God, worship on the Sabbath, spend time mentoring and consoling, ask the Father for guidance, listen to instruction and carry out commands. I can do all these things, especially since Yeshua promises to be yoked to me and help pull the load. He is my living model for behavior that will produce rest.

Of course, that means when I act in ways that are not consistent with His role model actions, I won't find rest. Do you believe that? Do you really believe that insofar as you do things that do not model Yeshua' actions, you are bound to dissatisfaction and stress? If you really believe that the only way to find refreshing work is to model Yeshua, then seeing His actions clearly is the most important thing you can do. You have to cut through the familiar and see how Yeshua really behaved. You have to understand how He responded to a wide variety of situations, just like the circumstances that you face. You have to know what He did when faced with accusation, betrayal, rejection, demands, loss, fear and temptation as well as victory, validation, joy, comfort and friendship. If you don't know what Yeshua did, you can't know the rest He offers.

Most of us think we can find our own way to the Promised Land. But we end up slaves in Egypt. If you want what Yeshua offers, you will have to follow by doing what He does.

29.

*"Take My yoke upon you, and **learn** from Me, for I am gentle and humble in heart, and YOU SHALL FIND REST FOR YOUR SOULS"* Matthew 11:29

Discipleship *Not* Required

Learn – This Greek verb *manthano* is not the same as the word used in the Great Commission passage. The verb in Matthew 29:18 is *matheteuo* (see February 16). The Great Commission is about *discipling* others. That means mentoring them in a way that *attaches* them to the rabbi. That means creating an apprentice relationship. But that is *not* what Yeshua says here. Right here Yeshua doesn't ask for discipleship. He asks for observation that results in moral responsibility and action. Do you see the difference?

To make someone my disciple is to *choose* someone to follow me. The teacher is the active agent, not the pupil. That's why the Great Commission is not focused on the *results* but rather, on the *method*. But in this verse, Yeshua changes the focus. Here the emphasis on is the student, not the teacher. It is the student's responsibility to carefully observe and copy the teacher. No intimate apprenticeship is required. No "teacher choice" is necessary. All that matters is that the student understand fully the obligation, the responsibility and the action. *Manthano* is a verb that says, "Just do *exactly* what I do."

Why does Yeshua use a verb that doesn't seem to require discipleship? The answer is buried in the structure of the universe. It's profound – and simple (most profound things really are simple). If I do *exactly* what Yeshua does, I will soon discover that my actions reshape my attitudes and emotions – and I will become His follower because I will discover the refreshment I long to have. I will experience something God built into creation – rest! When I do what Yeshua does, I discover my real purpose. I am satisfied at last. I am in-tune with the symphony of creation, in harmony with God's design within me. My life becomes a stanza in the poetry of the universe. I can never go back. I *make myself* a disciple.

It's such a subtle approach. Yeshua is so brilliant. Don't worry about getting all the facts right or having deep insights. Don't fret over theological puzzles or moral dilemmas. Don't be discouraged that you won't be chosen as an apprentice. Just copy Him. Just examine ever so carefully how He acts, and then do it too. And things will change. The more you do what Yeshua does, the more you will enter into the eternal flow of the Father's purposes. And things will change. Life will be much less burdensome – much more joyful. You will find the second wind.

Discipling might be up to the teacher, but learning (examining carefully in order to copy) is up to the student. Either way produces the same result. Pretty clever.

30.

*"Take My yoke upon you, and learn from Me, for I am gentle and humble in heart, and YOU SHALL **FIND REST** FOR YOUR SOULS"* Matthew 11:29

Yeshua and Yirmeyahu

Find Rest – What did the listeners hear when Yeshua quoted this passage from Yirmeyahu (see Jeremiah 6:16)? They knew it, of course, since they were schooled in the Scripture. All Yeshua had to do was quote one part of the verse and the audience could fill in the rest. It's the rest that matters, the part that we don't see in this text from Matthew. So, do you know what Yeshua *didn't say*?

Yirmeyahu 6:16 is God speaking to the wayward house of Israel. It's a very timely passage. All around, says the Lord, people are crying "Peace, peace." But there is no peace. Why? Because the children have abandoned the good ways, the path of the Lord. They were not even ashamed to forsake God's ways. They wanted to be relevant. But God says, "Walk in the old paths and you shall find rest." Don't walk in them, and you will find destruction!

Yeshua cites just enough of this prophecy in Yirmeyahu to get the attention of the audience. But here's the real barb. Yeshua is telling His audience that if they want to see what it means to walk in the old ways, the good path, *they need to look at Him*! If you want to see what it means to live according to the commandments, look at Yeshua. Do what He does and you will automatically be faithful to God.

In Yirmeyahu, the Hebrew words are *va umitsu margoa* from *masa* (to find or attain) and *margoa* (a state of refreshment and life). In other words, seek first the kingdom of heaven, and all these things will be added. Sound familiar? There is a reason why Yeshua had an electrifying effect on His audience, but it's not because He was presenting novel material. It was because He portrayed Himself as God. Jeremiah's verse is God speaking. No one in the audience could possibly doubt that. Now Yeshua proclaims that *He* is the pathway to the rest that God offers. Could anyone miss the point? Not a chance! Yeshua takes the role of God by quoting just enough of Jeremiah to make it obvious to anyone who really listened.

If you want rest, that state of refreshment in life, then you will have to come to Yeshua and follow His pathway of obedience. If you want to know the Father's blessing and the Father's delight, then you will have to take the yoke of Yeshua upon you. In other words, if you want to know God, you have to look at Yeshua.

If you can't feel the electricity running through the crowd when Yeshua said these words, then you must be dead (or sufficiently insulated so that nothing gets to you). Now you know one more reason why you can't read the New Testament without the Old, and you can't understand what Yeshua is saying without understanding His view of Scripture. Yeshua is not only the *only* way to the Father. He is also the *only* way to refreshing life.

Have you carried the load long enough to know this?

31.

that He will set you high above all nations which He has made, for **praise, fame, and honor**: *and that you shall be a consecrated people to the LORD your God, as He has spoken.* Deuteronomy 26:19

Tactical Instructions

Praise, Fame and Honor – This is the "big picture" verse. In order to understand it, we need to take a step back before we can take a step forward. The step back puts this verse in its proper context. First, God chooses some to reach many. God *elects* Israel in order to bless Israel so that His blessings will act as a magnet for the rest of humanity. Those who submit to the God of Israel take on the same mission – to live in obedience so that God might be glorified and, as a result, all the nations will come to Him. That's the plan. Election has nothing to do with merit. It is simply God's way of executing His plan.

Secondly, no true follower of YHWH ever thinks that God's love depends on his obedience. Love is determined by election.   Completion of the *mission* depends on obedience. Israel's failure to obey does *not* change God's election. It only affects the mission. Israel's failure to act as a magnet means that God uses the Gentiles who are *in the house* to accomplish the mission. Neither God's love for Israel or for the adopted Gentiles who come into the house changes as a result of this failure. The strategy is the same. The only thing that changes is the tactic.

Once we understand this big picture, we can understand this verse.   Favoritism is not part of the plan.   God chooses for His own reasons. He doesn't set Israel above other nations because they deserved it any more than He blesses you because you deserve it. Israel didn't deserve it and neither do you and I. God loved us *when we were still His enemies.*   God sets Israel above the nations in order that they can fulfill His mission. That is exactly what He does with us. The only reason God pours out His blessings on us is so that we can act as magnets. And, of course, we sometimes have a stronger magnetism in adversity than we do in prosperity. That part is entirely up to God.   After all, it is *His* mission.   How He accomplishes it through you is up to Him.

However, in general, God loves to make life good. So, in this verse, He says that keeping His commandments will result in praise, fame and honor.   That attracts the nations. Of course, these words in Hebrew don't quite mean what they do in English. They are *tehillah, shem* and *tiph'arah.* We can fill them out a bit.   "Praise" is really genuine adoration and thanksgiving due to the worth of the object. False praise means nothing, since it doesn't match the quality of the object.   But when God stands behind a nation, it is praised because it reflects His character. When a nation doesn't reflect the character of the One Who made it, no praise is due.

"Fame" is the familiar word, *shem* (name). It is good reputation. How will that occur? By being in alignment with the character of the Most High God. There is no better reputation than being God's regent in the world.

Finally, "honor" is *tiph'arah*. It means beauty and glory. When we fulfill God's mission, His glory shines right through us. That is the glory of transparent creation. When God's glory radiates through His people, we become invisible. He gets the glory.

So, the Commandments are the instruction manual for spiritual magnetism. Follow them and you will attract others to Him. Don't follow them and your magnetic quality will be passed to someone else. It's up to you.

32.

*You are our **letter**, written in our hearts, known and read by all men;* 2 Corinthians 3:2

The Company You Kept

Letter – It's a question of endorsement. Paul says that he could have used credentials, certificates, resumes or letters of credit. But they are unnecessary. Why? Because Paul's real endorsement comes from those whom he mentored in Yeshua Christ. If you really want to know the character of a man, look at those who follow him.

I wonder if we would be comfortable with such a claim.

Can you point to the ones who follow you as endorsements for your life? Can you demonstrate your integrity, credibility and covenant character by doing nothing more than pointing to those who come after you? We say that the apple doesn't fall far from the tree. What we mean, of course, is that the fruit resembles the fruit tree. Could I look at the ones you are most closely associated with and see them display characteristics that tell me what kind of person you are?

In our Greek-based world, we like to think that a man stands on his own. We want to believe that my *personal* standards are not to be confused with those of my closest associates. But that isn't Paul's point of view. Paul is so confident in his discipleship of others that he can point to them as evidence of his own walk with God. That's an amazing claim. It says that he has done such a thorough job of bringing others into alignment with what he believes and how he behaves that I am seeing Paul in his apprentices. Could I say that about myself? Have I done that kind of journeyman work with those who are under my care? Are my letters of recommendation inscribed on the hearts of others?

The Greek word here is *epistole*, the usual word for "letter," but here is it used as a synonym for *sustatikos*, (from the preceding verse). It means a letter of commendation. On a job application, this is the section called "References." Here's the insight that Paul gives us. A written letter of reference is simply a snap-shot of a person. It's usually a glowing recommendation about the person in question, but it doesn't really tell me much more than what I expected. What if my letter of recommendation was *your life*? What if I pointed to the transformation in *you* as my credentials. That really says something about me! If I am going to an effective biblical leader, if I am going to be a true servant-follower, then I must have *living* recommendation letters. I must have fruit that shows up in others. Without it, I'm just a poster child, no matter what the resume says.

The Hebrew worldview is a connected community. Everything touches everything. What I do today has ripple effects across the world far beyond my lifetime.

Just think of the impact of that Man Who hung on the cross. There is no such thing as an isolated person, a separate individual. What Paul says about his letters of recommendation is just as true for us. So, I ask you again, when you look at the lives of those closest to you, do you see the person that you really want to be?

33.

For we maintain that a man is justified by faith apart from **works** *of the Law.* Romans 3:28

Simple Ergonomics

Works – If I am reconciled to God by His credit-only gift, then what is the role of the Law? If God chooses me *before* I am obedient, they why give the Law at all? If justification is completely separate from my efforts, then doesn't the Law just confuse the whole issue?

Here's the shocking truth: the purpose of the Law is evangelistic. God desires our obedience *in order that* we will become His signposts in the world. In other words, the Law is not for believers. It is for unbelievers. The reason we keep the commandments is so that unbelievers will see what God is doing in our lives and turn to God. By keeping the Law, we allow God to bless us and use us to reach the rest of the world.

This is the only conclusion that we can draw. If the Law is not about earning righteousness, then keeping it has nothing to do with appeasing God. God doesn't need appeasement. But that doesn't mean the Law is useless. Everywhere you turn in the Bible, you are exhorted to be obedient. Yeshua is no different than Moses on this point. Keeping the commandments is critical. Why? Because unless you keep the commandments, you can't fulfill the mission that God has given you as one of His chosen. You can't be the city on the hill, the light on the lamp stand, the salt of the earth if there is no difference between the way you live and the way the world lives. In fact, you can't be God's human evangelistic instrument unless you live precisely according to His plan. That doesn't mean that you are just a good person. God doesn't need good people. You weren't a good person when He picked you. God needs sinners who are willing and able to live His way. God needs people who will follow the Law *in order to be useful to Him.*

James and Paul agree. If my faith isn't exhibited in active obedience (works), it's dead! It's good for nothing. The purpose of active obedience is *not* to get me to heaven. The purpose of active obedience is evangelism. This is God's simple *ergonomics*, from the word that Paul uses in this verse (*ergon*, Greek for "works"). Ergonomics is the study of work efficiency. That's why we have the Law. Following God's plan for living is the most efficient way to bring others to Him. Did you get that? Evangelism is not about preaching the message, handing out tracts or running crusades. That kind of evangelism is based in the Greek model of communicating information, what we call the "saving knowledge" of Yeshua Christ. God's plan is not about communicating information. It is about *living transformation.* St. Francis was right. Communicating the gospel is living in such a way that words are unnecessary. If you want to see others come to Yeshua, let them read your *life.* And the only way you can do that most effectively is to live according to God's instructions, in other words, follow the Torah.

You are saved by faith. You are used by works. Don't confuse the two – and don't ignore them either. God saved you to use you. Did you think that He rescued you so that you could go on vacation?

34.

Do we then nullify the Law through faith? May it never be! On the contrary, we **establish** *the Law.* Romans 3:31

Back to Moses

Establish – Christians tend to think that the death and resurrection of the Messiah means that the Law is no longer valid. Of course, this conclusion starts with the erroneous premise that the Law has something to do with appeasing God in the first place. Thinking that the Old Testament is a religion based on "works" leads directly to the current view that the New Testament is based in grace – and never the two shall meet. Then we read a verse like this one. Suddenly our conclusions don't look so solid.

Paul uses the Greek verb *histemi* here. It means, "to cause to stand, to confirm, to make permanent, to make enduring." That certainly doesn't sound like the Law is no longer valid, does it? In fact, Paul confronts this error.

Is the Law nullified? Never! Grace makes the purpose of the Law possible. Grace *confirms* the Law!

How can this be? Doesn't the New Testament teach that the death of Christ is the end of the Law? Doesn't Paul himself say that Christ is the end of law for righteousness to everyone who believes? Of course he does! The problem is that we think of "end" as termination rather than fulfillment. Christ is the fulfillment of what the Law is all about; namely living in a way that glorifies God so much that the world returns to Him. The Law points to Yeshua as the fulfillment of God's redemptive plan. Yeshua accomplishes His mission and satisfies the condition for righteous credit. But fulfillment does not mean finish. It means filled up. Yeshua "fills up" the Law by showing us what it was intended to do in His life. That does not set aside the Law as the means of evangelism. Faith justifies. Yeshua paid that price. But the Law sanctifies. Without righteous living, God's people can't fulfill their mission. So, says Paul, since faith brings me into the right relationship with God, I am now free to accomplish the mission God has for me – to let my obedience become the spiritual magnet it was meant to be. Grace establishes the Law as enduring part of the plan.

God made several covenants with His chosen. He established a covenant with Noah. He established a covenant with Moses. He established a covenant with Abraham. The sign of Noah's covenant endures. Rainbows appear confirming it. The sign of the covenant with Abraham endures. The faith-nation of Israel still exists. And God treats the covenant with Moses no differently. The Law endures. Yeshua Himself told us that not one letter of the Word of God would disappear even if the world stopped existing.

It's time to set the record straight, at least for those who think that the New Testament has no regard for the Law. Of course the Law doesn't save us. It never did, even from the beginning. It was never *intended* to save us. God redeemed Israel out of Egypt *before* He gave the covenant to Moses. The Law has a different purpose. That purpose is anchored in witnessing to the world. Yeshua showed us exactly what the purpose of the Law was when He lived a sinless life. It was to draw all men to Himself. So, is that what you're doing with the Law? Are you living according to the covenant to draw all men to God in Christ? Or have you forgotten why God gave the Law in the first place?

35.

*to the church of God which is at Corinth, to those who have been sanctified in Christ Yeshua, **saints** by calling* 1 Corinthians 1:2

Effective Inefficiency

Saints – When it comes to mass marketing, God doesn't seem to know much about getting the message out. If the fate of the human race really depends on knowing the truth about Yeshua, why doesn't God use more effective techniques? After all, how hard would it be for God to display a billboard across the sky, or send an internal e-mail to everyone on the planet, or cause some physical phenomenon that would undeniably convince the world of Yeshua' divinity? If the message is so important, why hide it away in the backwaters of history?

If these questions have never occurred to you, perhaps you haven't felt the agony of seeing people you know and love miss a vital relationship with God simply because they never had overwhelming evidence. If God is really not willing for any to perish, then why doesn't He just make a booming announcement?

The answer to all these serious concerns is found in the difference between effective and efficient. Ultimately, it's the difference between a Greek system that believes in communicating information and a Hebrew system that believes in causing transformation. If my worldview is Greek, then my evangelism will focus on the transfer of information. I will attempt to get others to understand what I think. I will appeal to others to come to a rational belief about the Christ. Of course, since the whole world needs this information, I will look for the most *efficient* ways to disseminate it.

Those efficient ways usually involve some sort of mass marketing. They end up in television and radio preaching, big campaigns, tracts, sinner's prayers and bait-and-switch techniques. The goal is to communicate the information to as many people as possible in the shortest amount of time with the least amount of effort.

All of this is noble. All of this is spiritually-minded. It just doesn't happen to be the method that God uses. God chooses to focus on *transformation*, not information. To do that, God chose a method that is gloriously effective but pitifully inefficient. God uses *saints*. The Greek word, *hagiois*, is applied to *all* believers. It's not a special category for the top of the spiritual ladder. If the Corinthians, with all of their real problems, are called saints, then obviously God considers you and I saints as well. These ordinary people have been chosen by God, set apart through Christ (sanctified), in order to bring others into the Kingdom. How do they do that? By demonstrating the character of God in the life they live. Sure, they talk about it, but what really matters from the Hebraic perspective is the demonstration of godliness in my ordinary behavior. If I want *effectiveness*, then I will need a lot more than simply words. I will need to model transformation and invite others to copy me. Oh, yes, and by the way, godliness is not limited to good ethics. Godliness means following God's instructions for living in all the areas of my life.

So, here's the question. Are you practicing the Greek method of efficient evangelism or are you living the Hebrew process of effective transformation? Only one works for the long run. Only one satisfies the requirement of *perseverance*.

36.

*and my word and my preaching was not in moving words of human wisdom, but in **proof** of the Spirit and of power.* 1 Corinthians 2:4

Back to Basics

Proof – "That was a great sermon, preacher. It moved me." Yes, that's what we want when we go to church. We want *moving* oratory. We want inspired eloquence in the pulpit. We want to be mentally entertained. It's unlikely that we would stick around to hear Paul speak because Paul tells us straight out that he didn't use moving words or demonstrate intellectual prowess. Paul had another purpose in mind. Not entertaining information but engaging transformation. Paul was all about proof.

What does this Greek word, *apodeixis,* mean? What is

proof? The first thing we must notice is that Paul's idea of proof cannot be the Greek concept of compelling argument. That is precisely what Paul *denies*! He didn't come with carefully crafted apologetics based in human wisdom. We have plenty of that, don't we? Books, tapes, video, seminars – it goes on and on – compelling rational arguments that attempt to convince us of correct understanding. In all of my years, I have never met anyone who became a follower of Yeshua on the basis of an intellectual argument. But that doesn't seem to dissuade us from using this approach, does it?

Paul offers a different method. He comes with *proof*. Now, if Paul's *proof* is not eloquent arguments and compelling reasons, then what is it? The answer is found in the Hebrew equivalent of *apodeixis*. This Greek word means "manifestation or demonstration." The Hebrew equivalent would be *hayah* – to come into being, to be manifest, to be. In other words, Paul's version of proof is the manifestation of life in the Spirit with power. It's much more than being a good person. It's the demonstration of God's action in and through me. Proof is God showing up in power. Proof is miraculous intervention, palpable presence of the Spirit and real transformation in the lives of disciples. Proof is what we find over and over in the New Testament church, and in the Old Testament church. Proof is what happens when God is in the midst. It's not words. It's action.

Paul didn't need stimulating arguments. He came with the power of God. Things happened. Things that couldn't be explained away. Jail doors were opened. Boys were brought back to life. People were healed. People were judged. Angels appeared. Dreams occurred. And everywhere there was prayer and praise.

Of course, it's nice to know about the evidence that demands a verdict. It's great to have an arsenal of arguments to combat Darwin or social immorality. It's fine to fiddle with figures and facts. But point me to the assembly that worships the God who comes in power and proof, and all the rest gets lost in the dust. If Paul says to the Corinthian church, a church with obvious flaws and failures, that God *manifested* power, then why don't we experience that kind of community now? Do you suppose it has something to do with leaning on human wisdom?

37.

*Now there were Jews living in Jerusalem, **devout** men, from every nation under heaven.* Acts 2:5

A Family Affair

Devout – Peter addressed the crowd and 3000 were added to the messianic community that day. Who were these people? The popular version suggests that these were non-believers, but that isn't what Luke tells us, nor is it what Peter says. Peter addresses 3000 *devout* Jews. The Greek word is *eulabes*. We might translate this as God-fearing men. It means those who rightly discerned and practiced proper attitudes and actions before God. In other words, these men were already *torah*-observant believers. Now you can understand why they had such a strong response to Peter's speech. They were following God in every detail of their lives. When they heard the truth about Yeshua, they immediately saw their guilt and repented.

Contemporary evangelistic methods like to point to Pentecost as the pattern for big crusades. It was a big day, no doubt, but it was not about reaching those outside the faith. It was not an attempt to preach to the lost. It was a day when "men of Israel" had their eyes opened to the rest of the story about the God they already served. In fact, the story of the expansion of the New Testament *ekklesia* is typically about going to those who were already worshipping the God of Israel and introducing them to the Messiah. In city after city, Paul goes to the synagogues to deliver his message. He rarely speaks to non-believers. Instead, his usual evangelistic effort focuses on those who worshipped the God of the Hebrew Bible. How else can you explain Paul's extensive use of Old Testament references and practices? You could draw the same conclusion from the writings of Peter, James and John.

Does this mean that there is no place for campaigns or crusades? Of course not! God draws men and women by all sorts of means. We do not dictate how God will act. If He wants to send a single prophet (Jonah) to an entire city, He is free to do so. However, if we are going to align ourselves with the New Testament pattern (and its Old Testament precedent), then we will have to pay a lot more attention to the process of intimate discipleship within Spirit-led communities. Our version of Paul's mission to the Gentiles overlooks the fact that nearly all of Paul's efforts were not with non-believers but rather with Jewish proselytes. They were Gentiles by birth, but they were already part of the community of Israel.

Evangelism today hardly bears any resemblance to the efforts of the early church. Today our outreach is focused on the "lost." We think of evangelism as the process of reaching the "unsaved" world for Christ. To do that, we adopt a Greek model of delivering correct information to as many as possible. We think that spreading the word is the equivalent of fulfilling the Great Commission. It's not. The Great Commission is about transforming lives through dedicated obedience and deliberate benevolence. It's a one-at-a-time delivery method because it can't be accomplished without long-term engagement. Did you notice that Paul often spent months or years with a Messianic community before he moved to the next city? A weekend blitz never crossed his mind. There are a lot of God-fearing men and women who need to know Yeshua. Pick one. Let them see your life poured out for them. That's evangelism.

38.

*And they say, "How could God **know**, and is there knowledge with the Most High?"* Psalm 73:11 (Robert Alter translation)

Absentee Landlord

Know – Put this verse into the ancient near-Eastern world. Is there *any* doubt that God knows? Of course not. God knows everything that happens. But in the ancient near-East, God (and the gods) don't really care. That's the conclusion of the wicked. So what if God comprehends all that happens on earth. He doesn't really care about all that human business. He is busy in heaven being God. On earth, He is an absentee landlord.

The conclusion of the wicked is more than justified. Think about the evidence. Wicked men are not immediately punished. In fact, sometimes they aren't punished at all. Lying, cheating, adultery, murder and all the other mortal sins continue unabated. Money buys immunity. And miracles? Well, they are explained by science. Only the weak-minded hold on to the idea of

God's involvement in the lives of men. Step back a few feet and you won't see any evidence for God in human history. You will see cause and effect, natural law, human will and fate. Nothing more.

Do you object? Do you still want to claim God is presently active? Then explain to me how a God of perfect goodness can allow so much human suffering? Explain to me why innocent children are tortured and die? Explain life's injustices? Where is God? Explain to me how it is that even I can commit sin after sin, day after day, and nothing happens? I can shake my fist at heaven, proclaim my own sovereignty and there is *no* reprisal. Where is God now?

Ancient near-Eastern religions absolutely believed that the gods existed and that they were responsible for life on earth. But the gods were fickle and self-absorbed. They didn't care what men did as long as it didn't interfere with their contentment. The wicked operated on the belief that God didn't pay attention to the tiny matters of human existence. Therefore, they were immune from prosecution, not because they were righteous but because there was no judgment. It is *exactly* the same today. Men still operate as if God doesn't care. How else can we explain that actions of the wicked? If divine judgment were instantaneous, no wicked act would even be contemplated. But since judgment doesn't seem to be in the cards at all, the only way to live in the world *successfully* is to get away with as much as you can – and then buy your way out of the rest.

This raises a question for believers: How do we know that God desires righteousness and punishes wickedness? Most of the time we can't point to tangible evidence. So how do we know? The answer is a paradigm shift. We *trust* what God says, even if we don't see the immediate evidence. That is the same as saying we have *faith* in Him. The statement that God cares about the actions of human beings is a statement of faith, not a conclusion from the evidence. It takes a change in paradigm to see the world this way. Perhaps that's why it is so difficult to explain to an outsider. "Come in and look at the world from my point of view. You will see it differently." Until the invitation is accepted, the wicked seem justified. Perhaps evangelism begins with despair over the lack of judgment instead of the offer for a wonderful plan.

Prayer

Prayer is the wine of the Spirit. Just like the finest of wines, it comes in many vintages. Unfortunately, the Church teaches neither how to pick a good wine nor how to enjoy the full variety of prayer. Most of us have lived on the common table wine from God's cellars. That's because most of us don't realize the rich-bodied vocabulary of prayer found in Hebrew. We have distilled everything to one word in English: prayer (Greek *proskuneo*). Greek provides us with a few words that cover the nuances of prayer, but in Hebrew there are literally dozens of words for prayer, revealing the subtleties of this engagement with the Spirit. God's wine cellars contain a wide array of vintages and varieties but most of us survive on a single mixed brew.

When the New Testament uses Greek words for prayer, these words are not used in the way classical Greek understands communication with the gods (or God). New Testament Greek finds its thought patterns in the LXX, the Greek used to translate the Hebrew Scriptures. This means that even though we find expressions for prayer in the New Tesament, we must attempt to understand them though the eyes of the Hebrew worldview. What we discover is that the Hebrew idea of prayer is much more tactile, more connected to ordinary life and human experience than it is contemplation and commuication with a transcendantal divinity.

In Hebrew, prayer is much like breathing. It is found in the most ordinary of human experiences in everyday life, in the range of emotions and, of course, in those glorified mountaintop encounters. When we examine the range of Hebrew expressions for what we categorize as prayer, we discover several important factors.

First, we find that emotions play a central role in the Hebrew idea of prayer. Unlike the Greeks, the Hebrews understood emotions as vehicles that brought them in contact with God. Emotions were the key to deeper life experience and in that experience, deeper appreciation of the Lord of life. The Greeks feared emotions, both good and bad ones, because emotions challenged the fundamental idea of human control. While the Greeks sought rational balance as a way to escape the pathos of emotions, the Hebrews sought life lived to the fullest, a pathway that engaged the full emotional spectrum. To *feel* is to engage in the life God has given us. To *feel* is to open the door for God's involvement. In this sense, to *feel* is to pray. If the Psalm provide any insight into life in the Spirit, they at least do this: they give us premission to *feel*.

Secondly, we find that prayer is more than set-aside ritual. In Hebraic terminology, prayer is the essence of being human. The rabbis taught that we are human insofar as we are in communication with our Creator. The man who does not pray is not a human being. He may be *homo sapiens*, but he is far from being what God intended. Prayer is more than communicating with God. Prayer is the vehicle that makes us human beings.

Finally, we find that prayer is not simply carefully crafted spiritual words expressed with appropriate ritual. In Scripture, prayer is growling, dancing, clapping, shouting (sometimes in anger), kneeling, weeping, arguing, collapsing and dozens of other actions. Prayer is *doing* something that connects me to the will of the Father, and this is not always verbal. Prayer's variety extends from the rich flavors of a Chateau Haut-Brion to the playful exhuberance of Sangria. By expanding our prayer vocabulary, we expand our appreciation for the multiple ways we adore our God.

1.

*Now we **pray to God** that you do no wrong* 2 Corinthians 13:7

What Only God Can Do

Pray to God – Just how much post-modern thought is infected with the consequences of a Greek worldview can be seen in our understanding of this simple Pauline statement. Even our prayers are tainted with unbiblical assumptions.

Paul uses the very rare phrase *euchometha pros ton Theon*. There is a lot involved in this phrase. *Euchometha* is a verb that means, "we ask, beseech, pray." It is associated with taking vows. The Hebrew root equivalent often involves formal temple prayer. Paul is using serious, holy language. But notice the second word in the phrase – *pros*. This preposition is primarily about direction. It can mean "toward" or "to," but here it has the nuance of a relationship of dependence. This is not prayer cavalierly cast toward heaven. This is prayer that utterly depends on God for its fulfillment. This is prayer of holy intercession.

Now think about what Paul says. He prays that, *as a result of God's sovereign action and in total dependence upon Him*, you will do not anything evil (*kakon meden*). It's too weak to suggest that Paul prays only to be sheltered from "wrongs." We lump everything excusable in that category. God is not protecting you from errors in your checkbook or failure to yield at a crosswalk. Paul prays that God will save you from *evil* in every form. And here's the kicker. If God doesn't act, you are doomed.

We don't think like this, much to our pity. We adopt a Greek view of prayer. We pray about those things that we think are beyond our control. We assume that God plays no role in those things that are within our control. So, we invoke the Deity, attempting to sway His options, when we no longer have any other influence. We endorse Seneca's comment: "It is foolish to pray for a right disposition when one can attain it oneself." Consequently, we take to God only those things that seem too difficult for us. Since we believe that we actually exercise control over our evil proclivities, it never crosses our minds that we would actually pray for *God* to keep us from evil. That is our business. With this twist, we neuter the hideousness of evil and deceive ourselves.

The Hebrew Paul knows better. Unless God deliberately intervenes in my nature, I will go astray. Only because of His divine mercy, grace and protection can I be spared the sin that lurks at my door. I am not capable of refraining from evil *unless God intervenes.*

Pray like a Hebrew. If God doesn't act, we are all lost. Nothing is really under my control except my need for Him.

2.

A voice is heard on the bare heights, the weeping and the **supplications** *of the sons of Israel; because they have perverted their way, they have forgotten the LORD their God.* Jeremiah 3:21

Basic Vocabulary

Supplications – This English word is a bit strange these days. We don't hear "supplications" very much in ordinary conversation. Perhaps that's why some Bibles translate this as "pleadings." The NIV uses the singular "pleading" but the noun is plural in the Hebrew text. This is the sound of many people, crying out with a single voice, each one bringing a fervent request before God. While the NIV helps, it still doesn't provide us with a readily understood, basic vocabulary of prayer. When was the last time you heard anyone say, "I have been pleading before the Lord?" No, we are more likely to think of words like asking, making requests, or seeking favor. All of these nuances are found in the Hebrew *tachanun*. But there is also a bit more. For that little extra, we need to do some digging.

Tachanun comes from a Hebrew root *chanan*. You might recognize the name *Hannah* from this root word. *Chanan* is the basic word for "favor" and is used many times in the expression, "found favor in the eyes of." This word is almost always translated into Greek as *charis* – grace. To find favor in the eyes of the Lord is to experience His grace. A petitioner can find favor in the eyes of another human being, but God is the only one Who can actually give favor, according to the Bible. This word is always used of relationships. You can't find favor with the stock market or the planets. Grace is always personal.

Two more elements are needed. First, *chanan* is not passive. It is the active, deliberate, voluntary choice of the stronger person to help the weaker person. Secondly, favor is incompatible with judgment. God cannot grant favor and at the same time pour out His wrath.

Now, how does all this help us understand a basic vocabulary word for prayer? This word teaches us that anxious, fervent requests made to God are quite literally attempts to see Him smile. If we could see His face in prayer, we would be looking for a sign of delight. We would want to catch the hint of acceptance. And the best part is this: God loves to smile and He smiles most often when He gives.

Cast away the mental imagery of a stern-faced cosmic judge. Substitute instead the radiant countenance of a loving mother, tenderly listening to the cries of her helpless child (Isaiah 66:13). Is there a bond deeper than that? Bring your pleadings to God. She's listening.

3.

*And it shall come about that when he cries out to Me, I will hear him, for I am **gracious**.* Exodus 22:27

Prayer's Assumption

Gracious – We come to God in prayer because we believe God is willing to give. That's the bottom line. If your god is reluctant, petulant, temperamental or immoveable, then you need to add this Hebrew word to your prayer vocabulary: *chanan*. God is gracious. But *chanan* has some implications that you may not have realized. God *gives* His grace. You do not earn it. You cannot negotiate it. You can't barter, bully, demand, claim or cajole God's grace. It is entirely His to freely give as He sees fit. Prayer is not a negotiating tool. It is an expression of human need, placed in the hands of the sovereign God. This means that prayer is followed by acceptance. There is no place for disappointed rejection of the Giver. When I come to God in prayer, I have no leverage with Him. Anything and everything He grants is pure gift.

There is another implication behind *chanan*. Since

graciousness belongs to God, all His gifts of grace also belong to Him too. God's gifts never transfer ownership to me. The gifts I receive are still His, and His alone. This idea is expressed in the ancient Semitic idiom, "to find favor in the eyes of the Lord." The favor I seek is *not* mine. The favor belongs to the one who grants it. I am merely the recipient of someone else's good will. Without voluntary benevolence, I walk away empty-handed. But even if I rise from my knees with God's gift in hand, it is still *His* favor. What I receive from God continuously belongs to Him. I am merely the temporary borrower.

Now we know why Paul tells us he can be content with much or with little (Philippians 4:11). The favor he receives is *God's*, not Paul's. Since the owner is the King of kings, whatever the King decides to lend to one of His children is entirely just and entirely good. When I understand *chanan*, my prayers result in contentment. God answers – always. And His answer is always enough for me.

Right?

4.

*Then he will **pray** to God, and He will accept him, that he may see His face with joy, and He may restore His righteousness to man.* Job 33:26

Verbal Advantage

Pray – Something quite unexpected occurs when the Old Testament speaks of praying. The only verb that actually means, "to pray" is this word, *athar*. It is used *less than twenty times* in the entire Old Testament.

Since there are more than 500 prayers in the Hebrew Bible, this seems quite odd until we realize that the Old Testament has a very different outlook on prayer.

Nevertheless, *athar* is still important (every word is important☺). But when we look at *athar*, we find something else unusual. In its root, *athar* means, "to cry out with a loud voice for deliverance." Such cries are always addressed to God. But *athar* is not used to describe the actual petition. Instead, Hebrew uses a whole host of other words to actually describe what the one who is praying wants. It might be a child (Genesis 25:21) or deliverance (Exodus 8:8), but *athar* is not used for prayer that focuses attention on the request. Instead, *athar* focuses attention on the Provider of the hoped-for request. In the Old Testament, *athar* is the word for praying *to God*. The actual request is secondary.

Does this make a difference in your prayers? When you come to the Lord, praying, are you focused on the hoped-for result of your prayer? When you pray for healing, does your attention fix on the repaired body? When you pray for financial stability, are you focused on the bank account or the job? When you pray for a spouse or a child, is your mind-eye occupied with a picture of that person? All of that is quite natural – and biblical – but it is not the realm of *athar*. If we are going to pray according to this infrequent verb, then we will need to remember that God accepts the one who prays with only the Provider in mind. To pray *to God* means that my prayer is focused on God Himself. I pray to my Sovereign Lord, the Creator, the Sustainer of life, the Alpha and Omega of all history, the compassionate, merciful and gracious King of kings. My God can and will intervene according to His plan, but *athar* tells me that Who He is, is far more important than what He does. I pray (using *athar*) in order to seek His face and find favor there. I pray (*athar*) so that the joy of His countenance turns toward me and He will restore my standing before Him.

Why is *athar* the only verb for the act of prayer? Perhaps it's because the true essence of prayer is not about us at all. It's about God and God alone. Perhaps, when I finally understand prayer, all I really need to know is that God is good.

5.

*Nevertheless, You heard the voice of my supplications when I **cried** to You.* Psalm 31:22

A Weeping Word

Cried – There is no better place to discover the range of prayer than in the Psalms. In fact, a great number of the Psalms are actually called prayers. But guess what? Yesterday's word "to pray" (*athar*) does not occur a single time in all the Psalms. Instead, we find words like this one – *shawa* – to cry out for help. In the English translation, *shawa* is transformed into a verbal expression ("I cried"), but in Hebrew it is a special form that implies two important things: first, it is an *intense, personal expression* and secondly, it is *a continuous action*. In fact, this form of the root is not treated like a verb at all. It is treated like a noun.

What does this bit of grammar mean? It means that the crying out is not something that *accompanies* prayer. It *is* the prayer! Treated as a noun, this word names the thing called prayer and what it names is my intense, personal, emotional, continuous crying out for help. My prayer is the agony I lift to God. I may weep. I may not. But the fact that I bring my cry (noun) before God is my prayer in a weeping word.

Most of the time prayer in the Old Testament is vocalized. It is spoken prayer, not the "silent" prayers that dominate our idea of speaking to God. In fact, the expectation that prayer will be spoken and heard is so strong that the priest condemns Hannah for her silence, believing that she is not praying at all. The Bible never explains this assumption. But maybe we can add some insight.

The vast majority of prayers in the Psalms use words like *shawa*. These words are sighing, groaning, roaring, grieving, pouring out one's soul, thanking, praising, magnifying, singing, shouting and rejoicing. Can you imagine any of these acts done *silently*? The point of these words is that they express overflowing emotions. They are not intended to be bottled up. God wants to hear them out loud because out loud they identify you as His dependent child for the entire world to hear.

But, of course, we have opted for order. We can't have everyone praying out loud all at the same time. It would be chaos (really? – then who are we praying to?) and confusion (did we think God couldn't sort it out?). But mostly it would upset our impotent, milk-toast version of prayer where we sort of fiddle around while some paid professional utters eloquently practiced verbiage for *us* to hear and approve. You get a choice. You can pray like the Pharisees – sound and fury signifying nothing – or you can pray like David - out loud, from the heart, to God alone, in continuous, personal crying.

I recommend *shawa*.

6.

*They have heard that I **groan**; there is no one to comfort me.* Lamentations 1:21

Oppressed Prayer

Groan – If this word has never been part of your prayer vocabulary, I wonder if you have really experienced fatal dependence. Every biblical character whom God used to accomplish His purpose seems to have been intimately familiar with *anaw* – the groaning prayer. Even Yeshua, who certainly was never outside the will of the Father, had times of praying agony – and not just in the Garden of Gethsemane! Until our inner spirits confront *anaw* prayers, we do not come to grips with the desperation of life.

Who groans? The Bible uses this word when Israel faced oppression and despair in Egypt. We find the word when the wicked occupy positions of political and social power. *Anaw* is the companion of those who are treated unjustly. It accompanies descriptions of people who are judged by God. It is the corollary of corruption, addiction and self-serving pleasures. Animals groan over Man's wickedness (Joel 1:18). Even the earth knows *anaw* (Romans 8:22). In a creation subject to futility, *anaw* hides around every corner.

But that does not mean it is to be avoided.

God uses *anaw* to bring us to the place where no one can comfort – except the Lord. *Anaw* identifies us with the destructive power of sin. It drives us to brokenhearted pleas for God's justice. It reminds us of our constant need of His righteousness. It destroys our self-confident

106

arrogance. It unlocks our need for compassion and mercy. Let the agony come. Let me sweat drops of blood in the face of a universe gone mad. Then I will know the heart of my Savior. I will recognize my desperate undoing. I will know what the jailer knew – that only God can save. *Anaw* is the sister of *'atsav* (sorrow), introduced to us when Man decided to play God in Genesis 3. When you feel the twinge of *anaw* and when you know its overwhelming torrent, do not run for cover. Groan to God. He listens.

7.

*When I kept silent about my sin, my body wasted away through my **groaning** all day long.* Psalm 32:3

When The Lion Speaks

Groaning – We have all kept quiet about sin. And we have all suffered the consequences. David is absolutely right (and he would know). When I close the closet door on my sin, when I cover it up and pretend it will go away, I might as well drink poison. The body knows something is wrong. Today we would call it psychosomatic. In David's day, he used a much more descriptive term – she'agah. But don't be misdirected by the English translation "groaning." This word is the sound of a lion's roar. It is not a muffled groan. It is a terrifying howl, a deep, ominous growl.

"When I kept silent about my sin, the lion inside was let loose. My body howled in my agony all day long." That is the prayer of torment. It is the prayer of a man who refuses to bring confession to the light. And it is eating him alive.

Did you expect the biblical vocabulary of prayer to include

the roar of the lion? Probably not. You probably thought prayer was quiet adoration, acceptable accolades, timid petitions and occasional outbursts of thanksgiving. The Hebrew view of prayer is a lot more uncivilized. It is emotional, overwhelming, dynamic, unpredictable and terrifying. It even includes the king of beasts released within the beast of kings. Wherever the heart travels, prayer should be there.

Sin will not be hidden. The Bible is quite clear about that. When your mind tries to cover it up, your heart roars like a caged lion. It howls for release. The only prayer that sets the lion free is the prayer, "Lord, have mercy on me, a sinner."

Let the lion out today. When it comes to confession, pray with a roar.

8.

*You will have plenty to eat and be satisfied and **praise** the name of the LORD your God.* Joel 2:26

Prayer Ratio

Praise – The most common Hebrew word associated with prayer is *palal*. In most contexts, it means "praise." Think about that for a minute. Hebrew prayer is eight times more likely to be about praise than about petition. Even when *palal* is not used for praise, it is used for intercession. That means if *palal* is not adoration for God than it is intervention for another.

Do your prayers have the same ratio as the Hebrew mindset? Are you eight times more likely to burst into praise or make intercession for someone else than you are

to pray for your own needs? In the Gentile world, this ratio is rare indeed. Have you ever wondered why?

We live in a culture that is very much the product of a different worldview than those ancient Semitic people whom God chose as His vehicle of salvation. Roots of individualism and human achievement dominate our worldview. Sandwiched between political autonomy and personal freedom, we have come to believe that the center of the universe is *me*. This personally focused orientation expresses itself in all kinds of ways, even religious ones. We even pray with an "I, me, mine" attitude. Do you need some examples?

When did you last intercede for your *enemies*?

When did you last praise God for eight benefits before you made a single request?

When did you last thank Him for every single trouble you are experiencing?

When did you honor Him for every single success you enjoy?

When was the last time your church spent eight times more minutes praising Him than sticking to the order of service?

When was the last time you spent eight times as much time glorifying His name in your daily devotion than you did telling Him all your troubles? (And, by the way, isn't it interesting that we call this time "devotion" when in fact it is usually nothing more than complaints and requests?)

Want to pray like Moses or Daniel or Elijah? Want to have fellowship with the Father like Paul or even Yeshua? You'll need a change of perspective. You'll need a transformation of mind. You'll need some adjustment in the prayer ratio. Right?

9.

*A **psalm** of praise, of David* (notation before Psalm 145:1)

What The Title Says

Psalm - Our title, "Psalms," comes from the title found in the Greek translation of the Old Testament (the Septuagint). In fact, it is a *transliteration* of the Greek word *psalmoi*. That means the Greek word is *not* translated. It is simply phonetically moved into our language. Since it is plural in Greek, we get the plural English word *psalms*. Transliteration is not uncommon when it comes to biblical terms. Baptism is a transliteration of the Greek *baptizo*. Hallelujah is a transliteration of the Hebrew *hallelujah*. But what would happen if we did translate these expressions? How would a translation help us understand what these words really mean?

Hallelujah actually means "Praise Yah" (the shortened version of Yahweh). *Baptizo* really means, "to be immersed." But, what about *psalmoi*? In Hebrew, the title of this book is *sefer tehillim*. What does it mean? It means, in translation, "book of praises." David uses the singular expression as the title of Psalm 145 (*tehillah le-david*), literally, "a praise of David," not as the NASB translates "a psalm of praise, of David." The expression, "psalm of praise," is redundant.

There are 150 psalms in the collection. The title of all of these psalms is properly *tehillim* – praises. Every psalm, no matter what its content or emotional tenor, is considered a *praise* to God. Let that sink in for a while. There are *tehillim* of remorse, of joy, of confession, of complaint, of struggle, of victory, of glorification and of questioning. All are *tehillim*. All are praises.

How can all of these be praises? It's because the Hebrew mind views all of life in the hands of God. There is no compartmentalization. There is no "religious" sphere. God made Man to enjoy Him – in everything. All of life is a praise to the Creator, the Sovereign Ruler, the Compassionate Father. In the final analysis, your life is either a praise or a problem.

Now go write a psalm.

"Preach the gospel at all times, and when necessary, use words." (St. Francis of Assisi)

10.

O give thanks to the LORD, for He is good; for His lovingkindness is everlasting. 1 Chronicles 16:34

What We Know

O Give Thanks - David knew what he was doing when he assigned Asaph the task of giving thanks to God. Asaph's prayer, recorded in 1 Chronicles 16:8 to 36 is a powerful example all of us. In the final stanzas, we find this single word, *hodu* (from the root *yadah*). Jews would read this phrase as *hodu la adonai*, substituting the word "Lord" for God's name (Yahweh) out of respect. You might consider remembering this phrase. It introduces us to another aspect of the Hebrew idea of prayer because the root word, *yadah*, means an acknowledgement of what is true about God, expressed in praise and thanksgiving.

Yadah is also found in Leviticus 26:40 where it implies a right relationship before God. Prayer is pointless if the one praying stands outside of God's goodness. Prayer assumes that I am obedient to the faithful God. God doesn't answer the prayers of rebels. *Yadah* shows up in the prayers of the whole congregation (Psalm 100:4), but it is also a part of prayers for personal rescue (Psalm 88:11).

This is what we know: God is good. My prayers begin and end with this fact. God is good. Prayer flows over and around and through this proclamation. God is good. When I pray, I confess and acknowledge the goodness of God. That's really the reason that I pray. If God were not good, prayer would be pointless.

Hodu la adonai is well worth incorporating into your prayer. In fact, without it prayer is worse than pointless. It is worthless. In the end, all prayer depends on the goodness of God and all prayer accepts God's response as the expression of His goodness. Prayer confesses that I *don't know* anything except what I know for sure: God is good. He always acts according to His character. His answers are always in line with Who He is. Prayer is my way of saying, "Father, may Your goodness be the guide of my life. Not my will, but Yours be done, for I know only this – that You are good."

11.

*Let everything that has breath **praise** the Lord. **Praise** the Lord!* Psalm 150:6

The Last and the First

Praise – In the end, it's *haleluya*. If my life amounts to nothing more than praise for God, it will have reached its zenith. In fact, David tells us that the purpose of *all* creation is to praise Him. The Hebrew is beautifully poetic: *kol han shama tehalel ya haleluya.* The last word of the last *tehillah* of the book of praise can be nothing other than *haleluya.*

Think about the biggest picture of your life. It's not the picture of your years here on earth. It's not about your achievements, your reputation, your legacy or your beliefs. The biggest picture of your life is about the praise of your creator. You exist because He cared. You have a purpose because He is willing to include you. You matter because He redeemed you. In the end, all that you are is designed to praise Him. So, David says, let *everything* that has breath utter the Hebrew words *tehalel ya.*

Have you considered your life from the biggest picture point of view? Are your thoughts, actions, expression, emotions, purposes and plan worthy of His praise? Anything less is demeaning to the God of all creation. Anything less is a form of rebellion and idolatry. You were created to praise Him. Anything except praise denies the purpose of your existence.

When we stop long enough on our mad rush toward self-significance to consider the biggest picture, our preoccupation with self-actualization is unveiled. What arrogance to think that our agendas for life are so important that we will not yield to Him! Who do we think we are? God? Well, yes, unfortunately, until we recognize the cosmic nature and origin all of praise, we really do think we are gods. We might be more polite than to say it out loud, but our behavior speaks the truth. When did we last consider whether or not our concerns exhibited praise for the King of glory? Most likely we keep on keeping on without a single second's pause to ask about praise. Yes, life is full of frenzy and fury. It is out of sync with its Creator. But that is hardly an excuse for any breathing being. Only those who are comfortable praising Him will find heaven a joyful place. This life is practice for the concert.

12.

*I remember the days of old; I **meditate** on all Your doing; I muse on the work of Your hands* Psalm 143:5

Soul Prayer

Declare – Prayer proclaims. In praise, in cries, in pleas, in exultation, we have discovered that most prayer in the Hebrew world is vocalized. Prayer is the personal, announced testimony of the grace of God. Once that concept is firmly locked in place, then we discover another layer of prayer – the prayer of silent speech.

This verse uses the Hebrew verb *hagah*. The same verb is found in the introduction to the *sefer tehillim* (the

Psalms). In Psalm 1:2, the writer says that the righteous man "meditates on the Law day and night." It has the same meaning in Joshua 1:8 and Psalm 63:6. But in many Psalms and the book of Isaiah, *hagah* describes a different kind of sound. In Isaiah 8:19, 16:7, 31:4 and 38:14, *hagah* describes the mutterings of witches, the moans of judgment, growl of a lion and the cooing of doves. *Hagah* is not the sound of words, carefully articulated in proper grammar and syntax. *Hagah* is the sound of the human

spirit when words fail. And when *hagah* is applied to prayer, we are transported from our carefully constructed containers of organized observation into a world where the mystery of God overshadows us. We utter sounds that never found their way into dictionaries. We groan our troubles, project our delight and move lips to our deepest thoughts. We come in contact with something Paul describes in Romans: " but the Spirit Himself intercedes for us with groaning too deep for words."

Hannah knew this kind of prayer. So overwhelmed with sorrow, she could not vocalize her agony. David knew this kind of prayer. He must have experienced it when he prayed for the life of his unborn child after the adultery with Bathsheba. He certainly wrote about it in many psalms.

Hagah is not the common verb for speaking. There are many other choices in Hebrew if I wish only to describe intelligible, audible sound. *Hagah* implies something else. It is the language of the soul. It may be completely silent, inarticulate noise or actual speech, but it is always the vocabulary of a soul consumed with the things of God.

Hebrew prayer is incomplete without *hagah*. Meditation is not sufficient to describe the range of *hagah* prayer. But consecration is. When we reach the end of ourselves, when there is nothing left of human being to fill the chasm of our hearts, then we are ready for the abyss of *hagah* where God can speak His own language of love in words we cannot comprehend. "How I delight to meditate on You, O Lord!"

Leave some room for *hagah*.

13.

I remember the days of old; I meditate on all Your doing; I **muse** *on the work of Your hands* Psalm 143:5

Customer Complaints

Muse – If you want to see the primary meaning of this word, you'll have to look at the Bible's longest complaint – the book of Job. Job 7:11 says, "Therefore, I will not restrain my mouth. I will speak in the anguish of my spirit. I will *complain* in the bitterness of my soul." Job uses the verb *siyach*. He refuses to remain passively silent while his world falls apart. In spite of his profession of obedience, he has reached the breaking point. Now he wants to know, "Why, God?"

How does a word like this get into the language of prayer? Isn't prayer supposed to honor God, glorify Him, trust in Him and *accept* what God decides? With the background of *siyach* in Job's accusation, why would David use the same word in a verse that introduces a pantheon of praise? The verb *siyach* offers an umbrella of meanings generally determined by context: "to ponder, converse, utter, complain, meditate, speak and, finally, pray." Except for "complain", we can easily see how these meanings are linked. If it weren't for the fact that "complain" is the primary meaning, we might just note it as an aberration. But we can't. There is something about "complain" that is essential to the use of this verb. We need to think a little deeper.

Bring your complaint to God. Then notice what is implied in this action. First, you have to assume that God can do something about it. No one complains to a customer service department that is closed for business. Secondly, you have to assume that God will listen. Then you'll notice that a complaint is usually carefully considered before it is voiced. There is some thought given to a formal complaint. Finally, complaints before God are one of those Hebrew kinds of prayers that make us uncomfortable, but are consistently voiced in the Bible. If praying is like breathing, so much a part of life that without it I suffocate, then there will be plenty of times when my breathing is rapid and heated. I will sometimes pray in *anger*. I will sometimes pray in *frustrated lament*. And I will sometimes pray in *accusation*. Read the psalms without your evangelically tinted glasses. You will find all these emotions, and many more. *Siyach* is me standing before God *just as I am*, even when my emotions boil over.

Then I discover something else. God still loves me. He would rather have me come complaining than not come at all. Why? Because He delights in my interaction with Him. When I pray with *siyach*, I am revealing my raw self. It's OK. God can handle it. He's an expert in customer service.

14.

*so that I may **declare** all Your praises in the gates of the daughter of Zion*   Psalm 9:14

The Arithmetic of Prayer

Declare – When David declares the praises of God, he uses the Hebrew verb *saphar*. It implies a great deal more than a simple announcement. *Saphar* is the verb for "to count." To *declare* all God's praises is to *count* everything that praises Him, one by one. This is biblical arithmetic. In fact, the Greek equivalent of *saphar* is *arithmein* (that makes it pretty obvious, doesn't it?).

Prayer without arithmetic is like painting without a palette. It all turns out gray. Prayer includes the *counting* of all God has done, not just for me but also for all of creation. Notice that David does not say, "Count all Your blessings." David is much more spiritually attuned than those who simply look for God's personal benevolence. David is interested in counting all God's praises (*tehillim*). And what sort of things count as praises? Well, David elaborates in another *tehillah*, Psalm 111:10. It's a familiar theme in an unfamiliar context. Reverence for God is the beginning of *all* human wisdom. All who keep His commandments are benefited. And His praise endures forever. In Psalm 111, David helps us see that it is God's very character that deserves praise. If I want to count what counts for praise, I will begin with these two things: 1 – God is my sovereign. Until I understand, acknowledge and live by that fact, I am foolish; and 2 – God is good. Therefore, all my discernment of the correct pathway depends on living according to His commandments. No wonder David praises God just for Who He is.

Already in this New Year you have undoubtedly had enough time to know that you are not sovereign lord of your life. Not everything has gone your way. Praise God for that. He has something far more significant in mind for those who follow Him. Now when you pray, instead of issuing God a summons to explain your situation, start with arithmetic. Count out His praises. Oh, and by the way, His praises extend to all that He is sovereign over and all that is connected with His goodness. It's a long list. If you're going to declare the praises of God today, you might not have time for any of the other things that were on your petition list. But don't worry. He knows what you need.

15.

Abraham said to his young men, "Stay here with the donkey, and I and the lad will go over there; and we will **worship** *and return to you."* Genesis 22:5

The Prayer of Faith

Worship – How unfortunate it is that we are confined with this English translation of the verb *shachah*. Yes, it's true that Abraham took Isaac to the mountain to *worship*. But because we gloss over the underlying imagery, we fail to see what Abraham really has in mind. *Shachah* is a word that describes an act of obeisance. It is the word for prostrating oneself on the ground before a superior. But it is not simply an outward, physical act. *Hishtachah* describes an inner attitude of worship even when there is no associated outward ritual. We see this attitude in the servant of Abraham when he meets Rebekah (Genesis 24:26). We find it in the Ten Commandments (Exodus

20:5), in David's desire to seek God's face (Psalm 5:7) and in the final purpose for all men (Isaiah 66:3). Yes, it's worship, but it is not the kind of worship that we typically find in today's congregations. *Shachah* is your soul, spirit, mind and strength facedown on the ground, in humble adoration, and total commitment to the only One Who is worthy of worship. *Shachah* is prayer permeating life.

The paramount place of *shachah* is verified by the fact that this Hebrew verb is translated by the Greek *proskuneo*, used throughout the New Testament for "to worship, to prostrate oneself before." Prayer in the biblical paradigm is worship! Worship in the biblical paradigm is prayer! Now we can appreciate the fact that one version of the Hebrew Scriptures defines Man as the *praying* being and considers prayer the vehicle that makes a man human.

How could it be otherwise? When we come before the Lord of hosts, we are undone. Isaiah knew it. So should we. There is no prayer (and no worship) without bowing down. Any man who thinks he can *stand* before the Lord has never understood Who God is. It's time to leave behind our preposterous assumptions about "praise and worship" and realize that worshipping the God of all creation occurs in prostration. There is a very good reason why the fathers of the faith fell to their faces. Our lack of humility and fearfulness before the God of life only compounds our spiritual ineffectiveness. We have not because we do not ask from the dirt. When prayer takes over your life, you will find yourself face down, terrified. Then He will gently lift your eyes to His – and declare you His friend.

16.

By faith, Jacob, as he was dying, blessed each of the sons of Joseph, and **worshipped**, *leaning on the top of his staff.* Hebrews 11:21

The Greek Equivalent

Worshipped - Jacob certainly wasn't Jimmy Hendrix, but you would be on the right track if you thought of this word with the lyrics "kiss the sky." *Proskuneo* literally describes throwing a kiss toward someone adored. You can imagine standing next to the road as the king passes by in his golden chariot. Flowers and kisses are thrown in his path to demonstrate affection – and obedience. If you come from Italian or Greek or many other cultural backgrounds, greetings are often accompanied by kisses on the cheeks. But worship is more than affectionate salutation. It is the sign of surrender, of prostration before a sovereign ruler, and of humility.

Don't imagine that worship is repeated choruses or hands held upward or vocalized praises. Worship, at least as far as *proskuneo* is concerned, is face-to-the-floor homage in utter abandonment of one's own desires. Jacob worshipped *leaning on his staff*, a translation that comes from the Greek Old Testament of Genesis 47:31 (through a mistaken reading of the Hebrew *mattehu*, meaning "bed"). Jacob is on his deathbed but he knows enough to turn his face toward the ground and submit to his God.

Notice that the author says that Jacob worshipped *by faith*. So must we. We do not live in the full reality of the Kingdom. Therefore, we submit, bow and serve looking toward the time when the Kingdom will become the *only* visible reality. Worship today is based on *hope*, just as it was in the days of Jacob. Worship is our prostrated declaration that God will prevail, that His justice will come, that His kingdom will reign and that His Son will return. We worship because we trust that His word is true and all that He says will come to be.

Jacob never saw the full reality promised by the God he served. So far, neither have you or I. But that does not lessen any part of the promise. Quite the opposite. Christ's delay strengthens my worship because He gives me opportunity to prepare, to confess, to repent, to transform and to redeem this world for His purposes. I used to think that accepting Yeshua as my Savior should be quite enough. I wanted to be instantly whisked away to heaven. Now I know better. Worship begins in the valley of the promise. That's where kissing the ground beneath His feet matters most.

17.

With all prayer and petition **pray** *at all times in the Spirit*
Ephesians 6:18

New Testament Summary

Pray – All of the ideas associated with prayer in the Old Testament are captured in the New Testament with a single word. That word is *proseuchomai*. It covers thanksgiving, confession, adoration, intercession and supplication. Notice that it is *not* the same as the word for "worship." Worship involves a mental and often physical attitude before a sovereign ruler. Prayer is the result of worship. Prayers without the right attitude are fairly useless. Yeshua commented on such prayers when He pointed out the hypocrisy of the proud Pharisee's prayer. Worship brings humility, and in the New Testament, humility is the foundation of prayer.

Proseuchomai is not the only word used for asking in the New Testament, but it is the word that is used when the author wants to emphasize the fact that the request is made to God. Fundamentally, this Greek word means, "calling on God" no matter what the content of the prayer happens to be. You might think of it is the summary of all our conversation with God. If you talk with the Father, you would use the Greek word *proseuchomai*.

Notice that Paul exhorts us to converse with the Father *at all times*. You might be easily discouraged by such a command. After all, there are plenty of times in human experience when God is not uppermost in our minds. Of course, if we begin to practice His presence, we will discover that He is available for conversation in every moment. But we are so easily distracted. The day brings many circumstances when we lose focus on the Father's presence. Are we to be castigated because we don't spend every moment in divine conversation? No, we aren't. If
we only knew that Paul uses the word *kairos* instead of *chronos* for "time" in this verse, we would realize that what he is saying is this:

"Every opportunity to experience the intervention of the divine into your ordinary, counting time is an opportunity to connect with the Father. Take it!"

Be on the look-out for *kairos* invasions. They can occur in any *chronos* moment. When they occur, call out to God. Prayer is God's triumphal entry into any and every human experience. Once you realize what is really happening, you are invited into a conversation with Him. Open your mouth and RSVP.

18.

*That I may proclaim with the voice of **thanksgiving** and declare all Your wonders.* Psalm 26:7

Sub-Categorical Prayer

Thanksgiving - Prayer is designed by God. Does that surprise you? Everything that works according to His purposes is designed by Him, so why should prayer be any different? Did you think that just because prayers come from your mouth that the structure and operation of prayer was your invention? David knows better. In this psalm, he uses a word to remind us that prayers are part of a categorical system that God alone put in place. Once we look at the Hebrew word, we discover something else about prayer. It's part of a much bigger picture.

David uses the word *todah*. It's the same word found in Leviticus 7:12, where we see it in its proper context. It is the word for a sacrifice offering under the category of the peace offerings. In other words, thanksgiving is a sub-category of *shalom* (peace).

Let that sink in. Thanksgiving belongs in the realm of *shalom*. That means it is part of the experience of well-being and right fellowship. It is expressly personal. Oh, I can be thankful for a good job, a great school, a neighborhood or security, but these are merely *circumstantial* occurrences. If my thanksgiving is based on only these sorts of things, then I will never be able to thank God when Job's messengers come calling. That's why the biblical perspective about thanksgiving is grounded in a relationship that does not falter or fail. Ultimately, my thanksgiving must be about the character of God. All the rest is subject to change, as life clearly demonstrates.

Read the verse again. Do you notice that David proclaims *God's* wonders – not David's benefits? David knew that life could take you from the cave to the throne and back. He knew that life twisted the greatest warriors for God into disobedient adulterers. He knew that no man governs his own destiny. So, he thanks God for Who God is. And he does it with a word that reminds his readers that God's real wonder is always found in the divinely established, personal relationship that *guarantees* well-being no matter what the circumstances are. Thank God for God. Without Him, there is no hope of *shalom.*

When you offer thanksgiving in your prayers, are you thanking God for the benefits you have received? Are you able to thank Him for your trials and failures too? Do you thank Him with an eye toward the *shalom* He is willing to give?

19.

"Did he not fear the LORD and **entreat** *the favor of the LORD, and the LORD changed His mind about the misfortune which He had pronounced against them?"* Jeremiah 26:19

Personal Passion

Entreat – What does it mean to *entreat* someone? Even in English we have a difficult time expressing this thought succinctly. Certainly the concept involves a gesture of respect, an act of petition, a plea for assistance and a hope for benevolence. But this does not exhaust the extension of the idea in the Bible. In fact, this word is the beginning of a special idiom (*chilah phanim*) that we translate "entreat the favor of." It is literally "make gentle the face." In other words, this phrase introduces an act that attempts to make God smile. That's why you find it used in particularly stressful circumstances when it is very important that the prayers of men cause God to change His mind.

There's something else that's interesting about this phrase. It is not part of the specialized religious language of the Hebrews. It is not found in the temple language or the language that surrounds the sacrificial system of worship. It is a phrase that it used by *common people*, not by the priests. *Making God smile* is part of the prayer language of the non-professionals. It is the kind of thing that you and I do.

Just think about that. Why do you suppose the religious aristocracy of Israel doesn't use this phrase but the laity does? Do you think it might be because this kind of action is like the action of a child before a father? You wouldn't expect to perform an act of humbling petition in front of a stranger, would you? No, it is far more intimate than that! To come before God with prayers that hope to make Him smile is to assume a deeply personal and intense bond. It's far more than asking for a favor. It emphasizes an inner expectation that God *wants* to listen and help. But it also has desperation in its mood. I entreat God when I am up against it, when I have reached my last resource. Did you notice that the verse suggests that attempting to make God smile is associated with the *fear* of the Lord? Of course it is! To fear the Lord is to honor Him as the ultimate authority and supreme ruler of my life. More than that, He is my loving benefactor. I seek His face because I know it is good for me to do so.

Have you prayed like this, detaching yourself from the religious rituals, the expected, sanctified vocabulary you hear in church, and opened your heart to the desperation of your soul? Have you come before your Father expecting to see Him smile? Have you asked God to change His mind on your behalf because your heart is breaking? Or are your prayer just to passive too be noticed?

20.

Exalt *the LORD our God and worship at His footstool; He is holy.* Psalm 99:5

Prayers of Altitude

Exalt – "See Him high and lifted up." Yes, songs can also be prayers. The Old Testament sees no distinction between songs of praise and prayers of exultation. We need to blur that distinction too, for prayers that rejoice in the Lord and lift up His name are often jubilant and

melodious expressions. Go ahead. Sing a prayer to God. Contemporary churches might seem less entertainment if we just became more Hebrew. The artificial distinctions we place on religious activities would be erased. We would discover that prayer spills over from prostrate confession to exuberant singing. We might even dance before the Lord (careful now ☺). With *kairos* attention, we would suddenly see God's hand in the strangest places, like parking lots and choir rooms, street corners and budget meetings. Any place we can lift up God becomes an act of impassioned prayer.

David danced naked before the Lord. He was soundly criticized. Today he would probably be excommunicated or arrested. We have become so *civilized* that we have forgotten we serve a dangerous and unpredictable God. Just look at His record - leveling a city with a shout, fighting an army with a handful of men (or even one), sending a messenger who ate locust and, finally, bringing redemption through a Son who was tortured and died. God is always surprising. When David says, *Rom mu*, he emphasizes God's magnificence. He shouts it out. "There is no One like You, O Lord!" David is on the top of the mountain with the God of the heavens. I can see him, hands raised, shouting, stomping, jumping, singing at the top of his lungs, making a spectacle of himself – because the glory of God has overwhelmed all his restraint.

Ever pray like that? You would be in good company. Set aside all those inhibitions that come with civilized prayer. Go for God's gusto. Make a joyful *noise* to the Lord. You might even hear Him laughing and dancing along with you.

21.

Because He is at my right hand, I will not be shaken. Therefore my heart is glad and my glory **rejoices**   Psalm 16:8-9

Prayer in Context

Rejoices – If you're going to make a joyful noise to the Lord, then you might be interested in the context of rejoicing. Every kind of prayer has a context. Sometimes it's desperation. Sometimes it's trauma. Sometimes it's thanksgiving. Rejoicing is no different. David gives us the proper context for rejoicing in this verse and in Psalm 2:11. Both are essential.

In this verse, David tells us that rejoicing (*giyl*) is motivated by the unfailing presence of God. When I realize that God is at my right hand (an idiom for support and strength), I know that the course of my life depends entirely on Him. That is a foundation that cannot be moved. Therefore, I will not waver. Fear of circumstances can be thrust aside. While the future is not up to me, it is up to God and since He is my strong shield, I have nothing to fear. From face-to-the-ground humility, I can leap up, raising my hands to heaven in honor of the One Who favors me. That is my motivation for rejoicing. The context is all about Who He is, not where I am. Rejoicing comes about because God can be trusted regardless of my situation.

Yeshua in the Garden. Paul in prison. Steven about to be stoned. Joan of Arc at the stake. Bunyan in prison. The list goes on and on. Followers who *rejoiced* in God's character in spite of their dire circumstances. You and I can live in exactly the same context of rejoicing prayer. God doesn't change, so why be crushed by life's trials? No matter what, it is always worth rejoicing over Him.

To see the other half of the context of rejoicing, take a look at Psalm 2:11. Rejoicing has some compatriots. They are called "fear and trembling." You see, dancing and shouting and rejoicing before the Lord never loses sight of His awesome majesty. When we truly rejoice in Who He is, we discover we are in the presence of blinding holiness. So, sometimes rejoicing feels a lot like terror, not of fear, but of unworthiness. You might think of

Isaiah's opening words. Woe is me! That is also rejoicing. It is exuberance over the unimaginable power of the God Who calls me His own.

When you pray, do you pray in context? Are you aware of the surrounding angels singing, "Holy, holy, holy is the Lord God Almighty?"

22.

*"or do you think that I cannot **appeal** to My Father, and He will at once put at My disposal more than twelve legions of angels?"* Matthew 26:53

Unexpected Absence

Appeal – The Hebrew vocabulary is rich in words for prayer. Every nuance of our relationship with God seems to find its own special word. So, when we come to this statement by Yeshua, clearly indicating a request of the Father, we expect to find a similar breadth of meanings in Greek. But, amazingly, we don't. The word we find here is familiar. It's *parakaleo* (to call alongside), the same root word that Yeshua uses to identify the coming Holy Spirit (the Paraclete). But when we investigate further, we discover the amazing fact that *parakaleo* is almost never used for calling on God or Christ in prayer. It finds most of its usage in the action of salvation, calling on Yeshua to rescue us from our pitiful, sinful condition. The idea of exhorting, quite common in ancient Greek literature, is virtually absent from the New Testament. Instead, we find this word used in connection with calling for aid in missions and admonitions.

Just for a moment, consider how unusual this really is. Here is a word that could have been incorporated into the prayer language of the New Testament. It has parallels in Hebrew (like "entreat," and "cry out"). But it finds another specialized use – a use that is associated with a particular event rather than with a continual request. The paradigm of *parakaleo* is not prayer but rather redemption. In the New Testament, this Greek word is lifted out of its wider context of making a request and applied to the much narrower context of divine aid of salvation through Yeshua. When *parakaleo* is used for "asking," it is found in the act of asking for grace. When it is used for "exhorting," it is found in the context of salvation already granted. Either way, *parakaleo* becomes a word that defines God's truest form of comfort – redemption.

It's such a shame that we are left without a way to clearly see the Greek words behind translations like "appeal." That particular translation does help us identify that Yeshua is using a word with carefully defined connotations. If we knew this, we might understand just a bit more the role and the responsibility of the Spirit. The Spirit does not come alongside for any reason whatsoever. No, the *Paraclete* is about *parakaleo* – ushering in salvation and sanctification, the once-redeemed, daily delivered process that summarizes what it means for God to shed His grace upon us.

Is *parakaleo* a prayer word? Yes, it is. But is it not the kind of prayer word we might imagine. It is not about asking for our needs. It is about the specific action of the Spirit, given in grace, which brings us into fellowship with the Father. So pray with *parakaleo* in mind, and let the Spirit work in you.

23.

*pray **without ceasing*** 1 Thessalonians 5:17

The Middle

Without Ceasing – Doesn't this command from Paul make you feel inadequate? I know that I don't *pray* constantly. I am quite sure that the vast majority of Christians don't either. That makes me feel as though I just can't live up to the standard. And I probably never will. I am defeated before I begin. Or so it seems.

But Paul is not Greek (how many times have you heard that?). He is Hebrew, and in Hebrew there are more than 40 different words for prayer. English and Greek are, unfortunately, abbreviated languages when it comes to prayer. We have but one word, and that word often carries with it a particular imagery associated with the formal prayers of worship. When you think about "Let us pray," you probably envision the congregation bowing their heads while some professional invokes eloquent words toward heaven. You may think of kneeling, folding hands (or lifting them up) or some other prescribed posture. And then you think, "I can't do that 24-7." In fact, even if you allow *silent* prayer, you will probably agree that there are long periods of time when you just aren't saying those reverential words even in your mind. It's OK. That is *not* what Paul has in mind. Paul uses the Greek *adialeiptos* (literally, "not leaving a gap"), but he is thinking from a Hebrew perspective.

You know, of course, that the original manuscripts of the Bible have no chapter and verse numbers. Erase them. Then read this again. You will discover that it is the *middle* of one continuous thought. Rejoice always, pray without gaps, in everything give thanks. That's the whole picture.

And that picture is part of the advice on *practical actions toward others* (read verses 12-15). If praying without gaps is the middle of an *attitude of thanksgiving*, set in the context of *commitment to others*, then how do you suppose this kind of praying will manifest itself? Do you suppose it will be a constant stream of silent words cast toward heaven? Or is it more likely that it will be displayed in the other 39 words in Hebrew thought used for praying? Those words include weeping, crying, dancing, blessing, lifting, calling, summoning, entreating, groaning, roaring, praising, confessing, meditating, declaring, remembering, counting, and a dozen more *actions* that belong to everyday life. In other words, prayer is not a specific religious ritual as much as it is a life-orientation that permeates all our thoughts, words and deeds. In fact, if praying happens continuously in all that you do, you will experience the reality that work and worship are the same word in Hebrew. You will *live* in prayer because you will be in constant engagement with God, even if it is in dancing, crying, declaring, meditating or all the rest.

And we will all see that you are praying without gaps because we will see that your *external* acts toward others reflect constant contact with God. Now go ahead. Live prayer without gaps. Oh, and by the way, the idea of prayer without gaps is a Hebrew expression about making every action of life full of God's direction and purpose.

24.

*"So shall My heavenly Father also do to you, if each of you does **not forgive** his brother from your heart."* Matthew 18:35

Prayer and Retribution

Not Forgive – Yeshua' parable of the wicked servant who refused to forgive the little owned to him after the king forgave an enormous debt is a chilling story. It begins with a question each of us asks. "How many times am I required to forgive someone?" Peter suggests seven, the perfect number of completion. Certainly if I forgive someone *seven* times, I have done my duty! But Yeshua responds with a humanly impossible answer. No, not seven times but *seventy times seven*. Then Yeshua tells us the story of this ungrateful slave. What is the result of the slave's unwillingness to shed forgiveness on others? He is handed over to the *torturers* until the debt is paid in full – in other words, for the rest of his life.

We nod our heads, agreeing that this ungrateful slave needed to be punished. And then we come to this verse. It scalds our hearts. Yeshua says that God will deal with us in the same way, delivering us to the torturers, unless we forgive from the heart. If this doesn't make you shudder, then you aren't listening.

The words in Greek are *ean me aphete* (if not you forgive). The construction is important. This is forgiveness conditioned upon real circumstances. Yeshua is not offering a *hypothetical* example. This is not *hyperbole*, as we are usually led to conclude. Yeshua is quite literally saying that, in real life situations, you are required to forgive over and over and over, just as God, the King, has forgiven. Why? We see the answer in the middle of the parable (verse 32). "I forgave," says the King, "because you entreated me." We know this word. It is a prayer word. The slave begged to be released from his obligation and because he begged, the heart of the King was moved to compassion. The King does not forgive for any other reason. But here is the twist. To forgive from the heart is not to forgive simply because compassion compels me to do so. To forgive from the heart is to forgive because I stand in a relationship with God. I am asked to act as God does. I do not forgive because it is the *right* thing to do. I forgive because God forgives.

How difficult it is for us to respond like God does! We have built-in personal advantage tendencies that we must deliberately set aside. In fact, if we find that we are calculating before forgiving, we will not fulfill Yeshua' requirement (and the torturers will await us).

There is another implication in this parable that cannot be ignored. Forgiveness is not conceivable without retribution. Do you understand this? Buchsel points out that love is not opposed to retribution. To claim that the God of love is incompatible with judgment and punishment is to misunderstand the entire gospel. It is the *expectation* of retribution that fuels the need for the good news. And when we forgive, we must never lose sight of this connection. There is no forgiveness without the possibility of retribution. To pray for forgiveness is to ask that inevitable retribution be set aside. God does just that. So should we.

25.

*Therefore, I will rather gladly **boast** in my weaknesses, that the power of Christ may overshadow me.* 2 Corinthians 12:9

Upside-Down Prayer

Boast – First, Paul *entreats* the Lord. We know what that means. It is *parakaleo* – to call for aid alongside. In one of those rare occurrences where the word is a synonym for *proseuchomai* (to pray), Paul tells us that three times he pleaded for aid. And then he received God's triumphant answer, "My grace is sufficient." Paul realizes that God's answer requires a different kind of prayer – the prayer of *boasting* in his weakness.

The word is *kauchaomai*. It is almost always used in a bad sense, denoting that self-glorifying proclamation that accompanies arrogance and pride. Paul himself speaks against prideful boasting in Romans 3:27. His Jewish heritage reinforces this idea in Proverbs where the Hebrew equivalent is often ascribed to fools and the ungodly.

With this in mind, imagine how startling it is for Paul to say that he *boasts*! Is Paul a fool? The answer, of course, is, "Yes, I am a fool for Christ." Paul takes a word that we would never have associated with godly attitudes and turns it upside-down. He shows us that when we have nothing of merit in ourselves, God uses our empty worthlessness for His glory. We can boast as fools, as long as we are boasting in the complete reversal of human effort brought about by the Lord.

What Paul discovered, and what we must also learn, is that prayer is often answered with foolishness. Prayer is not about me becoming stronger. It is about my weakness becoming the vehicle of God's strength. I do not pray, "Lord, give me power." I pray, "Lord, use my weakness to manifest Your power." "Lord, I am *not* able, but You are. I am *not* smart enough, but You know. I am *not* unwavering, but You are faithful. Lord, my weakness will overwhelm me unless You manifest Your grace.

I am nothing without You, so use this weak servant who struggles just to be obedient as a vessel of Your glory. Let me never forget that my weakness is the sacred curse for Your purpose. And, Lord, let others see Your hand because they recognize my inability."

It's not about me. It will *never* be about me. That is why His grace does not repair my weaknesses. God is most glorified in my flaws.

26.

*So we fasted and **petitioned** our God about this, and he **answered** our prayer.* Ezra 8:23 (NIV)

Open Answers

Petitioned .. Answered – Ezra's statement shows us the proper protocol for answered prayer. It does not *guarantee* that the answer we receive is the answer we hope to receive, but it tells us that answers do come. What is the proper protocol? It is captured in two Hebrew words we already know. They are just disguised from us in this English translation.

The first word is *baqash*. We *petitioned*. But now we know that *baqash* is more than requesting. It is asking with full submission. It is coming to God as His completely obedient servants, ready to do *whatever* He decides, without argument. It is the word for the full reign and rule of God's authority. "We fasted and came to God fully surrendered to His will" is the essence of Ezra's statement. Why fast? Because denying my physical well-being is a *symbol* of my submission. I show that I am willing to go to extreme measures in order to be obedient. Without *baqash*, prayer is just mouthing religious words.

Now we come to the second word. It's the unusual word *athar*; the seldom used official word for prayer. Here is it used reflexively. The verse doesn't actually say that God "answered our prayer." What it says is that God was "entreated on behalf of us." In other words, this verse simply says that God heard and acted. When His people come before Him with a demonstration of full commitment and the willingness of total surrender, God hears and acts. How God acts is entirely up to Him. But since we know that God is good, we know that all of His actions are destined for the completion of His good purposes. And, for those who are fully surrendered, *that is enough*! Prayer is completed when God hears and acts. Nothing more is needed. Prayer does not demand as its result a *specific* action. It does not dictate to God what must occur. It simply calls to God to hear and act, leaving the nature of the response entirely in His hands.

There is a deep, theological reason to leave your prayers open-ended like this. You don't know what is the best course of action for the purposes of God. You don't have an eternal perspective on things. You don't see the full picture. You are a very limited creature. He is the Creator, the Ruler, the All-mighty and Omniscient One. So asking Him to act with an open-ended agenda is *trusting* His decisions. Furthermore, God is full of surprises. He is the constantly creative God, not limited to the solutions that men devise. He is glorified when His answers are something we could never have imagined.
Ezra knew the secret - total surrender, evidenced by action; then open-ended acceptance. God hears those prayers – and acts!

27.

*Now to Him who **is able** to establish you according to my* *gospel and the preaching of Yeshua Christ* Romans 16:25

May The Force Be With You

Is Able – *Star Wars* is Greek. The idea of an impersonal cosmic force presiding over life and death is as old as Pythagoras. George Lukas might have been enthralled by the concept, but Paul wasn't fooled. Paul's view of power is not at all like the ancient Greeks, nor is it like our contemporary mythology about power. Paul is Hebrew – and that means that power is God's prerogative, not mine.

Our word is *dynamai*. You will recognize it in the words "dynamic" and "dynamite." It's about power. But in the Hebrew mind, power resides in a personal God who controls, sustains and directs all of creation. More importantly, power is *not* the goal of active creation (unlike the hope of politicians). Ultimately, the universe is about the *will* of the Father, not about the force required to accomplish that will. So, Paul is being entirely Hebrew when he suggests in this closing doxology that it is God *alone* who is able to bring about His will in your life. A Greek mindset would suggest that you have some divine spark within that needs to be nurtured in order for you to experience the "force." Don't be fooled by all that mumbo-jumbo. Unless God provides you with His energy, you are just a depleting battery.

Why don't we see this truth more clearly? The answer is simple: we experience personal power in life, so we conclude that it must reside in us. We can do things, so we think that our activity proves we have resident ability. And God accommodates this illusion by allowing life to operate as if the force is with us. He accommodates this illusion because He is interested in our personal decision to refuse this myth and submit to His authority. God is not interested in forcing me to see the truth. He requests that I voluntarily accept the truth. And the truth is that life is in Him, and no other!

Once I see that my life is simply woven into the fabric of His will, then I will recognize that all quests of individual power are an affront to God. They are also, ultimately, useless and stupid. God is the true source of all power, but it is always power conditioned by the purposes of His will. If I am not in His will, then my experience of power rests on quicksand. It will lead to nothing.

How can I be grounded in the power of His will? Ah, that's what prayer is for.

27.

*Shout for joy, O daughter of Zion! Shout in triumph, O Israel! **Rejoice** and exult with all your heart, O daughter of Jerusalem! The LORD has taken away His judgments against you,* Zephaniah 3:14-15

Moved By God's Grace

Rejoice – When God's amazing grace overwhelms you, it is nearly impossible to hold back your emotions. That's perfectly OK. God intended us to *feel* His goodness. Sometimes we weep with joy. Sometimes we sing praises.

Sometimes we dance and shout (but only if the church allows it ☺). All of these jubilant motions are part of this verb, *samach*. You can easily remember it if you think of the moving emotion of *smack*! When God's grace comes to town, things happen – on the outside and the inside.

But there's something interesting about this Hebrew word that we wouldn't see without investigation. When Hebrew scholars translated the Old Testament into Greek, they translated this word with the Greek word *euphraino*. That's not what we would have expected. *Euphraino* means "to be glad." It emphasizes emotional moods and is usually associated with physical events like festivals. It's a word for carnival happiness. We would have expected *samach* to be translated with the Greek *charis*, the usual New Testament word for "rejoice." *Charis* is also the word for "grace." In Christian circles rejoicing is usually thought of as a reaction to God's forgiveness. Even in this verse from Zephaniah, the reason for rejoicing is just that – God has forgiven. But in the New Testament, *euphraino* fades into the background while *charis* leaps forward. Why?

Here's one possibility. In the Old Testament, rejoicing occurs over specific events when God demonstrates His benevolence toward His people. Rejoicing is a one-at-a-time deal. Mixed into the sorrow of life are those moments when God breaks through and our hearts are thrilled. But in the New Testament, something even more amazing has happened. Yeshua' arrival signals a permanent presence of God in our midst. Yeshua, the Son incarnate, has become one of us, abides with us and never abandons us. Rejoicing is an emotional response that is no longer limited to God's temporary invasion. We rejoice now because *everything* has changed. The Anointed One has come! No circumstance in life is beyond rejoicing, for Emmanuel is here.

When the Hebrew scholars translated the Old Testament into Greek, they were still looking for the coming of the Messiah. But when He came, the face of the universe was permanently altered. *Samach* and *euphraino*, temporary exclamations of God's glory, disappear in the dazzling presence of *charis* – permanent gladness.

Have you moved from *samach* to *charis*, or did you get stuck at *euphraino*? Is your rejoicing permanent? Are you an over-the-horizon person?

28.

*For you know that when your faith is tested, your endurance has a chance to grow. So let it grow, for when your endurance is fully developed, you will be perfect and complete, **needing nothing**.* James 1:3-4 (NLT)

Much Prayer About Nothing

Needing Nothing – How often our prayers are motivated by circumstances in which we are acutely aware of our insufficiency! We run into something that is beyond us. We lack the skill, temperament, motivation or resources to overcome. So we pray. "Lord, help me." What we really mean is something more like, "Lord, bring Your power and will and knowledge to bear on my problem and fix it for me." Just listen to the standard community prayer in your church. It is probably filled to the brim with requests for God to fix things that we can't.

James has a different perspective. For him, *medeni leipomenoi* (literally, not one thing lacking) has a very different goal. James tells us that the presence of adversity (of all kinds) is food for spiritual growth. It is the *necessary* nutrient of grace. Without adversity, we fall prey to spiritual atrophy – or worse. Contrary to liberal theological opinion, God knew precisely what He was doing when He told Adam and Eve that they would have to complete their mission in the context of suffering and sorrow. Adversity fuels dependence – and inoculates us to the sin of self-sufficient pride. We need it, unfortunately, because we are deeply diseased at heart. However, the very stuff that results from disobedience – the trials and adversity now a part of the fallen world – can become the vehicle of God's unfailing grace. This is James point: The purpose of prayer is not to get God's answer. It is to draw close to God. The answer, whatever it is, is simply a by-product of being in His presence. The real answer to prayer – all prayer – is God. The answer is not the results brought about by God but rather God Himself. And anything that enables us to come closer to Him is useful – even if it is heartache and trials.

Today I am visiting with a family that survived hurricane Ivan. Its force submerged their home in a wall of water and sewage, destroying all that they possessed in a matter of minutes. Two years later they are still working to recover. But they are grateful to God. They are alive. They know His grace. They are stronger, closer, more aware. Next door is a neighbor who does not understand the meaning of adversity. He has never recovered in spite of his repaired home. He is shattered – the shell of a man who believes life should have been under his control. The difference is dramatic – and heartbreaking.

What about you? Is adversity your breakfast of champions? Do you see that the answer to prayer is never really about fixing anything, but rather about coming into His presence? Will this change your praying?

29.

*You ask and do not receive, because you ask with **wrong***

motives, *so that you may spend it on your pleasures.*
James 4:3

Too Hard To Hear

Wrong Motives – James is pragmatically focused. He doesn't mince words. What he really says is a jab to the solar plexus of our selfish desires. Maybe that's why we soften the blow with a modified translation. The Greek is *kakos*. It is literally, "evil." Maybe we should have listened to the original. "You ask with *evil intent.*"

James has a perfectly sound answer to the question, "Why doesn't God give me what I ask for." His answer is, "Your request is to satisfy yourself. You don't understand a thing about the character of God. You are asking with an evil heart. You only want what you want." How does James know this? It's obvious. He points at the goal for asking. If the reason you ask is to satisfy a desire that serves your self-glorifying agenda, then what you ask is as evil as any sin ever committed.

"But I don't ask for things that only serve me!" you complain. "I ask for help for others. I ask for good things. I ask for increases in God's kingdom." Really? Be ruthlessly honest. Was that prayer for healing just for your spouse, or was there a little motive in there about getting back to the life you want? Was that request for church growth really only about the horrible fate of the lost or was there just a hint of pride in the size of your congregation? Did you really think that praying for victory before a football game serves *God's* interests? Do you think that God listens to prayers for the hungry in Haiti when you have so much food in your cupboard you could feed an entire village and not bat an eye? Who are you kidding? Certainly not God!

144

Here's a thought: God answers every prayer that is in alignment with His will. He *never* dismisses a single one. So, if your prayers are not getting answered, what does that say about the motivation behind them? Maybe we need to take a much deeper look at *why* we ask, not what we ask.

I'm afraid that James is just too hard for us to hear these days. He is likely to point to our bank balances, our vacation packages, our multiple televisions and over-stuffed closets and say, "What's the matter with you? When you get honest about your own self-serving agendas, then maybe you will discover God's replies. But don't expect Him to give you anything when you are all about accumulation."

Today, God is moving in powerful ways in this world. Almost none of these are found in the affluent societies. Did you ever wonder why?

30.

*Moreover, as for me, far be it from me that I should sin against the LORD by **ceasing to pray** for you;* 1 Samuel 12:23

Why Do I Pray?

Ceasing to Pray – Anyone who claims that prayer is easy hasn't carefully observed human behavior. Prayer *should* be easy, but it certainly doesn't appear to be so. If it were, we would see prayers on the lips of *every* believer *all* the time. After all, it is the open channel of communication with our God. But when we look at real behavior, we find that prayer is not a common and consistent daily experience. We discover that most people struggle with prayer. They are uncomfortable

145

when asked to pray publicly. Prayer is one of the *last* things on their priority lists. They pray when distress comes, but most of the time prayer is only routine thanks at meals and routine supplications in church. Prayer is real work, but it is such strange work that we often have no idea how to effectively accomplish it. We need to listen to Samuel's voice, *"me'khadol le hit'palel."*

Samuel condemns the people of Israel for their insistence on establishing a king. They want to be like other nations. They think that if they have a king, they will gain power, prestige and protection. Samuel knows better. He chastises them, pointing out that God is and always has been their king .. to no avail. They demand a new ruler. God grants their wish, but with terrible consequences, for now they become subjects of *human* kings. They live under the government of fractured men. They will soon discover that power corrupts.

Samuel sees their folly. He warns them. Then he does something else. He commits himself to prayer on their behalf. In spite of their disobedience, he will not stop praying. The reason he will not stop praying is not about the *result*. It is about the *motivation*. Samuel will not stop praying because if he did, he would sin against God. Not to pray is sin! Samuel knows that the tide has turned against God's order for government. He knows that the days of the theocracy are over. He sees only heartache and ruin in the future. But this does not stop Samuel from praying because to stop praying, in spite of everything, would be sin against God.

There are plenty of days when my prayers seem entirely ineffective. There are seasons when I know that the present choices of others will lead them to terrible consequences. But if I stop praying on their behalf, I commit sin myself, because prayer is not about achieving results. It is about honoring the desire of the Father to communicate with me. Prayer ceases when it is used only as a means to an end. But prayer will never cease if it is the end itself.

God asks us to pray. Make prayer itself your offering to God and you will not sin against Him by withholding what He commands.

31.

Thy kingdom come Matthew 6:10

When?

Come – Yesterday we discovered that sometimes the verb tense makes a huge difference. Do you remember "revile" and "persecute?" Both were in the aorist tense. That means they are about a particular, limited point in the past. The actions do not go on and on. Aorist actions are like a single point on a page rather than like a line across the page.

Now we can use this knowledge to unravel something startling. The verb "come" (*eltheto*) in Yeshua' model prayer – a prayer which we say over and over – is also in the aorist tense. But this is quite strange. Does Yeshua mean that God's Kingdom has already come? No, not quite. The form of this verb is an imperative – a request and command that God's Kingdom arrive. But the perspective is that this is a *fait accompli*. This prayer is the prayer of absolute and total confidence that what God has determined to be is as good as already done. That's power! That's faith. The kingdom, which I cannot see, is guaranteed to arrive because its arrival date has already been fixed.

Is that what you thought when you last prayed the Lord's Prayer? Did you realize that you were endorsing the *past* guaranteed arrival of the kingdom? Or did you think you were imploring God to somehow bring about all the blissful changes you thought you needed in order for His reign to being here on earth? The difference is important. If you thought that you were imploring God to somehow bring His Kingdom into reality, you might be tempted to think that the arrival is the slow transformation of this world into the reign of God. You might be tempted to think that you have a hand in bringing the Kingdom along. You might think that the Kingdom is *progressive*. But once you realize that the arrival of the Kingdom has been fixed at a certain point by the guarantee of God in the past, you see that only God brings the Kingdom. It arrives fully formed. You are not praying that someday in the future this world will become holy. Your hope is not fixed on an unknown and unknowable arrival of the King. Your hope is fixed on the unwavering character of the God of history Who has already ordered His rule in place. You stand on conquered ground. Celebrate! It is finished!

The arrival has nothing to do with you. God will overthrow all the forces that hold this world captive. He will not convert them; He will destroy them. Only those who do not know the character of the faithful God waver under the apparent onslaught of the enemy. If you know Who God is, there is absolutely nothing to fear. Yes, the enemy is raging like a hungry lion, all the more so as his time draws to an end. But, so what? "Thy kingdom come" is firmly anchored in the past. Nothing and no one can change it now. Victory is His – and ours.

Pray it with me again. "Let come the kingdom of You." Hallelujah!

32.

*As it is written in the law of Moses, all this calamity has come on us, yet **we have not sought** the favor of the LORD our God by turning from our iniquity and giving attention to Your truth.* Daniel 9:13

Relent, O Lord

We Have Not Sought – If you knew Hebrew, you would shudder at the sound of this phrase. It uses the great prayer word *halal*, the basis of our transliterated word, *hallelujah*. But *halal* has three separate (though perhaps related) meanings, any one of which strikes terror in the heart of men. The first is used in 1 Kings 20:1 where it means "to become sick unto death." The second is found in Isaiah 17:11 where it describes a disease brought on Damascus as the punishment of God. And finally, there is this verse and many more (Exodus 32:11, Psalm 45:13 and Proverbs 19:6) where it means to beg God for a stay of judgment, to make entreaty or appeasement in order win favor and forestall calamity.

Have you prayed a prayer like that? "O Lord, please don't let this terrible thing happen. Please hear my cry to You and withhold Your judgment. Forgive, Lord, and restore. Do not cast us off." Go back and read this little story (it begins in 9:1). Daniel is not praying for himself. He is praying on behalf of the entire nation, crying out to God to relent from the terrible judgment that has befallen Israel. Why is Israel in such desperate straits? Daniel knows why. Israel is experiencing the fulfillment of Moses' prophecy – the curse that would come over any nation that knew God's law and yet refused to abide by it. As surely as the sun sets in the West, the order of the universe is built on God's rules. Disobey them and suffer the consequences.

149

Don't you wonder why we just don't get it? God's governance of the moral universe hasn't changed in spite of all our efforts to rewrite the code. Any nation that attempts to displace God's view is bound to feel the fire. But we go right on thinking that somehow this time it will be different. We are self-delusional saboteurs, providing evidence for our own condemnation as we march merrily toward destruction with evolved, educated egos. We look back on the past with disgust, but that will not matter when the past revisits us with the same situation that Daniel faced. Throwing himself on the mercy of God, he pleaded for a reprieve. Where are the Daniels of this age? Do we no longer believe we even need them?

One of the biggest roadblocks to true restoration is the heresy that God forgives all, as if to imply that once I am "saved" I no longer have any need to conform my life to God's law. Somehow we fool ourselves into believing that grace sets aside law. Can you imagine that? Keep thinking that way and the first two meanings of *halal* will undoubtedly arrive in due course. Yeshua died to remove my guilt, not to change God's law. Yeshua died so that I can now obey. That was the whole purpose all the time. Obedience first, last and in-between.

There is no other way. *Hallelujah!*

33.

Search me, O God, and know my heart. Try me, and know my thoughts Psalm 139:23

Elective Surgery

Search – Unless you're crazy or a fanatic, you won't

repeat David's plea without a great deal of hesitation. This is no casual request. Do you really want God to *search* your heart? Do you really want Him to turn over every rock, examine every tiny detail, look into every closet? The very idea brings many to sheer panic. Of course, we already *know* that God knows it all. But most of the time, we deny the reality of His knowledge. We pretend that our secrets are safely tucked away – until we meet someone like David.

David is crazy. Imagine a man who is guilty of immense pride (resulting in the death of thousands), sloth (staying home from battles), adultery, deceit, murder and cover-up – imagine a man like this *asking God to search his heart*. Don't you think David had some idea what God would find? Don't you think he spent night after night weeping over his sins, afraid to look in the reflecting pool for fear that he would see a man condemned by his own lusts? If the Psalms are any indication of the inner agony that haunted David in his worst hours, then we know that he was a man who experienced tremendous emotional pain. Why would a man like that plead for God's surgical examination?

The Hebrew verb is *haqar*. It is used in military applications for scouting out enemy territory. It is used to describe seeking the truth behind something. And, of course, it is used here to ask God to cut open the recesses of my secret life.

Every addict knows that the power of the addiction is in the secrets. Brought to light, the power evaporates. But, oh, how painful it is to bring these humiliating secrets to the light! How much ego loss, how much deflated image must occur to bring the light on our deep, dark secrets?

Once, David was forced to confront his actions. That lesson stayed with him all of his life. Now he says, "Lord, I am submitting myself for elective surgery. You know exactly what I am like. You know precisely where I am still holding on to personal pride and sinful denial. So, Lord, cut into me. Look for any tiny indication that there is still diseased thinking and attitude. And, Lord, in Your infinite mercy, remove it from me."

David knows it will hurt. It *always* does. Confession without pain is nothing more than lip service. God won't stand for it. Neither should you. Real confession, the result of open-heart divine surgery, is *life-threatening*. Without confession, I will die. With confession, I will also die – but the part of me that will die needs to die if the rest of me is going to live. I can't make it if the cancer of sin stays alive in me, but taking it out feels like going to the grave along with the tumor.

My hope is that God is the perfect surgeon. That is my *only* hope! Don't ever think there is another alternative. Cut deep or die.

34.

Search me, O God, and know my heart. **Try me**, *and know my thoughts* Psalm 139:23

The Acid Test

Try Me – "*bekhaneni*," says the Psalmist. The verbal root (*bakhan*) is direct, powerful and compelling. Put me to the test. Prove me. Throw me in the crucible of life's fire and see if I emerge refined and pure. If you thought asking God to perform heart surgery was insane, just imagine what is implied in this!

Let me tell you a secret. The measure of God's trust in *you* is determined by the amount of trials and hardships He allows you to bear for His glory. God knows exactly how much we can take before we break. God is not interested in crushing us. He is interested in providing us with just the right amount of testing so that we can emerge victorious, glorifying Him. He doesn't need to see how much we can handle on our own. That is never His plan. He wants us to learn the exact measure of our total dependence. We'll need to know this when we assume our roles in His eternal plan. Now is the time to find out just how much we *can't* handle.

God promises never to give you more than is essential for your perfect growth. He promises to always provide an exit door leading straight to Him. But remember, no pain – no gain. Stop praying to be removed from trials and heartaches. Don't you know that they are precisely what is needed for your painful growth? Stop asking God for the easy path. Don't you realize that if He grants your request He will have to shelter you from all you needed to become like Him? Why are you so intent on finding a way out when you should be pleading for God to give you a way in – into the *via Delarosa* – the way of the cross? Your perfection cannot be accomplished until the nails are driven home.

Did Yeshua plead to avoid the hard way? Did He beg God to give Him peace and tranquility? Not a chance. He knew that the pathway of obedience was bloody.

When you're ready (or, maybe, when you feel the least ready), say this – *bekhaneni*. Try me! Ask God to bring it on. Tell Him you want to be all that He wants you to be. Give Him the green light for proving your worth. He honors that kind of prayer. In fact, nothing pleases Him more. What is devoted to destruction is sacred in His sight.

35.

*"And all things, whatever you ask in **prayer**, believing, you shall receive."* Matthew 21:22

Dispelling Confusion

Prayer – In the midst of a long fast, I read this verse. Since it comes from the mouth of Yeshua, it must be true. But so much of the time, it seems as if what I ask does not come to pass. I know that the problem is not on God's side. He is *El Shaddai*. So, what am I missing? Perhaps I need to think in Hebrew, not in Greek.

The Greek word here is *proseuche*. It is a combination of *pros* (to) and *euchomai* (to wish). In the New Testament, this combined word almost always means prayer, rather than wish. It is more or less the *technical* word for prayer to God. But when we look at which words it translates from the Hebrew Bible, we find that it covers both *tephilla* and *techinnah*. A little detective work reveals that *techinnah* is used only 23 times, 14 of those concerning Solomon's temple. This rare word means "to request favor, to ask of God." We would use the English word, supplication, but *techinnah* is a bit more formal than that. *Tephilla* is used about 80 times, but even this is fairly rare. *Tephilla* carries the same nuance as *techinnah*, that is, it is a pleading prayer to God (for example, Psalm 4:2). Since there are more than three dozen different words for prayer in Hebrew, these two words barely scratch the surface of the Hebrew view on prayer. But Greek and English are both compressed prayer languages, with just a few words for describing all communication with God.

"So what?" you might say. "It's nice to know all this, but how does it help me understand what Yeshua means and why my prayers seem so anemic?" Here's some help. Since Yeshua isn't speaking Greek, we can't be sure exactly what Hebrew word He really used. All of the vast vocabulary of Hebrew prayer-words get compressed into this rather formal Greek word, so we don't know precisely what nuances Yeshua had in mind. Therefore, we are required to expand our understanding of prayer by doing our best to gain a Hebrew perspective through an investigation of the full range of Hebrew words – and then decide which word best fits the context here. What we discover is that there are several Hebrew words associated with pleading prayer (you can read about them in the *Today's Word* devotionals from January 4 to 26 of this year). All of them rest on the idea of absolute trust in the character of God. My plea is not the basis of God's answer. The fuel for divine intervention is my complete *abandonment* to Him. Pure prayer of supplication is stripped of any ego concerns.

When I look at the Old Testament context of pleading prayer, I find men and women who cry out to God in desperation. They use Hebrew words that imply agonizing speech, groaning, travail, lives stripped of every other option, and begging with faces to the floor. There is nothing casual about these kinds of prayers. They have life and death intensity.

Do you suppose that our failure to see God's hand comes from the lack of desperate dependence? We think Yeshua means "anything you want," but if He is saturated with Old Testament thought, maybe He means "anything you can't survive without." Would that change the way we pray? I wonder.

36.

*"And all things, whatever you ask in prayer, **believing**, you shall receive."* Matthew 21:22

The Long Run

Believing – Yeshua said it, and He doesn't lie. Yesterday we looked at the Hebrew idea of pleading prayer. It's not prayer for the impatient or the self-reliant. If you want to experience pleading prayer, you have to be desperate. Those kinds of prayers God hears. Now Yeshua adds this one condition – believing. Notice first that this is an on-going action. It doesn't stop when there is no apparent answer. It goes on and on and on until the answer comes. Daniel prayed every day until the answer arrived. Paul prayed again and again, waiting for God's timing. So did David, Jeremiah, Isaiah and Yeshua. Once we see that this kind of praying wears holes in the carpet, we realize that it is not appropriate for just anything. Yes, Yeshua tells us that pleading prayer covers "all things," but that doesn't mean it covers everything. It covers those things that warrant worn out carpets, sore knees and tears.

That doesn't mean we are not to pray about everything. God desires, and we need, communication about everything. After all, our shortsighted vision of the plan for life is just too restricted to know what really is happening. If you want to fit into the bigger picture, you better ask Someone Who can see the whole plan. So, pray without gaps (remember Thessalonians?). But not everything is worthy of pleading prayer.

The key is found in this Greek word, *pisteuo*. In the Greek New Testament, it means "to be firmly persuaded, to trust, in the context of confident expectation and hope." But we already know that Yeshua is speaking Hebrew (*'aman*). This is a word about stability and confidence. It's about things that can be relied upon; things that are solid as a rock. When you believe as a Hebrew, *you act according to the character of God.* Of course, that means that you must know the character of God. You must be immersed in God-thinking, God-doing and God-feeling. You must make the nouns of Exodus 34:6 your *only* measure of success. There is no point in wailing and weeping over wishes unless you are entirely anchored in godly actions. Do you want God to hear your pleading prayer? Then *act* like it. Do what He says without second thoughts. See the world as He sees the world. Feel the compassion that He feels. Speak as He speaks. Move to action as He moves to action. Then, no pleading prayer will ever be cast toward a leaden sky. God will send fire from heaven to lick the water around the altar.

Of course, if you're going to make the nouns of Exodus 34:6 your life's measure, a whole lot of things that you thought you needed to pray about might not be so important anymore. What will become priorities are the things that move God. All you have to do is look at what Yeshua prayed about to see how this all works out.

Do you trust God? Are you staking your life on Him? Without contingency plans? Without regrets? Are you willing to pray over the things that God cares about? If you are, be prepared for answers. And keep praying until they come.

37.

*It is written, "My house shall be called a house of **prayer**," but you have made it a den of thieves.* Matthew 21:13

Praying Naked

Prayer – David danced naked before the ark. Although Scripture doesn't comment on it, I am quite sure that David also prayed naked. I don't mean that he fell to his face without clothes. I mean that David understood the connection between "house of prayer" and "nakedness." I'll bet that Yeshua did too. In order to see why prayer is barrenness, we have to dig into Hebrew.

Yeshua actually quotes two prophets in this verse. The first is obvious. "House of prayer" comes from Isaiah 56:7. The second comes from Jeremiah (more about that later). Isaiah uses the Hebrew word *tefillah* (prayer). It's a fairly standard Hebrew word describing a cry or plea to God. That much is easily discerned. But when we examine the idea of a cry to God, we run across Psalm 141:8 - "But my eyes are on You, O Lord, my Lord, in You I take refuge; do not make my soul naked". David cries out in prayer. He is exposed to the searching eyes of the Lord. More than anything else, he feels naked. Nothing is hidden because his prayer invites the Lord's inspection. In the house of prayer, we stand without covering. That is one of the aspects of prayer woven into *tefillah*, our pleading cry. David's word for "naked" is *'arah*. In the vocabulary of prayer *tefillah* and *'arah* are connected. In the fallen world, naked prayer frightens us. But, of course, in the Garden of Eden, naked conversation with God was gloriously unashamed. Perhaps prayer should be the place where we return to Garden dialogue. *tefillah* and *'arah* are connected in other ways. *'arah* is also found in Isaiah 32:15. "Until the Spirit is *poured out* upon us from on high, and the wilderness becomes a fertile field, and the fertile field is considered a forest." When Isaiah describes the day of justice, he uses *'arah* ("poured out"). My nakedness, my uncovering is connected with the idea of being poured out. Prayer should empty me. Just as the Spirit is poured out when justice arrives, so my very soul is poured out when I come to the house of prayer for in the house of prayer I meet the holy God. Isaiah had it right. "Woe is me."

There is one more connection. "Therefore, I will allot Him a portion with the great, and He will divide the booty with the strong; because He *poured out* Himself unto death, and was numbered with the transgressors" (Isaiah 53:12). *'arah* is associated with dying. In the house of prayer, you and I must be sacrificed. The house of prayer is no place for posturing. Eloquence means nothing. Drama is deceptive. In the house of prayer, we are naked, poured out and dying until the Spirit speaks justice into our lives. It's hard to imagine that Yeshua, Old Testament scholar that He was, would have been unfamiliar with these connections. He is the poured out One. He is the epitome of *'arah*, and in Gethsemane we see just how naked one can be before the Father.

Why is Yeshua so angry when He discovers what has happened in His Father's house? Perhaps it has something to do with the hypocrisy of praying covered. Until you are spiritually undressed, you really have nothing to say to God. Pray like you are walking naked in the cool of the evening.

38.

It is written, "My house shall be called a house of prayer,"
*but you have made it a **den** of thieves.* Matthew 21:13

The Big Show

Den – Yeshua quotes Jeremiah. No doubt about it. "Has this house, which is called by My name, become a den of robbers?" (Jeremiah 7:11) The metaphor underlines the fact that the people come to God's house with deceptive words on their lips. They speak eloquent praises while their lives are filled with lies, adultery, stealing and murder. Yeshua recognizes that the people in His day fit the times of Jeremiah. They come saying, "the temple of the Lord," but their disobedience disrobes them. They pray with protective coverings, hoping that God will not see their naked hypocrisy.

The word in Greek really doesn't matter. The word from Jeremiah is *me'arah*. Do you see something familiar here? Remember the word for "naked"? *'arah* was connected to being naked, poured out, exposed. Here we have a possible derivation of the word. It means "cave" or "den." Scholars debate if this word is derived from *'arah* or *'ur* (they both mean naked), but we shouldn't miss the phonetic beauty. It helps us remember that God's house is a place of exposure, even when it is turned into something profane. If prayer is ultimately about walking naked in the Garden in conversation with the Lord, then how disturbing must it be to God when we attempt to converse with Him while we are clothed in deceit and disobedience. It's enough to make Him walk away.

Notice that Yeshua considers this outer court a "house of prayer." That was a particularly unusual sentiment. The outer court was specifically for Gentile believers. The "real" temple was for Jews. Did it really matter what happened in the courtyard of the outsiders? Obviously, Yeshua thought that it did. What disgusts Yeshua is the fact that merchants have turned the outer court of the temple into an emporium. It was the place for those who came to the Holy One of Israel by faith, not by lineage. To turn this court into a big display scandalized God's plan of evangelism. A place of prayer was for pouring out my soul, for kneeling naked before my Lord. A place of prayer allowed me to speak with God in the cool of the evening. How could that happen when I was surrounded with the big show?

There is a reason why the prayer of Hannah is considered the epitome of prayer by the rabbis. Hannah's prayer is so emotionally taxing, so completely a pouring out of her souls, that she can't even vocalize it. How different this prayer is from the ones we are used to. How different are our surroundings, filled with performers, technology, orators and programmed sequences. Even when we embrace "moment of silence," the musical interludes never stop. We might not be selling sheep and turtledoves, but our houses of prayer are just as much an emporium as that outer court. We Gentiles know what it takes to do business, even if it is the business of the church. We seem to have learned a lot from our Jewish merchant brothers.

It's time to let Hannah be the model. It's time for God's house to truly be a house of pouring out, of nakedness, of emptying. Then it will become a house of glorifying.

Justice

The Western world's system of law and justice is based on the Greek idea of the state. Law is the will of the people, tempered for the good of the majority and collective society. As such, the law stands above every citizen, dictating acceptable civil and moral practice in order to insure the continuance of the state or nation. Law opposes anarchy because anarchy ultimately destroys the state and the continuation of the state is the most important goal of the law.

While no citizen stands above the law, the law is not a fixed and permanent reality. Laws can be changed, and often are changed, to reflect the contemporary values of the state. That is the situation today in the conflict over the definition of marriage and the laws governing abortion and homosexuality. When the will of the people endorses these behavioral changes and they are determined not be to harmful to the existence of the state, they may become law. When democratic republics like the United States promote "law and order" around the world, they do not promote the Judeo-Christian view of law. They promote the Greek view of law based in the collective will and best intentions of the represented people. The Bible does not endorse or promote democracy as a political or judicial system. In fact, the Bible actually opposes the idea that the will of the people should be the rule of the land.

Infractions of the law challenge the authority of the state. Since the concept of criminal is defined by the laws of the state, it is possible to commit a crime in one nation that is legal in another nation. Punishment of crimes is often viewed in terms of a "debt to society", and while there are allowances for personal damages against victims, more often than not the required penance is determined by that state, not the injured party, and paid to the anonymous conglomerate called "society." Under these circumstances, it is quite possible to serve time for a crime, fulfill the required punishment and never make any restitution to the victim at all.

The Hebrew view of law and justice is quite different. The Hebrew concept of law is based on the character of God. Since God's character never changes, law in the biblical world is permanent, fixed and inviolable. What God deems unholy is unholy and will always be unholy, even if every man and woman on earth thinks otherwise. Hebrew law is not concerned with the will of the people nor the continuance of the state. It is concerned with actions that are acceptable to God. It is about obedience to a fixed code, not because the code insures tranquility and civil order but because the code reflects what God declares good even if His declarations stand in opposition to everything the society considers acceptable.

Hebrew justice is rooted in the idea of the tribe. God, as chief of the tribe, determines the governing principles of the tribe. As long as God is chief of the tribe, these governing principles remain in force. This is precisely what occurs when God establishes the covenant with Moses at Horeb. God proclaims the system of jurisprudence that will govern Israel. Of course, none of these instructions are new. They have been the governing principles of the world since God formed it. At Horeb they are simply codified into a national constitution.

Finally, the personal God focuses the attention of law on the personal implications for the victim. Reading the laws of the Torah drives the point home. In example after example, restitution and punishment are determined directly by the effect on the victim, not the state. For example, in the law concerning murder, the injured party is God Himself since the crime of murder steals a life that God ultimately owns. The focus of the law is always on the relationships between God and people. This is why there is no "jail time" in biblical thought. What matters is the restoration of the relationship between the offended and the offerder. Everything is very, very personal.

Today we are quickly approaching a time when the Greek model of what is legal is beginning to expose the vast difference between the Hebrew view and the Western view. The Judeo-Christian morality that was once taken for granted is under attack on every front, principally because the Western world has always had a legal system with a Greek philosophical foundation. Judeo-Christian ethics were merely icing on top of a Greek cake. The icing has been eaten away. Now the true texture of the cake is being revealed. Believers in the Holy One of Israel will find this a very uncomfortable and difficult time.

Let's look closely at some passages that will help us understand the enormous difference between the Greek and Hebrew views of justice.

1.

*You shall not show favoritism in **judgment**; you shall adjudicate exactly alike for the small and the great. You shall not be afraid of man, because **judgment** belongs to God.* Deuteronomy 1:17

Alien Justice

Judgment – In Hebrew thought, no principle of justice is more important than this one. This verse removes judgment from the realm of men. All judgment belongs to God. He sets the standard. He holds men accountable to it. He administers it. Even though He may appoint human agents and even though He may specify particular consequences, in the end all justice rests on His shoulders.

Why does this matter to us? The answer is startling. In our contemporary society, we no longer act as though God retains justice as His own. We live in a Greek-based culture where the rule of law is the final arbiter. The problem is that in the Greek system, law expresses the will of the people. That means that the law is subject to change – and we have clearly seen that occur over and over as we move further away from the Commandments and their application. Under the Greek system, the people exert pressure on legislators to alter the law to fit their desires. Under the Hebrew system, men were not to cower to such pressure because God owns judgment. When I succumb to the will of men rather than uphold the law of God, I act as though God is no longer Lord of all. I insult the Lord of the universe. He does not forget it.

Mishpat is translated almost 300 times in Scripture as

"judgment." This might make us think that God exercises the *court* functions of government, but that would be misleading. In ancient tribal cultures, the figurehead of the tribe (the tribal chief) was not simply the final arbiter. He had oversight of all aspects of governance. All branches of civil authority were his. This is the context of *shapat*, the verbal root of "judgment." God is the chief, the elder of His people. His word rules every aspect of governance. He speaks the law, administers the law and executes justice under the law. He is the ultimate and final patriarch. To violate His law is tantamount to committing treason.

Because we live under a Greek legal system, we can hardly imagine the God would not be "democratic." What a fatal mistake that is! God is King, not President. His subjects do not have the right to ignore, question or excuse His governance. Yet we routinely act as though God's revealed truth in the *torah* (instructions) no longer has relevance for us. Who are we kidding? Are you going to stand before the One Who owns justice and say, "But I didn't think it mattered anymore?"

2.

If, however, you are fulfilling the royal law, according to the Scripture, "You shall love your neighbor as yourself," you are doing well. But if you **show partiality***, you are committing sin* James 2:8-9

Face Time

Show Partiality – James was still a Jew. When he wrote his letter to the first century Christians in Greek, he still used ancient Hebrew expressions. He just converted them into Greek words. Once you see what lies behind the idea of "partiality," you will be amazed at the wisdom of the ancients. You might even wonder if evolution isn't backwards. Those who lived closer to the Creator (in temporal span) just might have greater insight than we do. Wouldn't that make an interesting headline?

The Hebrew idea behind partiality (and the parallel in ancient Greek) is all about the face. To be partial is to show deference to one person over another. In both ancient cultures, this is literally, "to receive the face." It should remind you of the modern Oriental cultural expressions of "saving face." It quite literally is about turning your face *toward* some people but turning your face *away* from others. In Greek, the expression is *prosopolepteo*. In Hebrew, it is *paniym*. When you give or grant "face time" on any basis other than God's grace, you show partiality.

Now, you're probably thinking, "Hey, I knew that! What's the big deal?" The big deal is that in both Hebrew and Greek, the original words are *plural*, not singular. The word that describes your countenance is not "face," but "faces" (if we were to translate literally). That causes us to reflect. Why would these ancient cultures view the countenance as a *multiple* object? Perhaps the answer reveals something deep about being human. Perhaps we are a lot closer to exhibiting *masks* to the world than we would like to believe (by the way, the Greek word is *also* the word for "mask"). Perhaps what these ancient societies recognized is that we all portray *multiple* faces. We pick and choose the one we wish to show depending on the circumstances or the audience. Of course, it could be as simple an explanation as the fact that the face is made up of multiple expressive elements (eyes and mouth). Or it just might be that in a world where I had to read the character of a man with a glance, where I didn't come with a background check, a resume or a Google search, I learned a very important lesson: every man carries *faces*.

Now apply this verse. How many different faces do you show to your Christian brothers and sisters? How many masks do you put on in order to hide the dark side of your soul? If your Christian colleagues could peel back *all* the faces, who would they really find?

Yes, you might skate by this verse if it is only about not showing discrimination. But what if it's about *face time* with those inside your circle? What if it's a sin to wear a mask? Then what will you do?

3.

*He has told you, O man, what is good; and what does the LORD require of you but to **do justice**, to love kindness, and to walk humbly with your God?* Micah 6:8

Intentional Transactions

Do Justice – Don't be fooled! The Bible never suggests that doing justice is haphazard, accidental or purposeless. You don't *do* justice by simply being a good citizen and minding your own business. If you're going to *do* justice, you will need to be deliberate, focused and goal-driven. You'll never get there without some serious attention to intentions.

The Hebrew phrase, *im-asho ot mishpat*, consists of two words, *'asah* and *mishpat*. We know this second word, *mishpat*. It is court language, often describing the accurate and proper decision of a judge. But it is more than that. It is the term for the execution of *righteousness*

169

and *divine orderliness* in the creation. It is God's character made manifest in deliberate decisions. It is *redemptive* living.

This word is combined with the verb *'asah*, a verb that covers the range of performing all sorts of activities characterized by deliberate purpose, moral obligation and goal orientation. In other words, doing justice requires intentional action to bring about right relationships and order. It will never happen by fortuitous serendipity. If you want to do justice, you have to *plan* to do justice.

This changes things. God *requires* me to act with deliberate intent to bring about righteousness and order. That means He expects me to plan, purpose and perform actions that cause real change in this fallen world. I do not meet this requirement if I am unconsciously just going about my life, fitting in to the moral society as needed. I do not *do justice* unless I am quite specific about my actions that are designed and determined to redeem the world for the Kingdom. There is no such thing as *passive* compliance with this command.

Are you *doing* justice, or are you simply taking care of your own morally insulated life? Have you made reconciliation, recovery and redemption a *deliberate* goal? Do you have an action plan for Kingdom regeneration? Or are you just floating along with the good graces of the moral majority, keeping your nose clean but never getting your hands dirty in the work of bringing God's will to earth?

God tells us *exactly* what He requires. Not one tiny fragment of His expectation involves passive compliance. If you are doing justice, you will instantly be able to bring to mind specific redemptive acts. If you can't think of any, you'd better start asking for forgiveness.

4.

*He has told you, O man, what is good; and what does the LORD require of you but to do justice, **to love kindness**, and to walk humbly with your God?* Micah 6:8

Intimate Delight

To Love Kindness – Micah's choice reveals a deeper meaning. You see, Micah does not choose a verb (to love). Instead, he chooses a noun. It isn't grammatically correct in English, but it communicates something absolutely vital in Hebrew. If you want to know what God really wants, then you better pay attention to the *Hebrew* version.

The phrase is *ahavat hesed*. Once again, we are familiar with the second word. *Hesed* is that powerful umbrella covering concepts like mercy, goodness, faithfulness, kindness and steadfastness. Read Psalm 136 where *hesed* is used twenty-six times. *Hesed* is ultimately a description of the loving character of God, seen in every single act He performs. If you love *hesed*, then your life is a mirror image of the Creator. His attributes shine right through you, radiating the world with the glory of His person.

So, why does Micah choose a *noun* to describe this requirement of the Most High? The answer is this: *ahavat* is a noun that is often associated with the deep intimacy of love between human beings (Jacob and Rachel, for example). This word is used ten times in the Song of Solomon (nearly one-third of its occurrences). It

171

covers the emotional and volitional aspects of the closest taste of heaven given to men and women on earth. It is the noun of personal delight in someone else. And, it is used to describe God's particular enthusiasm over His people (Deuteronomy 7:3).

Do you *love* kindness like this? Do you delight in mercy and faithfulness? Are you thrilled at the thought of delivering your enemies, providing for the needy and weak, lavishing mercy and goodness of those undeserving, maintaining steadfastness in the face of betrayal, and, more than anything else, upholding the covenant commandments with your Lord? Do you look upon the redeeming work of the Kingdom with the same intensity that you have when you look into the face of the one you love here on earth?

Micah picked the right word. We can't skate by with some watered-down sentiment of general goodwill toward kind acts. To *love* kindness is costly. Those who understand *ahavat* know that the symbol of *ahavat* is the cross. That's what is required of you, O man.

Now what are you going to do?

5.

*He has told you, O man, what is good; and what does the LORD require of you but to do justice, to love kindness, and **to walk humbly** with your God?* Micah 6:8

Before A Fall

To Walk Humbly – What does Micah have in mind?

What characteristics and actions demonstrate walking

humbly? Do you think it means self-effacing, modest, submissive or unassuming behavior? Do you get mental pictures of the unimportant, demeaned or servile? You might list all these as contemporary synonyms, but the meaning of the Hebrew word Micah uses is very narrow. It is only found in one other place in the Bible. That is in Proverbs 11:2 where the word is used in contrast to the fatal flaw of humanity - pride. So, if we know what the Bible means by "pride", we will have a pretty good picture of this word too. It will be just the opposite.

"To walk humbly" is the combination of *tsana* and *yalak* (the Hebrew is literally "to be humble to walk"). The opposite is *zadon* – a presumptive arrogance that relies on human cunning, engineering and effort to secure personal status. In the Bible, this kind of pride is marked by an inflated sense of authority ("*I* am in charge of things around here."), a rebellious disobedience ("*I* don't have to listen to you!") and willful selfishness ("It's my life. I can do what I want."). Pride is more than *hubris*. It is an attempted demonic *coup d'etat* of God's right to reign and rule.

What, then, is walking humbly? Now the answer emerges with startling clarity. "You shall love the Lord your God with all your heart, and with all your soul, and with all your strength, and with all your mind; and your neighbor as yourself" (Luke 10:27 from Deuteronomy 6:5 and Leviticus 19:18). To walk humbly is to deliberately place yourself under the complete reign and rule of God and then, act accordingly in every aspect of life. Humility encompasses heart, soul, mind, strength and relationships. Anything less is *zadon*.

Micah railed against the Israelites for their pretentious

religious practices, mimicking worship without total surrender. Are we any different? Don't we espouse humility at the same time that we withhold that smallest part of obedience and surrender? Don't we claim humility while we continue to act as though we are really in charge of our destinies (and those of anyone we can command)? Don't we laud humility but still think that life should be lived the way we want it to be?

Micah gives us the right word, boiled down to its pure essence. Not one of us walks humbly if there remains a place for pride in the corners of life. And pride, we have discovered, is a good deal more subtle than strutting our stuff. Pride simply asks God to step down from the throne, just this once, just for a moment. No man walks humbly unless he is fully obedient.

6.

Evil men do not understand justice, but those who seek the LORD understand all things. Proverbs 28:5

A Closed Universe (1)

Evil Men – What did you expect? Did you think that men who do not pursue an intimate relationship with God nor seek His counsel will give you justice? How could they? They live in a closed universe – closed to their own best guesses about what is right and wrong. Their justice is stirred, and shaken, with personal motivation, leverage, influence and pressure.

The Bible calls these people *anshei-ra*. The critical term is *ra*, an adjective that covers a very wide range of bad and evil behaviors. In this context, it is used to describe people who do not subject themselves to the authority of God, who spurn His law and character and rely on their own system of assumptions to render judgments. These are not necessarily people of the court. The Bible is clear. Anyone who rejects God's rule is blind to true justice.

Followers of the Way will certainly not be surprised to find themselves in conflict with these people, even when *evil men* are in positions of authority and are supposed to represent what is just. But the proverb applies across the board. We find miscarries of justice at all levels of society because men and women who live without an active presence of God are simply not able to discern good and evil – and act accordingly. Jesus called them "the blind leading the blind." We, the followers of the King, are usually the victims.

Today is the day for adjusting your view of justice in this world. Peter calls us alien residents. Abraham shows us that we are wanderers. Jesus invites us on a long journey of suffering in the same direction. But the Bible never suggests that we will experience heaven on earth. This world has fallen. It can be restored, slowly, carefully and in great agony and struggle, but it will never be the *new heaven and the new earth*. Joy is not the same as justice. When every knee bows and every heart proclaims that Jesus is Lord, then justice will rule the earth. Until then, *anshei-ra* will live in the dark, and expect you to do the same. You will be ill prepared for life as it is if you expect of men what only God can give.

Of course, you could decide to participate in the closed universe model. But then you would have to be blind, wouldn't you?

7.

*Evil men do **not understand** justice, but those who seek the LORD understand all things.* Proverbs 28:5

A Closed Universe (2)

Not Understand – Why don't evil men understand justice? Can you answer that question – biblically? Oh, we are quick to give a lot of reasons. They are self-possessed. They are morally blind. They lack real compassion. They are "bad" people. All of these may be true, but when we realize that the term "evil men" applies to *everyone* who is not in alignment with the Lord, then our usual explanations begin to falter. Don't use the worst examples of human depravity in your thinking. Use the *best*! Take a look at those paradigms of human goodness, those people known for altruism and self-sacrifice, and apply this verse. The biblical view of evil extends to *everyone* on the other side of the fence, regardless of their morality. Jesus demands radical allegiance. "If you are not for me, you are against me." There is no neutral ground to plead the cause of the "good" people.

The implications of *o-ya vinu* (the verb is *biyn* - to understand), tell the story. The primary meaning is to give heed, to discern, to distinguish. But the biblical use is never concerned with intellectual knowledge alone. *Biyn* is connected with hearing and obeying. In the Bible, understanding without application is pointless. Worse than that, from the biblical perspective, *I do not understand until and unless I am obedient to what I receive.* We think understanding is the collection of correct information regardless of its application. I can

176

claim to understand justice, but I mean only that I know all the rules and the case law. The Bible never allows such foolishness. Understanding is *personal application of revealed and accepted truth.* I don't understand until I put it in action.

But there's a catch. No man has the ultimate perspective needed to be able to perfectly discern right from wrong. The world is simply too complicated. Therefore, the kind of discernment essential for justice can come from only one source – God Himself. Unless God gives me correct understanding, all of my knowledge will be incomplete and flawed. Jeremiah makes it clear (Jeremiah 9:11). If you aren't listening to God, and being obedient to what you hear, real justice alludes you.

Will you throw up your hands in despair? Do you feel as though it's hopeless since you can never know *exactly* what's right? You missed the point. God has already *revealed* what constitutes justice. Only God can do such a thing. All you have to do is understand what He has already said by doing it!

The Bible is the source book for God's perspective on life. If your idea of justice is not in alignment with the Book, then your god is not the God of Scripture. But the Bible is not a rule book. It is a cook book.. So, start baking. No one eats the recipe. Good food is the result of putting the recipe into action.

8.

*Evil men do not understand **justice**, but those who seek the LORD understand all things.* Proverbs 28:5

A Closed Universe (3)

Justice – Pilate asked one of the truly great questions: "What is truth?" You have a chance to ask another one: "What is justice?" Both questions are answered from the same source. Truth is found in the character of God. It is much more than not lying. It is representing the holiness of God in word and deed. Justice is also found in the character of God. It is *mishpat*, the Hebrew word that connects truth with action. Justice is the discernment of God's will and its application to human society.

Old Testament justice has a forensic base. That means it comes from the arena of the court. It is about applying the law. It is connected to the role of the king and the officials. God puts people in these roles in order that His moral order may be exercised in the human community. In particular, the Old Testament considers action toward the poor, the disenfranchised and the afflicted as the best example of justice. That tells us that justice is deeply interwoven with compassion. God puts things right. Where circumstances and situations are not right, God expects those who are under His authority to do all they can to make things right, not according to the way we see things, but according to the way He sees things.

Let's be clear about this. Justice is not the same as fairness. God is not fair. He is just. God perfectly applies the attribute of moral perfection in every situation. If we followed His direction perfectly, we too could exercise justice without a flaw. But that does not mean that God intends life to be fair. Fair is a measure of the will of human desire. Fair is a term for majority (usually) opinion. When I complain that things aren't fair, what I mean is that I am not treated the way others are treated. I want to be treated the same. If I were foolish enough to demand that God be fair, I could never experience His forgiveness. Redemption is not fair. It is undeserved favoritism applied to those who should to be treated according to their moral efforts. A doctrine of fairness sends us all to hell.

Fortunately, God is just. He does what is right, in spite of what is fair. He shows compassion instead of wrath. He redeems instead of condemning. He lifts the downtrodden when they do *not* deserve it. Would you rather that He be fair? Not me. I need justice, the application of God's love to my unworthy life. Now that I know what justice looks like for me, am I willing to apply it to others? Am I ready to give compassionate benevolence to those who do not deserve it? Will I uphold the character of God by acting with grace and forgiveness? Or will I complain about the fact that life isn't fair, and in my complaint, deny God's sovereignty?

9.

Those who abandon instruction praise the wicked, but those who keep instruction ***strive*** *against them.* Proverbs 28:4 (Waltke)

The Dividing Line

Strive – The world is divided in two. There is no middle ground. The line cuts through every social and economic group, every ethnic and national background, every political affiliation. You are on one side or the other. And your actions are the badge of your allegiance. You either fight against the wicked, or you join them.

This verse is sometimes translated "strive with them," but, of course, the thought is not that you are in league, fighting alongside the wicked. Citizens of the

Kingdom are the opposition, facing the wicked in battle. The Hebrew verb *garath* can mean to provoke or to strip up or strive. Context tells us how to apply the phrase.

What's important here is who ends up on each side of the line. This verse gives us just one of the delineation criteria. In this case, the line is drawn over the "law." That's the word *torah* – instruction. Those who abandon God's instruction are in league with the wicked. They praise God's opposition. They emulate God's enemies. They submit to the patterns of this world's system. Don't think that these people are reprobates. They are your neighbors, your officials, your teachers, your friends, your relatives – anyone who determines that life should be lived *my* way, anyone who does not recognize God's authority over every decision. You know these people well. And they know you. In fact, they might consider you one of them, unless your life demonstrates in tangible form that you are submissive to God's instruction. One of the great tragedies of the church is that those on the inside don't appear to be very different from those on the outside. Both groups strive for the same things – success, happiness, acceptance, importance. That's why this line cuts right through the heart of every man and woman. If you are not standing up against what opposes God's instruction, then you are endorsing His enemies.

Are you ready to take a really hard look at your actions? Can you face the facts? Whenever and wherever you refuse to oppose those who flaunt God's law, you lose all credibility as a servant of the King. Even a choice with "insignificant" consequences is a telltale sign of your allegiance. What did you think God meant when He commanded us to be holy - to just improve our lot in life?

Or, did He mean for us to separate our attitudes and actions in such a way that everyone notices we are different?

10.

He has told you, O man, what is good Micah 6:8

Convert Your Thinking

Good – What is good? Well, if you subscribe to the Greek view of life, you will come up with a list that looks like this:
1. Exemplary effort
2. High standards
3. Self-discipline
4. Fairness toward all
5. Thoughtfulness and discretion
6. Moderation and capacity

In other words, the classical education that leads to praiseworthy life among the people, coupled with demonstrated skills and notable success. For the Greeks, the final phase was the link of *eros* with *kalon* (the love of the Good). Such a life led to the highest experience - a glimpse of eternal beauty. The Greek ideals still dominate our view of education, justice and economics, even if we don't live up to them. But they are miles away from God's view.

Our culture is saturated with the idea that God and classic virtues go hand-in-hand. Not so! We need Micah to remind us that God is the only One Who can tell us what is good. And He does, in great detail.

The fundamental difference between the Greek view and

the Hebrew view is this: Everything that is good in the Hebrew culture is determined by the will of God expressed in the Law. There is absolutely no room for any motivation that results from self-determination. Self- perfection is *excluded* from God's point of view. The Hebrew word, *tov*, is radically different than the Greek *kalos*. It is *kalos* that stands behind the Greek educational motto *"kalos kagathos"* – the combination of what is noble and useful with what is holy. This is an inward perspective, looking to the soul of Man to find the eternal. But the Hebrew *tov* looks first to the character of God Himself to determine what is good. The Hebrew view is simple: Man cannot be trusted to know what is good within himself. He must rely on the explicit command of God. Therefore, what is useful, suitable, noble and holy is all wrapped up in the same concept, *tov*. And that concept is defined and delineated by what God tells us to do. The good is finally what I do and what I say and what I think *according to God's Word*.

Isn't it interesting that Genesis 2:17 uses the word *tov* to describe the tree of *good* and evil? Good is doing what God commands. Evil is not doing what God commands. Simple. At least in principle. It is the *execution* of what God commands that becomes difficult, especially in a world that encourages you to "think for yourself." Now you have a chance to re-educate yourself. The Word is there to tell you what is good – and *all* that is good. Still comes down to trust, doesn't it?

11.

*You shall have no other gods **besides Me**.* Deuteronomy 5:7

The Ground of Morality

Besides Me – In Hebrew literature, this is the first *word* of the Ten Words; those saying that we commonly call The Ten Commandments or The Decalogue. The first *Word* is all about loyalty and exclusivity. This phrase in the first "word" is very difficult word to translate, even though the general meaning is quite clear. In Hebrew it is *al-panai*, a combination that could mean "beside me," or "above me," or "in preference to me."   What is clear is this: God will not share His glory with *any rival* (see Isaiah 42:8), whether man or beast or inanimate object. Spoken to a congregation that had just come out of a culture where men, beasts and objects all represented gods, this was a powerful declaration.

If we break down the two combined Hebrew words, we discover that the preposition *al* is followed by the word for "face" (*paniym*). Hebrew is a tactile language, rooted in practical experience. So, when Hebrew uses words to describe intangible concepts, it often turns to the *visible* symptoms of the invisible.   Thus, "before my face" describes the idea of presenting oneself in an audience with the King.   To stand before the *face* of God is to account for one's attitude and actions in the presence of the Holy One of Israel. This commandment implies that God will determine where our true loyalty lies in a face-to-face examination.

What He finds is of utmost importance.

Perhaps our Greek-based intellectualization of God's person (omniscience, omnipotence, omnipresence, etc.) could use a little "in-your-face" correction.   Imagine standing before the King, the Creator of all things, the One Who gives you your very breath. This is a fearful event since everything you are and everything you have is really a loan from the King. You exist only because of His grace. Now, while you are contemplating your essential dependence, God asks you about your loyalty. But, of course, He does not ask you what you *think* about it, or how you *feel* about it. He asks you what you have *done* to demonstrate this absolute loyalty. He asks you to give an account of your actions. Do they exhibit fidelity to Him, or do they point toward obedience to His rivals?

All men have gods. It is the nature of men to serve some higher power, whether that be a person, a cause or a dream. In the final analysis, there are no atheists. There are only those who refuse to serve YHWH, the God Who brings you out. The first *Word* commands clarity of devotion. Any substitution in public or private worship violates this commitment and denies the essential worthiness of the character of God Himself. This is the basis of *all* morality, for either I live according to the character of God or I do not. Therefore, every one of my actions can be measured according to His character. When I have no other gods, there is nothing in my life that points away from His holy being. The question is this: where do your actions point? No wonder discipleship requires such exacting assessment of our lives.

12.

*You shall not bear **false** witness against your neighbor*
Deuteronomy 5:20

Hitch-hiker

False – It's court language, but it's not limited to trials. The word picture recalls the witness stand. "Do you swear to tell the truth?" The answer better be "Yes." In front of the judge and jury, we want true testimony. So does God. But His reasons for demanding the truth are not always the same as ours.

We look for justice. We want satisfaction. God has a much deeper concern in mind. Lying disturbs the nature of the universe. Why? Because God is truth and whatever circumvents, diminishes or deflects truth attacks His very character. The universe reflects the glory of God, says the psalmist. Lying in any form damages that glory, and God will not put up with it.

Once we see the Hebrew word, *shaw*, we understand the hideous nature of lying. The word is not just about circumventing the truth. This is a word that also means emptiness, vanity, evil, ruin, worthlessness and uselessness. Lying fits all of those categories. It constructs a fictitious universe, a world where there is no reliability and no consistency. No wonder God tells us that He *hates* lying (Proverbs 6:19). Everything that results from lies stands in utter opposition to the character of God.

Take another look at the meanings of *shaw*. Did you notice how many are associated with *actions*, not just words? Did you see how *shaw* is rooted in the practical, not just the linguistic? Worthless, useless, empty and vane – lying gets you exactly nothing. It moves you in the opposite direction from life itself. It sucks the blood out of relationships and drains the world of meaning. Lying is a step toward chaos and away from the God of order.

It's popular to suggest that life requires little white lies. After all, just shading the truth a bit here and there seems to ease things along. Transparency and brutal honesty are not virtues in a Greek-based world of image management.

185

It's far easier to side-step the conflict with a tiny, little lie. But now you see why even the whitest of white lies comes from the blackest pit of hell. Every lie moves me away from the living God. That means it removes me from my own real life. No matter how "justifiable", a lie attacks the glory of the Creator and the handiwork of His image in me. Lies send me right back to the second verse of the Bible, when the world was without form and void.

The choice is yours. Lies always stand at one-way streets waiting for a ride. You can stop and pick them up, but you will have to travel toward the dark if you do. Or, you can see them for what they are - and turn around.

13.

*I will **bear** the indignation of the Lord because I have sinned against Him, until He pleads my case and executes justice for me. He will bring me out to the light, and I will see His righteousness.* Micah 7:9

The God of Justice (1)

Bear – God is just. We acknowledge the absolute truth of this claim. After all, doesn't Abraham say, "Shall not the Judge of the all the earth deal justly?" No surprise here, until we ask, "But what does it mean to say God is just?" Then we begin to stumble. Certainly it has something to do with the law, with fairness and with punishment, but how do all these things come together? I don't see much justice in the world, so how can I proclaim that God is both sovereign and just? Micah's statement will get us started.

Micah starts where we must all start – with sin. He uses the Hebrew verb *nasa'*. This verb is used nearly 600 times in Scripture (that means it's important). It covers three different categories of meaning, but these three are tied together. *Nasa'* can mean "to lift" as one would lift a stone or lift up the face. It can mean "to bear or carry" and is particularly associated with bearing guilt. Finally, it can mean "to take away", both in the simple sense of carrying something off or in the metaphorical sense of taking away guilt by forgiving. Exodus 19:4 shows us just how important this verb is for understanding the role of God as the *ezer* (help-meet) of Israel. God says that He lifted up and carried Israel to Himself. This is more than empathy. This is active support, assistance and provision.

But Micah gives us the dark side of *nasa'*. I will *carry* the load of my sin. That's where I start with God. Until I recognize my real condition, God really can't do much for me. As long as I think I don't need help, as long as I deny my guilt, God waits for the load to crush me. It will. It always does. But too often someone will come along and tell me to "get a grip" or try to keep me from sinking. That only delays the necessary. The first step toward understanding justice is intensely personal. *I* must bear His indignation. If you try to defer or deflect, you prevent God from lifting me, no matter how noble your intentions.

It seems to me that realizing the Hebrew verb means both "carry" and "take away" is very important. God cannot take away what I do not carry. There is no way to lift off a burden unless the weight of the load rests firmly on my shoulders. In Hebrew thought, these two critical actions are intimately related. I cannot experience freedom and release if I have never experienced slavery and restraint. What did Jesus say of the woman who wept over Him? "For this reason I say to you, her sins, which are many, have been forgiven, for she loved much" (Luke 7:47). God takes away in proportion to what I carry.

In a world of instant psychology, we are quick to rescue ourselves and others from distress and remorse. We pry away the load before it has accomplished its purpose. Then God has to re-engineer life to bring us back under the burden. We run interference and step on God's plan. Let *nasa'* become personal. Put the "I" back in carry, or God will have to start again.

14.

*I will bear the **indignation** of the Lord because I have sinned against Him, until He pleads my case and executes justice for me. He will bring me out to the light, and I will see His righteousness.* Micah 7:9

The God of Justice (2)

Indignation – The storm warnings are out. There is a fury in the sky, headed this way. This is the big one, a 5.0 tornado, a category 5 hurricane, a sandstorm that none will survive. That's the impact of the Hebrew word *za'aph*. God's fury has arrived. Most importantly, in the Hebrew Bible, this is the *first* word in the verse. *Za'aph YHWH* is Micah's cry. God's storm is pouring out on me.

Did you notice that Micah's real focus is not on his personal guilt but rather on God's anger? I just might be able to bear up under guilt. After all, I can always find excuses or resignation or denial. Guilt is internal psychological distress. There are pills for this. But there is no remedy for God's storm. No denial, no excuse, no deflection can remove the lightning and wind that will destroy me. There are no pills to keep the tornado from tearing my home apart. God's wrath is a cross no man can bear!

This recognition is crucial. Our world would love to just deal with the guilt. We could point to Jesus and happily say, "Oh, He paid for it all," as though His death makes us immune. We live in a religious atmosphere where believing is the equivalent of political endorsement. Just put a "Jesus" sign on your car or wear a "WWJD" bracelet, and life will be wonderful. We haven't heard Micah. It's not guilt that he fears. It's God's wrath. My sin might produce an inner discomfort that I call "feeling guilty," but it is not likely to place me in the hands of an angry God until I understand what justice means. That's a mistake Micah doesn't make. The *first* thing on his mind is God's impending storm. There is no avoiding the rushing disaster.

There are two results to *za'aph*. The first is unsettled anger. The storm clouds in the heart of a holy God will be unleashed. The Bible calls this rage. The second result is another emotional catastrophe. *Za'aph* can also result in dejection (see Genesis 40:6). There is a kind of hopelessness that comes as a result of those who refuse to act on the truth. I'm not sure if God ever feels this way, but it wouldn't surprise me. Remember what He said about the evil of men before He washed the earth of them? He *grieved* over their rebellion (Genesis 6:6). Then the storm came.

One more look will cement the picture. Jesus faces the same storm in the Garden on the night of His arrest. "If this cup can pass," is His recognition of the truth in Micah's announcement. The cup of God's wrath is beyond bearing. It took the life of the Son. It will most certainly take our lives since we are far less human than He was.

Justice begins here. It begins with the personal awareness that God's storm clouds are coming for me. Do you want to know what justice means? Are you willing to look into the gale and see yourself?

15.

*I will bear the indignation of the Lord because I have sinned against Him, **until** He pleads my case and executes justice for me. He will bring me out to the light, and I will see His righteousness.* Micah 7:9

The God of Justice (3)

Until – "How long, O Lord, how long?" Until. That's the word *'ad*. The phrase is actually *'ad asher* ("as far as when"). I will carry the impending storm of God's wrath as far as the point when *He* does something, not me. Do you see that calming the storm, avoiding the disaster, does not depend on my action? It depends on God taking up my case. No matter what I do, the storm will come because I bear His wrath for my sin. And there is nothing *I* can do to take it away.

Don't get confused. Asking forgiveness does not avert God's wrath. Begging for mercy doesn't change the direction of the weather. Unless *God* does something on my behalf, I am in for it. Salvation belongs to Him. Ultimately, it has nothing to do with me.

We learn two important facts about justice from the middle of this verse. First, we learn that God must provide the rescue. He is the offended one and only He can bring about the reconciliation. That's not the same as saying that we don't have to confess. Once we realize our situation, confession is the only reasonable response. But by the time we realize where we stand, by the time we see the storm clouds on the horizon, it's too late to do anything but confess. The rest has to be up to God.

Second, we learn that there is no rescue for those who have not embraced the consequences of their sin. God doesn't save those who think they can save themselves. God doesn't provide reinforcements to those who pretend they do not bear the burden of His wrath. God lets them sink. Why? Because only drowning men know they need a savior. Those who think they can tread water in the perfect storm haven't faced their reality yet. So, God applies *'ad* – until. David knew the truth of the matter. "Until I was afflicted, I did not follow You" (Psalm 119:67). Pain has purpose. Use it wisely.

It's easy to think that God will come to the aid of all who call on Him. We've been taught that God is loving and compassionate, so we conclude that this must mean He would never turn away from anyone in trouble. We see only one side of the coin. Mercy depends on wrath. If you don't like the pain, you will never experience the gain. God told Jeremiah *not* to pray for Israel before He sent them into captivity. Why? Because they thought treading water would save them. It's very easy today to pretend that God will not arrive in the storm clouds. We have been seduced by the "kindly old grandfather" theology. Our morality is mixed up with a doctrine of fairness. But Micah is beginning to clear our confusion. God isn't fair; He's just. And justice is tied to "until" He acts.

Is there a storm in your life? Have you tried to hold your

breath under the waves? Do you see that your salvation is delayed *until* He acts? What good is your remorse now? Rescue is God's choice to act, not mine to demand.

16.

*I will bear the indignation of the Lord because I have sinned against Him, until He **pleads** my case and executes justice for me. He will bring me out to the light, and I will see His righteousness.* Micah 7:9

The God of Justice (4)

Pleads – You're caught. You are arrested and charged. There's not much point in resisting since you know you are guilty. You stand before the judge, ashamed and humiliated. What can you do? There is no way out of this unless someone pleads your case. But who would plead the case of a man who has already confessed to the crime? Actually, only one person could do such a thing – the injured party. The only person able to speak for the criminal is the victim.

That's the scenario in Micah's courtroom description. I have offended the Most High God. He is the injured party. There is no question about my guilt. Therefore, only He is able to take up my case and bring about justice. The law demands punishment, but the victim can plead for mercy. If God doesn't act on my behalf, there is nothing ahead but wrath and misery.

The Hebrew word *riyv* comes directly from the courtroom. It means to conduct a lawsuit, to contest and dispute in legal proceedings. God Himself uses this word to describe His accusation against idolatrous Israel

(Isaiah 3:13). Now Micah says that unless God takes up our sorrowful verdict, we are lost. In the court of heaven, I need the best attorney in all creation, and that, of course, is the merciful Lord Himself.

This is a legal proceeding like no other. God is victim, judge and defense counsel. It may seem a bit strange to us, but this is the way it must be. God is judge by right of creation. He made it all. He owns it all. He sets the rules in place for the governance of it all. God is also the victim here because, in spite of His right to require obedience, I have spurned Him. I have refused to live according to the decrees of the Owner of all. He is the injured party in this proceeding.

But Micah also tells me that God is the defense counsel. I discover that God is not simply the moral policeman of the universe. He is exactly as He describes Himself in Exodus 34:6 – compassionate and full of mercy. God steps in to plead my case when there is absolutely no excuse for my actions.

So, what does pleading mean when I am a confessed criminal? From my perspective, it can only mean one thing – a cry for a merciful verdict. In these circumstances, that's all I could come up with. That, however, is not God's way. God's way is amazingly controversial, completely unanticipated and absolutely unique. The victim voluntarily dies in the place of the guilty. This is the whole creation turned upside-down. Nothing could have prepared us for this solution. The law is upheld. The judge is satisfied. The guilty are forgiven. Mercy triumphs over wrath without compromising justice.

This might be a good day to praise the God Who died in your place. It's the only reason you are free.

17.

*I will bear the indignation of the Lord because I have sinned against Him, until He pleads my case and executes **justice** for me. He will bring me out to the light, and I will see His righteousness.* Micah 7:9

The God of Justice (5)

Justice – Justice at last. The path to justice includes experiencing my guilt, carrying the impending storm of God's wrath, waiting for God to act and discovering that the holy Victim stands in my place. Now we come to the summary word, *mishpat*.

Actually, *mishpat* is the end result of justice. It is the legal decision, the proper claim and the correct verdict. Insofar as it is the result of the legal proceeding, it summarizes justice, but it does so in a very practical way. A *mishpat* is not an ethical theory. It's not a legal opinion. It is an *executed judgment*. In the Hebraic mind, the *mishpat* is the *action* of rectitude. This is God's intended goal for His people (see Jeremiah 7:5) – to *do* what is right before Him.

In our world, executing justice is often quite confusing. It seems that in many cases we simply don't know what is the right thing to do. Our view of justice is so mingled with the fairness doctrine, the "rights" philosophy and the blameless society that we walk away from case after case shaking our heads in disbelief. We know that the system failed us. We have an inner sense of injured conscience. But we don't quite know *where* we missed the mark. It's just one big muddle.

Micah (and God) calls us back to the original design. The solution to our muddle is really simple. Give up trying to figure it out. Abandon the Greek idea that reason alone can bring sanity and sanctification. No man is able to know the final truth in a world of dynamic relationships. If we want justice, we will have to turn over the legal proceedings to God. We will have to listen to His ethical instructions and adopt them as our own. Will a man negotiate with God? Apparently, we think so. We systematically ignore the clear directions God gives regarding everything from education to execution. We believe in ourselves. So, we try to figure it all out through legislation and case law. What insane arrogance!

The end of justice takes us right back to the beginning. How long will I bear the indignation of the Lord? As long as I continue to act as though His judgments do not matter any more. I can pretend that God has grown up and put the legislation of morality in the hands of those who have earned their degrees in the subject, but to do so insults the King of creation. How long will I bear His indignation? As long as it takes me to realize that my version of "legally correct" is a pitiful proclamation of self-independence. As long as legal technicalities prevent proper execution of God's moral standards. As long as I think that I can change the law to fit my desires.

Justice finally belongs only to God. It is nothing more than doing what He deems to be right. Maybe Micah wasn't far removed from the commentator in Ecclesiastes. "Fear God and keep His commandments. For this is the whole duty of humanity. For God will bring every deed into judgment."

18.

I will bear the indignation of the Lord because I have

*sinned against Him, until He pleads my case and executes justice for me. He will **bring me out** to the light, and I will see His righteousness.* Micah 7:9

The God of Justice (6)

Will Bring Me Out – There is nothing more destructive than secrets. In fact, you can probably measure the depth of your walk with God by the absence of secrets in your life. The more we hide in the closets, the less we find that perfect peace God promises. In this verse, Micah tells us that God's justice includes bringing us into the light. God intends to expose who we are.

If that sounds terrifying to you, you're not alone. In a world where personal reputation plays an enormous part in self-identity, most of us have more than a few things we would just as soon keep in the dark. Just thinking about exposing the secrets of our shattered lives sends shock waves of humiliation through us. We can't imagine the shame and embarrassment we would have to endure if *everything* about our lives came to light. That's why we need to pay very close attention to what Micah says.

First, we notice that *God* is the active agent here. In Hebrew, it is *yotsi.eni la.or* (He will bring me out to the light). The basic verb (*yotset*) has dozens of nuances surrounding the idea of go out or come in. Did you notice that the verb has a dynamic continuum of motion? It represents the *movement*, not the direction, so "going out" or "coming in" are tied together in the same kind of motion. It is God's action that carries me out or in. I don't do this myself. In fact, I am almost incapable of doing this. After all, I bear His wrath because of my sin. Not only must God plead my case, He must also act as my transporter. If He doesn't take me into the light, I will never get there.

Second, when I come out into the light, I do not see a purified "me". I am not suddenly transformed into a dazzling white, sinless person. No, what I see is *God's* righteousness, not mine. Why? Because the righteousness that I experience in the light is alien to me. It doesn't belong to me. It belongs to God. When He pleads my case and carries me into the light, when my secret sins are burned away by His holiness, then what is left is His righteousness. God deals with my sin by ushering me into His blamelessness. I am guilty of acting against His will. He knows that. But God acts as my advocate. He executes justice for me by taking the punishment on Himself and, in the process, He leads me into the light of His holiness. In the end, justice is only about the holy God of Israel. I am either carried into His blamelessness or I fall under His indignation. There is no other option.

So, what happens to those secrets? God deals with them as only He can. That does not mean that He won't use someone else as part of this movement into the light. He will do precisely what is necessary to bring me out of the dark. But only He can do this. No self-help regimen, no therapy, no confessional, no accountability group will ever remove the grip of the secrets in my life until *God* brings me out of the dark. And when He does being me out, I am a witness to His amazing grace.

19.

He waited for **justice**, *but behold, bloodshed; and for* **righteousness**, *behold, an outcry!* Isaiah 5:7

Words Within Words

Justice, Righteousness – When Jesus quotes this passage in Isaiah (Matthew 21:33-46), He applies it in the same way that the prophet did. It is a metaphorical description of judgment found in the parable of the wicked tenants. God in His goodness does everything necessary to prepare a place of harmony and fruitfulness. But the ones He leaves in charge of His carefully constructed garden not only refuse to use the vineyard as the Master wishes, but also seek to take possession of it for themselves. They kill the Master's messengers and eventually the Son. What is the result? The Master will come upon them with vengeance, destroying them and removing their authority. What was true of the leadership of Israel in the 5th Century BC is also true of the leadership in the 1st Century AD. Those who refuse to use what God provides for God's purposes will be removed. God's purposes will prevail no matter what.

Buried in this verse in Isaiah is a Hebrew word play that shows us just how razor sharp the edge between obedience and disobedience really is. The text reads, "He waited for *mishpat* (justice) but, behold, *mispah* (bloodshed), and for *tsedaqah* (righteousness), but behold *tseaqah* (outcry). Once you see it phonetically, you can understand how powerful the verse really is. The difference between obedience and disobedience is just a single letter. Leadership is granted to those who are meticulous in their obedience.

In Hebrew, meanings derived from these slightly altered words are fundamentally related. Justice has something to do with bloodshed. Righteousness has something to do with a call for help against iniquity. The difference is all important, but the difference is just a tiny shift. If my leadership is motivated by God's goodness, I will confront bloodshed, fight against bloodshed and abolish bloodshed. If I slip from exhibiting God's character in my leadership, I will end up on the side of bloodshed. The root word means outpouring. Here the message is that leadership devoid of God's justice will result in the outpouring of false judgment on the innocent. What this means in graphic terms is that a society without godly leaders will put to death those who do not deserve to die.

In the same way, leadership without blameless conduct and integrity will result in *tseaqah*, an outcry from the oppressed regarding the outrage of sin. This is the wailing cry of despair by those who are abused because of godlessness. Righteousness is the only protection against exploitation of the ones who have no voice in society. The role of true leadership is to act as the voice of these invisible members of humanity. Leaders who take advantage of the unnamed through their position and power are guilty of an enormous sin before God. And He does not forget!

We see God's word to Isaiah about the consequences of godless leadership. We see Jesus endorse Isaiah's pronouncement. Now the question sits with us. What kind of leadership do we endorse? What kind of leaders do we follow? If God did not overlook the sins of Israel, do you think that God will overlook ours?

Law and Grace

Everything about Yeshua's proclamation of grace was wrong, according to the legalists' religious view. Legalists believe that men need to merit God's favor by doing what God requires. Christianity is split right down the middle on this issue. Since the Protestant Reformation, those who broke away from Catholicism claim that God could never count as worthy those who were *essentially* unworthy. Protestants generally claim that every effort to earn God's blessing, every bit of striving to make myself into something acceptable to God – all of it – Yeshua cast aside. God is for those who know they don't have a prayer. According to the Protestant tradition, the *essential* element lacking in human beings is not performance, ritual or religion. It is righteousness – and only God can provide Man right-standing before Him.

The Greek word for righteousness is *dikaiosyne*. It comes from a Greek root that means "justice". The concept of righteousness is closely linked to the Hebrew concept of Torah. God's law (His *instruction*) is the most powerful expression of His covenant with His chosen people. The Torah is not just the legal proclamations of the Ten Commandants or the laws given in Deuteronomy and Leviticus. The Torah is God's rule governing all aspects of life found in the stories, the history, the poetry and the legislation of the first five books of the Tanakh (the Hebrew Scriptures). The Old Testament consistently affirms that God's rule is the proper order of all life. This concept is very different from our modern Greek-based legal system. The Greeks believed that Law was essentially a result of rational implementation of what benefited the state and its citizens. Law was what is proper and what is established for the good of the citizenry. This concept is not present in the Hebrew view of Torah. The Hebrew view of Torah begins and ends with God. Unlike the Greek concept of Law, God is not subject to some higher principle that He merely administers in the world. God Himself is the embodiment of righteousness. The Torah is simply an expression of His character as the Holy God. God is *The* Ruler Who establishes the conduct code of His kingdom based on what He knows to be true because it is the expression of His very being. Because He is The Ruler of all that is, He is the proper authority for the expression of all life-governing principles. His instructions are unchangeable and incontestable. God is the interrogator, prosecutor, judge and jury concerning conformity to His code of conduct. Righteousness is the term used to express the idea that God is both the Lawgiver and Judge.

Nevertheless, God's righteousness is not a static set of demands. God is actively engaged in the exercise and application of His righteousness. God's instructions for living are not like the Greek idea of conformity to what is proper. God's rule is the active involvement of His righteousness with our deficiency. In simple terms, God is holy. We are not holy and can never be holy based on our own efforts. We will forever fall short of God's standard. But this does not mean that God casts us aside as unworthy, nor does it mean that *all* of our acts are unworthy. We can do things that emulate the character and holiness of God even if we fail to meet the standard of complete holiness. Amazingly, in spite of our failures, He counts as righteous those who recognize their unrighteousness and seek His help. We can think of the stories of Abraham, Moses, David, Isaiah, Daniel and many others who knew they didn't meet God's standard and yet, God established them as righteous.

In the days of Yeshua, some of the rabbinical clergy believed that right standing in front of God (righteousness) was based on godly behavior. In other words, they thought that if they kept all the rules, their human efforts would result in a balance in their favor and God would reward them. For this reason, some scribes and Pharisees were meticulous about rule keeping. This was incredibly serious business. Their lives hung in the balance, both in this world and the next. Yeshua attacked this belief and practice over and over as nothing more than self-righteous sinfulness. No wonder these members of the religious establishment were so opposed to Yeshua. Yeshua proclaimed that no man could earn his way to God – a statement that challenged everything about the purpose of this rule-keeping religion. This is the same argument we find in Paul's letter to the Galatians. It's not about an essential tension between "law and grace." It's about the confusion of the purpose of "law" (Torah instructions) and grace. Grace saves! "Law" provides life direction so that our behavior will serve God's purposes. The authors of the New Testament material, and the majority of rabbinic teaching, did not suggest that a man can *earn* his way into God's favor. Both rabbis and Jews who followed Yeshua as the Messiah knew this was impossible. Grace is God's gift. It has always been God's gift, but it does not erase the need for God's instructions about how to live *after* one has received the gift. In the New Testament, the real theological battle was about the difference between this view of grace combined with Torah and the view of the legalists who claimed one must *first* keep the "law" before grace could arrive.

This chapter explores the unfortunate misunderstanding about law and grace. Far too often, we have been taught that law and grace stand on the opposite sides of the fence and that we must choose between them. This separation belongs in the legalist's framework, but it is not part of Yeshua's view or the writing of Paul. As we look deeper into the following texts, we will find that grace is the natural precursor to a life lived according to God's instructions (Torah), that grace and Torah fit together to produce a life that exemplifies the distinctiveness of God's community. We will discover that grace without the "law" is faith without works – and we all know where that leads.

1.

*For He Himself is our peace, who made both groups into one, and broke down the barrier of the dividing wall, by abolishing in His flesh the **enmity**, which is the Law of commandments contained in ordinances, that in Himself He might make the two into one new man, thus establishing peace.* Ephesians 2:14-15 (almost) NASB

A Comma Here, A Comma There

Enmity – What a difficult passage! Especially when various English translations *add* punctuation and dependent relative pronouns that subtly alter the meaning of the verses according to some accepted theology (e.g. *which is* has been added in this NASB translation). Once again we should be looking at the Greek text, not the English. In this case, the only way to understand Paul's Greek is to interpret what he says in light of other Pauline passages and the statements of Yeshua. The question is whether "enmity" refers to "the dividing wall" or to "Torah." Try reading the English text *without the additional words* "which is" and see if you can determine the proper reference. It's far more difficult. Here is the Greek text literally: "and the middle wall of partition having broken the enmity in the flesh of him the law of the commandments in decrees having abolished that the two he create in himself into one." Now what does "enmity" refer to?

David Stern offers perhaps the most reasoned explanation of this passage. He notes that no one considers the Torah to be enmity. Paul and Yeshua both declare the Torah good and holy. Furthermore, Yeshua expressly declares that He has not abolished Torah

(Matthew 5:17) and Paul refutes the idea that Torah causes sin (Romans 7:5-14). Stern argues that the sense of this passage is that Jews and Gentiles are separated from each other and express enmity toward each other as a result of the Jewish response to Torah. In other words, Torah "occasions" the opportunity for this enmity. As Jews express the truth of Torah and live accordingly, they stand opposed to the lives of Gentiles and call into question the gods of the Gentiles. This opposition creates enmity between Jew and Gentile. This enmity (not the Torah itself) is sin because it creates hostility between men.

Yeshua tears down the wall separating Jew and Gentile through the sacrifice of His own flesh. Because He died, Jew and Gentile no longer stand on opposite sides of the chasm of obedience. Both are given free access to God's grace. Both are empowered to follow Torah. Once enemies, they are now brothers. The share a common code of conduct and a common ability to keep it. Yeshua died for all so that all might enter into the Kingdom. The "law of commandments contained in ordinances" once stood as an occasion for hostility between Jew and Gentile. No longer. Gentiles no longer are excluded from fellowship. God's grace touches them too. Jews are no longer constrained from embracing Gentiles. God's grace includes all. The artificial wall constructed from ethnic animosity is gone. Yeshua has removed it. Therefore, what once looked like strife caused by Torah-observant living has been shown to be of no consequence to the operation of grace. Now all may enter into the Kingdom.

Many English translations portray these verses as if they suggest Paul considered the crucifixion to be the abolition of Torah. Nothing could be further from the truth. The ambiguity in the Greek text means that these verses *cannot* be used *by themselves* to argue for Torah nullification. We must look at this subject in relation to all of the New Testament writings (of course, we'll have to look at the Old Testament too, since the New Testament is commentary on the Old Testament).

Have you been disturbed by the English translations? Do they challenge your thinking? Let those questions drive you to dig. Look for the bigger picture. Listen to what Paul says about his own life after the Damascus road. Think – and learn. Ask yourself if you are ready to discover that Torah obedience is for *all* believers. Maybe your hesitancy is about the *implications* for your own life. Maybe the questions are not exegetical but rather personal.

2.

*But shun foolish controversies and genealogies and strife and **disputes** about the Law; for they are unprofitable and worthless.* Titus 3:9 NASB

Belaboring the Obvious

Disputes – Sermon after sermon, article after article, book after book – all about the place of the Law in the life of a Christian. I wonder if Paul wouldn't throw up his hands in frustration. Why all this controversy? Isn't the answer *obvious*?

Apparently, it's not.

We know that Paul was a Torah-observant follower of the Way. His own self-declaration confirms this years *after* his encounter with the risen Lord. We know that James,

Peter, John and the other apostles made the same claim. We know that Yeshua lived a life of sinless Torah obedience. Is there any question about this?

Both contemporary orthodox Jews and modern Christians (Catholic and Protestant) seem to think that Paul *rejected* the Law, that Jesus *replaced* the Law and that we Christians now live under the opposite of the Law – something called "grace." This doctrine is so powerful that it stands as the real issue of separation between Jews and Christians. In fact, the more we read from the pens of *Jewish* authors about the mistakes of Christianity, the more we realize that these authors are reacting to *Christian commentators* on Paul, not to the actual words of Paul. Neither side seems to have paid attention to the actual words Paul wrote. Instead, they react to the theologians who speak on behalf of the New Testament authors. As an example, we can consider this verse. Out of context, it could be read as "disputes about the replacement of the Law by grace are unprofitable because everyone *knows* that grace overcomes the Law." But the next verse dismisses this interpretation. Paul instructs his readers to reject the factious man after two warnings because such a man is "perverted and sinning." Paul assumes that we will *know* him by his behavior. How is that possible without the Law? If it's all grace, then why would behavior matter? If it's all about "Jesus in my heart," then why would Paul exhort us to *observe what the man does* and make a judgment based on that? If the Law really is set aside, then how will we know such a man is *sinning*? It just doesn't make any sense. And, in practice, we actually do just what Paul suggests. We actually look at the behavior of others to determine if they are meeting the "standard." That, of course, implies that there actually is a standard? To claim that the Law no longer applies is to endorse lawlessness, precisely the characteristic of those whom the Bible considers the enemies of God. One way or another, we all subscribe to some form of the Law. Our theology might deny it, but our lives don't. The only question is this: is our standard God's standard? If it isn't, then we have an issue to settle with Him, not with the Church or the theologians.

Perhaps we should start by re-examining the translation. The Greek phrase is *machas nomikas*. Theological dictionaries actually define this as "controversies respecting the Mosaic laws," but notice that the word *nomikas* is an *adjective, not a noun*. Therefore, the translation cannot be "about the Law." There is no preposition or noun here. The translation should be "legal fights." Paul is telling us to avoid court battles, something we can all appreciate.

How did this bit of practical advice turn into a statement about the *Law*? The only explanation is that the translators *read into the words of Paul what they wanted to say*, not what he actually said. Paul's point is obvious. No one wants a court battle. The translators' position is subterfuge.

Who told you the Law was set aside? Maybe the real question is "Whose Bible are you reading: the Bible of the translator or the Bible of the author?"

3.

*One ordinance shall be both for you of the congregation, and also for the stranger who sojourns with you, an ordinance forever in your generations; as you are, so shall the stranger be before the Lord. **One** Torah and **one** code* *shall be for you, and for the stranger who sojourns with you.* Numbers 15:15-16 (Hebrew World)

A Company of One

One – The redemptive plan of the Scriptures depends on the concept of *ehad* (one). This word about essential unity not only governs our thoughts about the single Creator and King of the universe (God is *ehad* as noted in the Shema), it also should direct our thoughts toward the unity Yeshua prays for in the Garden (John 17:22), the unity intended in the reunion of marriage (Genesis 2:24) and the necessary unity required to provoke God's people to stand apart as one Body (Romans 11:14). Just as God is one, so His plan is one. It is precisely the same plan for any child of Abraham, whether Jew or Gentile. Long before there was any division among followers concerning "law and grace," God already instructed His people that all who resided within the camp had the same ordinances and the same Torah. <u>Belief and practice didn't depend on the family of origin, only on the family of adoption.</u>

If God tells us that all those who are called by His name are to have the same worldview, the same code of conduct and the same understanding of His purposes, then can there really be any debate about diet, legal rulings, sacrifices, worship or social and civic responsibilities? If Torah is the same for anyone who is adopted into the family, does that mean we can pick and choose which Torah instructions we want to follow? Aren't God's instructions valid for everyone who claims Him as Father and King? It certainly seems as if this is the posture prior to Augustine, Tertullian and Marcion. If God tells Moses that everyone in the assembly (the *qehelah*) has the same code of conduct, why do Christians and Jews seem so different today? Could it be that *both* groups have departed from the single set of instructions?

From the end of the apostolic age to the time of Constantine, Hellenism made significant inroads into the mixed congregation of Jews and Gentiles who followed the Way. By 200 AD, Gentile believers far outnumbered Jewish believers. At the same time, following the destruction of the temple in 72 AD, Judaism began to move from its eclectic conglomeration of different schools. One branch of Pharisees became the voice of the people without a temple. These men redefined Judaism and established the trajectory that Judaism follows today. Neither Christianity nor Judaism attempted to maintain the unity found in the first century followers of the Way. In spite of the fact that there is historical evidence demonstrating that the early believers in Yeshua as Messiah were congregations of both Jews and Gentiles until perhaps the fourth century, contemporary Judaism and Christianity are now worlds apart.

But that isn't what God intended. What God intended is a Body unified by His Torah. The critical question for followers of the one true God today is this: Will I take steps in my own life to bring about this unity? If I am a Christian, will I begin to live a Torah obedient life so that I can recover the ground lost between my Jewish brothers and sisters and me? If I am a Jew, will I recognize that Yeshua is Jewish, that He advocated Torah obedience and that He calls all His followers to Torah? If I am a Christian, will I take on Torah as a sign of my commitment to the God of Israel? If I am a Jew, will I read Sha'ul without the baggage imported by theologians after Augustine?

How will I begin to heal the breach? How will I show that I understand *'ehad*? What must I do today to bring God's people closer to His purposes?

4.

*having canceled out the certificate of debt consisting of decrees against us, which was hostile to us, and He has taken it out of the way, having nailed **it** to the cross.* Colossians 2:14 NASB

The Certificate

It – What is "it"? What is nailed to the cross? According to the Greek text in this verse, it (*autos*) is the *cheirographon*, the hand-written certificate of debts. Isn't that clear enough? What Yeshua nailed to the cross (metaphorically) is our debt accounting record, the record of all our sins that condemns us. Yeshua took away that piece of paper that said, "You owe." But if you read this verse in the NIV, there is a *significant* change. The NIV says, "having canceled the written code with its regulations." According to the NIV, the Torah was nailed to the cross, not the debts we accumulated due to disobedience but the regulations themselves! This mistaken translation (or was it deliberate?) finds its way into popular Greek lexicons too. Thayer's Greek Lexicon suggests that Paul applies *cheirographon* metaphorically for "the Mosaic law." In other words, some Christian theologians and translators simply converted a document that specified our debts into the entire legal system of rules. That's like going to traffic court with a speeding ticket and claiming that the ticket in your hand is the equivalent of *all* traffic regulations, and then telling the judge that none of them are valid. What do you think the judge is going to say? The ticket might not be correct but that doesn't imply that the rules of the road are worthless. The fact that you hold a *ticket* in your hand means that the rules do apply. The only question is whether or not you are guilty of breaking them.

The idea that God instructions are "nailed to the cross" or discarded is based on ignoring the meaning of *cheirographon*, the debt certificate. My traffic ticket is a debt certificate. It is not a copy of the traffic laws of the state of Florida. I have the ticket because the laws are in place. If someone comes into the court and *pays the fine for me*, I am no longer held liable under the law, but that doesn't mean the rules went away. It only means that I didn't pay the fine! As long as a debt certificate isn't equivalent to the legal determinations it stands on, voiding the debt certificate will not erase the legal structure. And in the Bible, my sin is *not* the same as the Law that tells me I have sinned.

In the NIV, you are actually reading the interpretation and theological position of the translators. Unless you could read the Greek, you would never know this isn't a translation. Thousands of Christians have been taught that the Law was nailed to the cross when Jesus died. They have been taught that the Law was replaced by grace and that no Christian has any obligation to the Torah. How could they know anything different when the translators change the meaning of the verses? We are called to correct this. We must take a stand on *cheirographon*. The Law, the Torah, matters. God's instructions are firmly in place, written so that you and I and all the nations will know how to live. Grace is *insufficient*! Grace is completely sufficient for our redemption, our deliverance, but it is insufficient for instructions for living. We need God's instructions in spite of our sins. And fortunately, He provides them.

5.

*And I saw a new heaven and a new earth; for the first heaven and the first earth **passed** away, and there is no longer any sea.* Revelation 21:1 NASB

Shake It Up, Baby

Passed – Things aren't always what they seem. If we've learned anything from the last decade of New Testament scholarship, we've learned that the previous theological paradigm based on Greek metaphysics initiated by Augustine's love affair with Platonism has seriously misled the Church. We've learned that New Testament followers were the continuation of a thoroughly Jewish understanding of the world, of heaven and of God. We've learned that we have to rethink some very basic religious ideas, bringing them back into alignment with their Hebraic origins. This isn't easy. It is seriously disturbing to discover that we might have misunderstood major components like law, grace, baptism, sin, redemption, heaven and hell. But re-evaluate we must. The truth will not let us be free to continue to believe whatever Church ecclesiastics taught. We must know for ourselves.

N. T. Wright, a world-renowned scholar, recently published *Surprised by Hope*. In it he questions the usual Christian idea of heaven, particularly the idea that heaven is a place free from bodily restraints, completely unlike the corrupt earth and immediately experienced upon the death of the believer. Wright questions the entire theological focus on "going to heaven." Wright's contribution to our understanding of this very famous verse in John's apocalyptic vision is his remark about the *reunification* of heaven and earth. "At no point do the resurrection narratives in the four Gospels say, 'Jesus has been raised, therefore we are all going to heaven.' It says that Christ is coming here, to join together the heavens and the Earth in an act of new creation."

Of course, knowing that John writes from an Hebraic perspective already tells us that John views this act as *restoration and renewal*, not an absolutely new beginning. This stands in *utter contrast* to the Augustinian-Platonic idea that this world is essentially worthless since the Fall and destined to be *replaced*, not renewed. Based on the thought of *passing away*, the Church since Augustine has taken the Platonic idea of the ethereal, transcendental abode of pure Forms and used that to describe the other-worldly place called heaven. But that doesn't square with Yeshua's remarks nor any of the Hebraic teaching about *Sheol* or heaven. Furthermore, as Wright points out, there is no justification for the idea that we are instantly transported to heaven upon death. That thinking stems from Plato, not YHWH.

I know that this is hard to swallow. We have been part of the "go to heaven" crowd for so long that it's agonizing to realize we were duped. So many of our "sacred" myths seem to be dismantled when we read the Bible within its own culture. But it can't be avoided unless you just want to put your head in the theologically-correct sand. Even the verb should have warned us that the Platonic concept was suspect. "Passes away" is the combination of *apo* and *erchomai*, literally "to come or go near or away." It could be translated, "to flow past," or "to come to an end," but it also means "to disregard, to remain unnoticed, to depart." Read the verse again and ask yourself why John connects "going away" with the absence of the sea? Does that mean there aren't any beaches in heaven or is John using imagery that expresses the removal of *borders*, precisely the role ascribed to the land and the sea in Genesis? Is John poetically suggesting that this current arrangement   of boundaries will be replaced with a conjoining of heaven and earth into one cosmic Kingdom? Since Jewish thought was never preoccupied with getting out of this world, why do we think Yeshua endorsed an escape route? If God created the world good, and blessed it, why would He abandon it?

Maybe this is one more thing we need to rethink.

6.

And He saw a certain poor widow putting in two small ***copper coins.*** Luke 21:2 NASB

Affordable Charity

Copper coins – A *lepton* was the smallest coin used by the Jews. It had a value of about ¼ of a penny. In common parlance, it wasn't worth the paper it was written on. It's hard to imagine that you could buy *anything* for ¼ cent. But the two *lepta* that the widow deposited into the temple treasury far surpassed the large sums given by others. We have all heard this story as an example of giving, but we may have missed some of the details that make it so important.

First, of course, is that fact that the widow had *two* coins. She could easily have said, "I'll give half of my assets to God." Fifty percent! How many of us even come close to such a sum? If someone came to us and said, "I want to give half of my finances to the Lord," we would be amazed. Certainly no one would have begrudged the widow keeping only half. The opportunity was there, but she didn't take it. She gave it all. Everything! Why?

The only reasonable answer is that she had utter confidence that God would care for her. No one would give it all unless God's sovereign care dominated that person's faith. The watchword of such faith is *trust*. Period! Most of us would call such a woman an absolute fool, especially in the first century. A widow – that means no human support, without property rights, left to fend for herself. No welfare, no social services – you get the idea. Without *trust* in God, she dies.

Second, this story illustrates the Kingdom principle of giving. It isn't about 100% donations. It's about *tsedaqah*. Torah requires *tsedaqah* toward those in need (Deuteronomy 15:7-8), even if they are strangers (Leviticus 19:34). The prophets declare *tsedaqah* more valuable than worship rituals (Micah 6:6-8, Hosea 6:6, Proverbs 21:3). When the widow approached the treasury, *anyone* who witnessed her act should have stepped forward to assist. Allowing her to give all she had *without offering tsedaqah* exhibited the sinful insensitivity of the audience. The widow's action honored God and condemned the crowd.

As I write this short study, I feel that same condemnation. I don't give from my need. I give from my excess. Of course, that is a tithing principle. It's not 10% and it's not 100%. The measure of value is determined by the proportion of need. *Agape* is benevolence toward others *at cost to myself.* I don't need to ask the question, "Should I give?" *Tsedaqah* requires that I give! I need to ask the question, "What is the cost?" If the answer comes back, "I can afford that," then maybe I don't really know the value of a *lepton*.

7.

*By this you know the Spirit of God: every spirit that confesses that Jesus Christ has come **in the flesh** is from God;* 1 John 4:2 NASB

Flank Attack

In the flesh – Understanding the Bible requires placing the writings within their historical and cultural context. We have learned that it isn't appropriate to pull a verse from its *sitz im leben* (life setting) and apply it to our environment. So Paul's statement about women wearing head coverings is specifically about the situation in Corinth in the first century, not New York City in the twentieth-first century. Most of us get this. We realize that the points made by the authors have to be contextualized. Of course, that applies to both prohibitions and exhortations. While we are pretty quick to recognize Paul's cultural situation, we aren't quite a quick to recognize John's. The battle that John fought with false doctrine isn't quite the same one that we fight, but if we contextualize John's argument we might see how it applies today.

The big issue for John is whether or not Yeshua was really a human being. This heresy is called Docetism. It is the affirmation that Jesus was really God *disguised* as a man. He just looked human but he was really divine (God in the shell of a man). John counters this heresy by telling us that anyone who says Yeshua wasn't really human is from the antichrist. Yeshua was entirely human (and, as the Church later declares, entirely divine at the same time). He was God come *en sarki* (in the flesh).

The Church settled this issue centuries ago, but does that

mean we no longer have to contend with heretical statements about Yeshua? Unfortunately, no. The enemy simply attacks from the flank. Today we don't fight about whether or not Yeshua was human. Today we have a different version of the heresy. Today we fight about whether or not Yeshua was Jewish! The enemy lost the battle about his humanity, so the fight simply shifted to the next level. Yes, Jesus is human, but now some believe he is Greek-Indo-European. Think about all the portraits that fill the sanctuaries of Europe. Fair-haired, dressed in European royal robes, this Caucasian "Jesus" is a far cry from a Semite. Furthermore, since the Church moved away from a Torah-obedient Jesus, even the Christian Jesus' actions do not appear to be Jewish. The Church proclaims that Jesus came to do away with all those inadequate Semitic rules. Jesus is more like Socrates than Moses. He is one of "us." He certainly isn't Jewish.

John had to deal with the heresy of Yeshua as a disguised god. We have to deal with Yeshua as a disguised European, or worse, a conservative Evangelical. How should we counter such heresy? Perhaps we need to take a page from John's playbook. F. F. Bruce issues the warning, even though he never intended his words to be applied to this problem. "Because the philosophy to which [the antagonists] endeavor to accommodate the gospel, depriving it of what makes it the gospel in the process, is current secular philosophy, the prevalent climate of opinion . . . no form of 'worldliness' is so inimical to Christianity as this kind of 're-statement'."[1] We agree, except that the form of secular philosophy that perverts the gospel is not an attack on Christianity. It is Christianity – with its reformulation of the truth of Yeshua's origin, culture and spiritual perspective. Today

---

[1] F. F. Bruce, *The Epistles of John*, Revell, p. 106.

Christian thinkers are waking up to the fact that Jesus is a
Jewish rabbi and the His view of the world is wedded to
the Talmud, the Targums and the Tanakh. Yet how are
we to convince traditional Christian believers that Jesus
isn't German, Scandinavian or American?

What is the answer? Once again, Bruce provides the
needed insight. "The love of God displayed in His people
is the strongest apologetic that God has in the world."[2]
What is this love of God? It is "a consuming passion for
the well-being of others."[3] Do you want others to see the
vital connection between Torah and the Messiah? Are
you burdened by the disaster of the heresy of Israel's
replacement or the tragedy of opposing Law and grace?
Do you think that more words will win the day? No, they
won't. What wins the hearts and minds of those who are
walking in the dark is *compassion* for them, here and
now. Heaven can wait. By then, none of this will matter.
What brings the victory is not what we say. It is what we
do to bring the fullness of life to others. Yeshua doesn't
need another mouthpiece. He needs hands and feet
willing to carry someone else's load. How much are you
carrying?

8.

*as to zeal, persecuting the church; as to the righteousness
which is in the Law, found **blameless**.* Philippians 3:6
NASB

Liar, Liar, Pants on Fire

Blameless – If we were to use the Josh McDowell

---

[2] Ibid., p. 109.
[3] Ibid., p. 107.

technique of "Evidence That Demands a Verdict," we would have to say that Paul was either a liar, a lunatic or saying something that we can't imagine to be true. We could throw in the extra possibility that he was simply theologically in error, but since we want to hold that his words are inspired, that would be a hard one to defend. Do you think Paul was a liar? Was he telling the truth when he said he was *blameless* according to the standard of righteousness found in the Torah? The Greek word isn't ambiguous. It's *amemptos*, literally "without fault." The same word is used to describe Zacharias and Elizabeth (Luke 1:6) and the divine intention for every believer (Philippians 2:15). Obviously, human beings can be *amemptos*. (By the way, the word is only used five times in the New Testament and none of these are about Yeshua). The Hebrew parallel is *naqiy*, "innocent," "clean" or "free from blame" (e.g. Genesis 44:10 and Job 22:19). In either language, this is not something we readily attribute to ourselves. So, once again, was Paul lying? Was Luke? It seems that answer must be "No." Whatever *amemptos* means, Paul and Luke are using it correctly. Men and women not only should be blameless, they *can* be blameless.

Wait! What about "in sin did my mother conceive me" and all that Augustinian-Lutheran guilt and sinful nature stuff? Will we quickly rush to the solution that Paul is describing himself *before* he realized his true spiritual condition and his need for Christ? Was Paul just delusional? He thought he was blameless but he was really blinded by his sinful nature. But what about Luke? Were Zacharias and Elizabeth also insane? Maybe we need to rethink where this is going. Maybe our idea of "blameless" has been influenced by factors we don't find in the Scriptures.

What does it mean to be blameless? The Hebrew suggests that *naqiy* means free of liability for an offense (innocent). The word is used to describe proper conduct in normal life as well as ritual purity. It involves both ethical and moral immunity. In other words, it is the human condition that does *not* need forgiveness. But didn't Paul himself argue that everyone sins and deserves punishment? Didn't Paul proclaim that everyone needs forgiveness? Then how is it possible for him to say that he was *blameless*? Perhaps there is a difference between the righteousness found within the Torah and the idea of sin expressed in Romans 3:23. Could it be that even if I keep all of the Torah I am still in need of a savior? Could it be that my blameless state with regard to executing God's instructions doesn't actually have anything to do with my need for grace? Could it be that Torah-keeping is not an alternative to God's grace but rather directions for living that any man can actually fulfill? Then I could this day proclaim that I too am blameless as to the Law, but I still stand in need of His favor. Maybe, just maybe, we have so mixed up the needed distinctions that we no longer believe men can actually do what God wants. Wouldn't that be a convenient excuse?

9.

*"Take My **yoke** upon you, and learn from Me, for I am gentle and humble in heart; and you shall find rest for your souls."* Mathew 11:29 NASB

Reading the Shema

Yoke – Yeshua quotes Jeremiah 6:16 in this famous passage. The context of the Jeremiah citation should help us understand the key words here. Those words are "rest" and "yoke." But when you read the passage in

Jeremiah, there isn't any mention of a yoke at all. So why should we be looking for a Tanakh context to Yeshua's choice of the word *'ol* (Hebrew for "yoke")? The answer is found in the cultural ethos of the audience.

When we think of the yoke of Yeshua, what do we have in mind? Most Christians think first and foremost about the "law of love." We imagine that this yoke is the urging to live a morally upright life, to encourage good behavior and acts of grace. But it is highly unlikely that anyone in the audience that day would have had these thoughts. Why? Because the connection of Jeremiah and "yoke" could only have meant one thing – Torah!

Look at the context of Jeremiah. First notice that it is YHWH who speaks. He says, "Stand by the ways and see and ask for the ancient paths; where the good way is, and walk in it." What are the ancient paths? What is the good way? YHWH can only mean His instructions found in Torah. After we have found the ancient paths and walked in them, then "you will find rest for your souls." And what of the "yoke"? The Mishnah and the Midrashim call the Shema *kabbalath 'ol malkhuth shamayim*, "taking on oneself the yoke of the Kingdom of Heaven." Every Jew who said the Shema three times daily would have known what yoke Yeshua spoke about. It was the same yoke YHWH gave His people, the same yoke YHWH encouraged His people to renew in the prophecy of Jeremiah, the same yoke that governed the life of Yeshua. The only difference, and it is a very big difference, is that Yeshua calls this *His* yoke. No one except YHWH could ever make that claim.

The crowd understood. This was not a "new" commandment. This was a prophetic call that echoed Jeremiah. Come back to the ancient paths. Walk in the

223

ancient ways. Take the yoke of the Kingdom upon yourself. Follow Yeshua in learned obedience. And discover that this burden brings rest.

10.

Be not as servants who serve the master on condition of receiving a reward; be rather as servants who serve the

*master without condition of receiving a reward; and let the **fear of Heaven** be upon you.* Pirke Avot 1:3

Paul's Predecessors

Fear of Heaven – You won't find this verse in the New Testament. It's from the *Pirke Avot*, a collection of sayings of the greatest Jewish Sages. Designed as a practical guide to an ethical and holy life, this collection stands outside the Bible as a testimony to the similarities in thought between the great rabbis and the authors of the New Testament. In fact, with a little research you can find material here that looks strikingly similar to the words of Yeshua. And we should not be surprised. After all, Jewish consideration of the Scripture and its application to life situations has a very long history, well over three thousand years. All of this serves to demonstrate that our Christian New Testament is hardly new. It is the product of a long line of thoughtful, God-fearing men who experienced God's grace and wrote about it for those who followed.

Central to the thought of the Sages is the idea of the "fear of Heaven." This, of course, is a euphemism for "fear of God," typical of rabbinic speech and of at least one of the gospel authors. If the fear of YHWH is the beginning of wisdom, these men knew intimately that practical moral behavior was the outcome of awe and reverence, something that seems to be in very short supply among churches today. More importantly, the commitment to the fear of Heaven says something about the nature of the whole world; something that we cannot afford to miss.

Our Western culture is the product of Greek Hellenism. Chief among Hellenistic ideas is the *kosmos*, the orderly world of natural law determinism within a fixed universe. This means that for a significant school of Greek thought, individual happiness was achieved by understanding the natural laws that governed the operation of the world and using them to personal advantage. In other words, if I aligned myself with the way nature works, I had a much higher probability of success. I was going with the grain of the universe. So far this seems quite reasonable (another element of natural law – reasonableness), but then Stoicism (a form of Greek philosophy) introduced a corollary – virtue. According to the stoics, virtue was simply *working in conjunction with natural law*. This included accepting the patterns of the world and a man's place within those patterns. Consequently, the reward we receive from following the world's natural laws is *inherent* in the action itself. I don't need an external incentive to do what comes naturally. "Virtue is its own reward" is a direct result of this Stoic doctrine. That means that I should act according to nature simply because nature knows best.

You might say, "So what? I know there are natural laws. What does that have to do with my relationship to God?" Here is the implication. If I convert Stoic philosophy into religious language, then I would proclaim that I should serve God *without regard to personal reward* because serving God is reward in itself. God is the author of all nature. He designed the natural laws, in fact, the whole *kosmos*. So my serving Him should be based solely on my love for Him as the highest expression of alignment with His nature. If I serve God because I imagine there is some *personal* reward in the action, I serve Him with *lesser* motives, motives not truly holy.

Voilá. Stoicism reigns in the Church. It is simply disguised in religious garb. How many times have you heard someone say that we should serve the Lord out of love alone? How many times have you heard someone disparage personal reward as a motive for serving God, as if such feeling were somehow spiritually inferior? You are listening to Stoics in sheep's clothing.

This saying from *Pirke Avot* reflects a certain Stoic position. But does it reflect the Bible? Does God really expect us to serve Him without regard for personal reward? Or does Scripture teach that God intends me to be motivated by my hope of success? Does the Bible teach that I should look forward to His favor as a sign of reward for my efforts or am I to strip myself of these "selfish" desires and serve only for the sake of goodness?

You might need to answer this question for yourself before the next person suggests that God's plans are indifferent to your plans.

11.

"But you have turned out of the way; you have caused many **to stumble** *at the law. You have corrupted the covenant of Levi," says YHWH of hosts.* Malachi 2:8

Priestly Indictment

To Stumble – God calls our priests to be intercessors and proclaimers of His truth. He holds them *accountable* to that charge. God charges His priests with two sins. First, they themselves have turned away from "the way." What does that mean? It means that these priests no longer *practice* according to God's instructions. Go back to the instructions in the Torah. God is meticulously specific about the actions of the priest. He sets the standard and it is not subject to modification. To be a priest is to follow His directions *to the letter*. To corrupt the covenant of Levi is a serious offense.[4]

The second sin is a direct result of the first. When a priest of the Lord doesn't do exactly what the Lord asks, the people stumble. Do you remember that often quoted verse, "Where there is no vision, the people perish" (Proverbs 29:18)? What you might not realize is that Solomon isn't talking about foresight. Solomon is talking about *prophets and priests*. He tells us that unless we have *seers*, we are lost. We must have God's words, given faithfully to us, established in our behavior, if we are to survive. This is not about a five-year planning committee. It's about the faithful presence of our intercessors.

God charges the priests with personal disobedience *and* public misdirection. If the priest isn't living according to God's instructions, the people will stumble. The Hebrew verb here is *kashal*. This is a dangerous word. It is connected to falling by the sword, the collapse of nations and the rise of wickedness. When the priests don't do what God expects, the whole nation totters. Did you think the death of nations was the result of failed

---

[4] For the moment, we will ignore the requirement that a priest be from the tribe of Levi.

economic policies, corrupt judges or bad politicians? Think again! God lays the blame at the feet of the priests.

The pictograph of *kashal* is "the last to destroy authority." Stumbling is the last step that destroys control. What is left after stumbling is chaos. Did you notice the connection between "stumble" and Torah? When the priests are not true, the people destroy the authority of Torah. They stumble over God's instructions. A priest who does not live and speak as God directs takes down the house! Why? Because the people no longer guard, honor or obey Torah.

This is very serious business. In God's universe, the fate of entire nations rests in the hands and on the lips of God's intercessors. The spiritual condition of God's servants has a direct bearing on all God's children. No wonder His servants are called to *guard* the Way.

12.

What is man that You take thought of him, and the son of man that You care for him? Psalm 8:4

The Wrong Question

What – The Hebrew word *mah* is an indefinite interrogative pronoun that means "what?" But "what" isn't right in this verse. The Hebrew translation is correct, but the cultural transposition isn't. "What is man?" is the wrong question. You see, asking what man is can be answered by a list of reductions common to our way of thinking. Man is an upright, walking animal that is self-aware. Really? Man is a biological machine that processes food into thought. Really? Man is the end of the evolutionary chain. Really? You see, when I ask "what," I miss the point of David's question. David isn't asking for a biology lesson or a social-political theory. He is asking *who* we are from God's perspective. How is it possible that the God of all creation pays any attention to us? Who are we that this God should even notice? The difference between our understanding of "what" and David's understanding of *mah* is enormous – and critically important.

Abraham Heschel says, "It is indeed conceivable that man may continue to be without being human. . . . One of the most frightening prospects we must face is that this earth may be populated by a race of beings which though belonging to the race Homo sapiens according to biology will be devoid of the qualities by which man is spiritually distinguished from the rest of organic creatures."[5]

You may want to read that again. Three thousand years ago, David recognized that the truth about *who* I am is defined by my relationship to the Creator. It is not a matter of biology or politics or mechanics or any other factor. I am human *because* I am related to God and only in my relation to God can I become human. Soren Kierkegaard said it well: "Now with the help of God I can become myself."

Being human means being tied to God's path to life. It means standing against chaos and the forces that destroy life. It means sharing in a covenant guarantee. It means knowing what is permitted and what is not, and *acting* accordingly. Any behavior that denies, negates or rejects these images is not human behavior and the creatures

---

[5] Abraham Heschel, *Who Is Man?* (Stanford University Press, 1965) p. 29.

who exhibit non-human behavior are not creatures that exhibit God's image. Before sin entered the world, God made human beings as perfect representatives of His image and likeness. Now we discover that this is an *active* and *dynamic* condition. In the perfect creation, nothing prevented male and female from taking on the image and likeness of God. *They are human because they act humanly.* In the process, they continue to become human. But when sin entered the picture, something tragic occurred. Now it became possible to move in another direction. Over time, those who have been designed to become human can reject walking this path. Many do. They eventually arrive at a destination not intended for human beings. Human beings are intended to arrive at the full expression of "our image and likeness." But it is also possible to arrive at another destination.

The image of God is not a static element in being human. It is not something that we possess like flesh and blood. It is a dynamic activity. I carry God's image as the order-maker when I act as the order-taker. It is action within the relationship that constitutes the image. This is exactly what we expect from a Hebrew perspective. We are human because of and through our actions. We are manifest as human beings when we act humanly, when we act in ways that manifest the image and likeness of God. Just like God is a verb, the image of God is a verb. We truly are "works in progress," and the reason we are works at all is because God notices us.

13.

*as sin reigned in death, even so grace **might reign** through righteousness to eternal life through Jesus Christ our Lord* Romans 5:21

The Consequences

Might Reign – Mark Seifrid makes an interesting observation about Paul's tension between law and grace. He points out that the same tension is found in the apocryphal literature of Paul's time. Paul's choice of verb (*basileuse*)[6] seems to suggest that one of the functions of the law is "to provide a way to obedience that gives life in *the age to come.*"[7]   This echoes the thought of the apocryphal book 2 Esdras 3:20, "And yet You took not away from them a wicked heart, that Your law might bring forth fruit in them." Is Paul in line with the author of the book of Esdras? Is he suggesting that the law will guide obedience in the next age? Oh, there's one other question that comes along with this: Does Paul incorporate the theology of the apocryphal books in his writing?

Let's see if we can answer this last question first. Why wouldn't Paul be inclined to use thoughts from other literature in his letter to believers in Rome? Jude does it. Even Yeshua seems to use words and phrases that indicate his awareness of Greek culture. Paul's letters are filled with local references. Since Paul was a scholar, he would certainly know the literature of the period. He just used what was already part of his background. Perhaps that will help us take advantage of our own cultural elements. Wherever we find opportunity, why not use what the culture provides to further the message of the good news? We have the truth. There is nothing to fear from the opposition.

---

[6] This is the subjunctive aorist of the Greek verb *basileuo*, "to rule or reign." The subjunctive mood implies that something is probable or possible, depending on certain other factors.

[7] Mark Seifrid, *Romans* in Carson and Beale (eds.), *Commentary on the New Testament Use of the Old Testament*, p. 629.

What about the idea that the law has a place in the world to come? Doesn't Jeremiah's revelation of the new covenant say that in those days all believers will serve the Lord because Torah will be written on their hearts? That certainly sounds like the instructions of the Lord will continue "until heaven and earth pass away." As far as I know, that will be a long time! Should we be surprised that the same idea is found in books which are not included in our canon?

Now, just a minor addition. Yeshua tells us that God's Torah is eternal. Jeremiah writes that the Torah will be the operating system of the new world. Paul makes that same claim. But in one sense, the new world begins the moment God takes rule and reign in our lives. This is the "already" but "not yet" tension of the Kingdom. We experience it already, right now in our submission to His authority. But it is "not yet" fully arrived. We wait for the day that all the earth will be filled with His righteousness and everyone will serve the Lord. That is the essential tension of the Kingdom. So, while it is true that Torah will provide a way to obedience in the age to come, it is also true that Torah provides a way to obedience right now. Those who live by Torah will simply continue to enjoy its blessings. This is *practice* time for the real game; the one that begins when all creation worships Him once again.

Paul used all the literature at his disposal to communicate a message of hope. This world isn't the end. That message was, at the same time, a message of urgent appeal. Obedience is the watchword of the Kingdom, here and in the age to come. What are you waiting for? A second invitation?

14.

*And it shall come to pass, if you **carefully listen to** my commandments which I command you today, . . .* Deuteronomy 11:13

Graceland (1)

Carefully Listen To - Rabbi Joshua ben Karha said, "Why does the section, *Hear, O Israel* (Deut 6:4-9) precede the [section] *and it shall come to pass if ye shall harken [diligently to my commandments]?* – so that a man may first take upon him the yoke of the kingdom of heaven and afterward take upon him the yoke of the commandments."[8] What does the rabbi mean? He means that *grace* always precedes commitment to Torah. Every Jew knew that God chose *before* God commanded. Every Jew knew that keeping the commandments was a voluntary obligation taken *after* God's rescue from bondage. No Jew ever believed that being Torah-observant "saved" someone. God acts first. Torah observance comes later. It is grace, always grace, in God's land.

If Jewish rabbis knew that faith comes first and works come second, and if Jewish rabbis knew that obedience is an expression of devotion to the God who *already* saved us, then why is there such an artificial battle between "law" and grace? James makes it very clear that both are necessary. Paul says that grace and works go hand-in-hand. But somewhere along the line Christians began thinking that law was opposed to grace. Where did all that begin? You can't find it in the rabbis' writings and you can't find it in the Hebrew Scripture. Who started this debate?

---

[8] *Berakoth* 2.2

The answer is Augustine. When Augustine converted from paganism to Christianity in the 4th century, he read Paul's words in Romans 7 as if they described the *normal* process of conversion. In fact, he saw his own life in those words. As a result, he thought Paul was speaking autobiographically, contrasting the man who wished to do what is right with the man who was under the power of sin and could not do what was right. In other words, Augustine saw "sinful nature" hidden in this text – a sinful nature that was condemned under the law and set free under grace. Law became the enemy, existing only to make us more aware of our plight. Grace became the rescuer, setting us free from the awful verdict of the law. For Augustine, law stood in opposition to grace. To be free meant to be free of the law.

Augustine set the stage for nearly 1800 years. Luther followed him. So did Calvin. As a result, Christianity today is the product of Augustine's conversion experience, not the teachings of Jewish rabbis like Paul, Peter and John. Christians today read the Bible interpreted by Augustine, a neo-Platonist pagan convert. Even Jewish rabbis who don't embrace the Messiah know better.

If the "law and grace" dichotomy is the product of extra-biblical influence, what other Christian doctrines are also the result of men who did not write our Bible? Do you think baptism might be an issue? Or atonement? Or forgiveness? Or *salvation*? We need a much better historical awareness, don't we?

15.

*And it shall come to pass, if you **carefully listen to** my*

commandments which I command you today, . . .
Deuteronomy 11:13

Graceland (2)

Carefully Listen To – We have discovered that even
Jewish rabbis recognized the priority of grace. The false
dichotomy between law and grace was an invention of
Augustine. His influence spread through church history,
resulting in the current mistaken view that Jews believe
salvation comes by "works" but Christians have a
superior understanding of the role of grace. None of this
is biblical.

So, now that we have a corrected view of the biblical
position, let's take a closer look at this verse.
Immediately we see that the original is a duplicate word,
shama'. The text actually reads *"eem-shamoa tishmeoo"*
(if you *shama' shama'*). The verb *shama'* means "to listen,
to hear, to obey, to regard, to proclaim, to heed, to
understand." A pretty wide umbrella covering most of
what it means to know what God says and do it. In order
to emphasize the importance of this concept, the text
duplicates the word. This is like putting an exclamation
point behind the idea. It's not simply a matter of
receiving the sound waves with your ears. This is "Pay
attention!" "Do what you are instructed to do!" *Carefully*
give attention to God's Word and be sure that what He
says becomes the way that we live.

It's worth noting that there is a small Hebrew particle
proceeding the duplicated *shama'*. That particle is *eem*.
It is "if." God's instruction is *conditional*. "*If* you pay
attention and do what I command you to do, then certain
things will follow." Of course, conditional statements

require fulfillment. So, even though Israel is God's chosen people, they must still *commit themselves* to His ways. The covenant of grace contains expected obligations. God acts to save. Israel is expected to live accordingly.

"If you carefully listen and obey," says the Lord, "then I will deliver what you need to be prosperous, safe and satisfied." That sounds pretty good. After all, who is capable of bringing the rains, causing the growth of the plants, protecting the livestock and satisfying our needs more than God Himself? Do we really think that we can handle all the tasks and circumstances of life on our own? Are we really ready to say, "No thanks, Lord. I'll just make my own way in the world." Obedience has rewards – *if* we listen carefully.

Of course, there is the other side of the coin. We could act as if God's instructions for living don't apply to us. We could ignore the *if* and not listen or obey. I wonder what we can expect to occur then? Maybe we should ask Adam.

16.

For not the hearers of the law are justified with God but the **doers** *of the law shall be justified.* Romans 2:13

Order-Takers

Doers – This is a nearly impossible verse for Augustine and Luther (and those who follow their lead). It's impossible because Paul unequivocally says that those who *do* the commandments of God are justified. Actually, it's even worse than that. Paul says that those who merely *hear* God's commandments but do no do them are not justified. This is about as strong a statement about the necessity of following God's instructions in Torah as you will find in the New Testament. And it comes from the apostle of "grace." What can we say?

A quick look at the Greek confirms the dilemma. The word is *poietes*, from the verb "to make" (*poieo*). It clearly means someone who performs the required commandments. There's not much wiggle room here. Paul says it plainly: justification comes from keeping the commandments.

This conclusion is so antithetical to the long-standing Christian doctrine of *sole fide, sole gratia* that we are apt to do whatever we can to reinterpret Paul's statement. Unfortunately, we don't take Paul seriously. We retain the paradigm rather than recognizing that something doesn't make sense. It isn't Paul who is confused. It's our interpretive scheme. Thanks to Augustine, the early church fathers, the Reformers and the evangelicals, we would rather believe what we want to believe than listen to the apostle. Paul doesn't see conflict. Grace and works form a covenant *together*. We are the ones who split them apart – and we have struggled with this text (and others) ever since.

So, Today's Word is not about this text. The text is clear enough. Today's Word is about the paradigm that causes us to read the text as either a problem for our theology or a confirmation of Paul's unity of law and grace. This paradigm is based on an association between the general pagan religious requirement to placate the gods and the Jewish idea of works of righteousness. Pagan religions often view men as victims of the gods. In order to survive in this world, paganism requires that men offer sacrifices to appease the gods and gain their favor. We find this thinking in all kinds of pagan religions, from the worship of Ba'al and Moloch to the Greeks and native Americans. When thinkers read passages in the Bible that described sacrifices and worship rituals, they connected these with pagan appeasement. Therefore, they thought that Israel practiced a more sophisticated version of appeasement theology. This association became the opposing idea to Christian grace. In other words, according to this paradigm, Judaism developed from prior pagan rituals but was still connected to the basic idea of placating YHWH, an ancient god of anger.

Christianity takes a significant step forward by rejecting this ancient pagan idea. According to this paradigm, Christianity rejects any connection between "earning" God's favor and prescribed religious rituals. Therefore, Christianity stands opposed to Judaism.

This paradigm is not based on Scripture. It is based on a general concept of religion, independent of the actual prophetic tradition of Israel. Therefore, it reads the Hebrew Scriptures within the paradigm – and ignores or reinterprets contradictory passages to fit the paradigm. The biggest problem is really right in front of us: How do we take off the blinders?

Unfortunately, many wonderful and devoted believers will not be able to take off the blinders. The paradigm is so much a part of their way of looking at the world, and has been reinforced by the Church for so long, the very idea that there might be another way is so frightening they refuse to consider it. They are sure of their beliefs, so forget the problems and the text. This is the way it has always been. It takes enormous patience, gentleness, yes, and sometimes shock, to remove the fear of examining the text. For some, it just isn't going to happen.

But here's the caution. We can't make it happen either. This is God's arena. We live according to our understanding of His unity, and He uses us to bring about awareness and truth. Insistence will not turn the tide. Love will. It is important to be aware of the paradigm shift that brought about this unwarranted chasm. It is important to know that Scripture is consistent in its grace-Torah perspective. But "love your enemies" is still the authorized way of life. Seek truth. Live Torah. Hope in His faithfulness.

17.

Thus the priest shall make **expiation** *for them, and they shall be forgiven.* Leviticus 4:20

Clearing Up The Confusion

Expiation – For centuries we have heard Christian theologians proclaim that forgiveness comes by grace alone. Pastors and professors have driven a wedge between the teaching of Leviticus and the words of Paul. The Jews were under the "law." Christians are under "grace." This is a false dichotomy. Every Jew knew that sacrifice would not remove the guilt of intentional sin. But every Jew also knew that sacrifice was absolutely essential for life before God. Why? Because every Jew knew there was a difference between moral purity and ritual purity. In order to have fellowship with the Lord, a person must be cleansed on both counts.

Baruch Levine makes the point that the Hebrew verb, *k-p-r*, is often translated by a phrase such as "to cover or conceal." But this isn't correct. The idea behind *kipper* is to wipe clean, to remove defilement, to wipe off. We can think of ritual impurity as if it were contamination. The worshipper realizes that something done has contaminated his presence before God. The contamination must be removed if he is to enjoy fellowship and proper worship. God Himself has given the appropriate steps necessary to expiate (remove) this contamination. That's what Leviticus is all about. God tells us how to worship Him. We don't make up the process of worship as we go along. We don't decide what we will do to worship Him. He decides. If we want to worship Him properly, we will take the steps He commands. Some of those steps insure that we are *ritually clean* when we come before Him.

Too often we fail to distinguish between ritual purity and moral purity. So, when we read the word "forgiven," we think in terms of moral acts. We think the sacrificial system was about forgiving our immoral choices. Then we conclude that the Jews believed sacrifices brought redemption, and we reject that suggestion because it looks like "earning" salvation. Once we see that sacrifices bring *ritual* purity, our views are corrected. Every Jew knew that a sacrifice didn't bring *moral* redemption. Atonement brought moral redemption. But the sacrifices were needed to wipe away the accumulation of ritual impurity - the contamination of daily life - that made communion with a holy God impossible. Frankly, it's hard to imagine that these requirements have changed. Are we so ritually pure that we no longer need to be cleansed before we come into His presence? Does moral atonement cover ritual defilement too? Or are we really missing something here? Does our behavior really say, "Thanks for forgiving me, Lord. Now I will worship you in the way *I* choose to worship"?

18.

*When a person commits a trespass, being unwittingly remiss about any of YHWH's sacred things, he shall bring as his **penalty** to YHWH a ram without blemish from the flock, ...* Leviticus 5:15

Diet, Dress and Holidays

Penalty – A few days ago Matt and I looked carefully at the list of the 613 Torah commandments. You can find them here. We spent about an hour and a half going through each one in order to determine if it applied, how it applied and what we were doing about it. Of course, we immediately discovered that the vast majority of these 613 are things that we either already do or would have no problem doing. We don't lie, cheat, steal. We do love God. We honor His name. We know that He is the only God. We want to take care of others. We wish to worship correctly. When we were all done, we looked over the list of the ones we thought might present some debate. None of them included sacrifices before the priest at the temple (because there isn't any temple so we couldn't do them even if we wanted to). None of them included any commandment that presupposed inheritance of the land of Israel since we (as Gentiles) aren't part of that group. Of course, we also aren't Levites, so those didn't count either. When we were done with the list, we had about 12 commandments that *might* be controversial. Almost all of them were about what we eat, which days we celebrate and what we wear. That was it. Nothing theologically earth-shattering. Just diet, dress and holidays.

Then we realized that for us Torah observance simply meant deciding to eat what God tells us to eat, dressing as God asks us to dress and celebrating His festivals.

Everything else we already were doing or could quite easily do. Suddenly the very big issue about **law and grace** seemed quite inconsequential. It all boiled down to this: am I going to live the way God asks me to live even in these simple things, or am I going to offer any number of excuses for living some other way. There was absolutely *nothing* on the list that was impossibly difficult to do; nothing that would require a revolution in my life. Everything left on the list of the 12 things were simple, tiny, insignificant changes. If I did them, I would have the joy of knowing that I did them simply because I wanted to be closer to what He said.

This reminded us of Moshe Kampinski's comment when we heard him speak in his store in Jerusalem. He said, "You silly Christians. You think that keeping Torah is about keeping rules. We think that keeping Torah is about 613 opportunities to love God." It all depends on perspective, doesn't it? And that perspective is usually the direct result of an attitude of the heart. Look at this verse from Leviticus. It requires the one who has unintentionally offended God in some element of worship to bring a sacrifice as a *penalty*. Of course, we could react to this and say, "Penalty? Why do I have to bring a penalty? Doesn't God *love* me? Why do I need to follow some rule about removing guilt about something I didn't even know I was doing?" That is the same attitude that says, "Shrimp? Why can't I eat shrimp? What's wrong with shrimp? We have food processing today. Eating shrimp is my *right*." What's wrong with all this? It's the attitude – seeing God's instructions as impediments to my *freedom* instead of seeing God's instructions as opportunities to enter into His presence.

So, what will it be? Are they 613 ways to love God or are they infringements on my right to do what I want? How you answer that question will probably determine the direction of the rest of your life.

19.

*The land, moreover, shall not be sold permanently, for the land is Mine; for you are but **aliens and sojourners** with Me.* Leviticus 25:23

Grafted In

Aliens and Sojourners – All of God's children are adopted. It doesn't make any difference if you are Jew or Gentile. *All* of God's children become His because He adopts them. That was just as true for Abraham and Moses and those who left Egypt as it is for us today. We are all grafted in. The only difference is that some of us were grafted in before others. But from God's perspective, we (Jew and Gentile) depend on His gracious act in order to be included in His Kingdom.

The terms for *alien* and *sojourners* are *gerim* and *toshavim*. Literally, you are *outsiders* and *temporary visitors*. Why? Because the land belongs to God. The whole earth belongs to God, so our status as residents on the earth depends entirely on Him. It will *always* belong to Him. At no time will we ever be owners. We are the servants of the King, not the employees in management training. We don't hold stock options on heaven – or on earth. We don't get shares. We can't negotiate terms of purchase – or even terms of lease. We are here only because we were invited.

Sometimes it's important to be reminded about ownership. God owns it all. We simply manage it for Him for the time being. Ethnic background, spiritual condition, theological declaration or creedal beliefs don't change anything. We are stewards of His possessions.

This has profound implications for my life. I will be held accountable for my treatment of God's property. And the standards of my accountability are not determined by me. Perhaps we need to read the Beatitudes again, but this time with an eye toward God's measurements of proper stewardship. Maybe it would do us well to go through our lists of possessions and ask if they meet God's stewardship standards. Maybe what's on the list needs to change too.

Gerim and *toshavim* are invited into the Kingdom, but they come on the King's terms. Perhaps we need to read the Bible as if it were a conditional temporary occupation agreement. Yeshua has a lot to say about that kind of contract in His parables. I wonder if we aren't guilty of thinking that we *own* what God *loans*.

20.

*"Arise, go to Nineveh, that great city, and **cry out against** it; ..."* Jonah 1:2

The Punisher

Cry Out Against It – Jonah knew the heart of God. That's why he ran in the opposite direction. Jonah knew the power of God's word. That's why he refused to preach the message. But if you thought that the story of Jonah was about Nineveh, you have missed the point. The story of Jonah is about the conflict between punishment and atonement. Jonah rejects God's command because Jonah believes that only punishment can cleanse sin and he's afraid that God will relent and forgive. The forgiveness of God challenges all conceptions of justice for it subverts the law. Those who sin should die. That's the punishment for rebellion against God. So how can a God of justice also be a God of _hesed_? The conflict in the story of Jonah is the reconciliation of law and grace.

From Jonah's perspective, divine mercy shoots holes in the uniformity of divine justice. A judge who can be swayed by compassion is not the kind of judge who upholds the law. Such a judge is fickle, discriminatory and unreliable. Would you want a judge like that to preside over your lawsuit against a single mother who stole merchandise from your store? Wouldn't you be afraid that the judge would look on her condition and pronounce her justified in her actions in spite of the law? He might even tell you to give her more. Would that be just?

When Jonah considers that God too often relents, he wants nothing to do with the possibility that God might forgive Nineveh. It's not that he hates the people of Nineveh. They aren't the issue here. Jonah wants a God who stands for righteousness. Jonah wants a God who can be counted on to do the right thing – and that thing is to uphold the law. Most Christian theologians would argue that the book of Jonah surrounds the idea that the Jews didn't want the message of salvation to come to the Gentiles. But this can't be found in the text. The story of Jonah is about Jonah, not about Nineveh. It's Jonah's misconception about punishment and atonement that needs correcting. God just uses Nineveh to demonstrate the lesson.

The Hebrew text is _ookra aleha_ (cry against it). The combination of the verb _qara'_ and the preposition _'al_

245

indicates a proclamation of impending destruction (for example, see 1 Kings 13:1). Jonah is not commanded to simply preach God's message to Nineveh. The Hebrew phrase clearly means that Jonah is to proclaim *judgment* over Nineveh. This makes Jonah's response all the more curious. Everything about God's message speaks of punishment for sin, but Jonah doesn't *trust* God. Jonah declares that he knows God's heart better than God's own declaration. Jonah believes God's _hesed_ will override His wrath because Jonah knows the God of love. And love is an attack on justice. If Jonah thought that God's judgment would stand, he would catch the fastest plane to Nineveh and insist on prime-time coverage. Clearly, Jonah doesn't believe justice will prevail. But it might if no one tells

them of impending doom.

How God deals with Jonah's rigid justice is a lesson in compassion. Jonah's real problem is not justice. It is his failure to identify with fellow human beings. He is more concerned with the sanctity of the law than he is with the life of the sinner. Perhaps he's a great deal more like us than we wish to imagine. Rule-bound behavior, especially from those who preach a gospel of grace, often separates the common fellowship of men. We are *all* in the same boat and until we come to really understand that other person by walking in his shoes, we will have the tendency to view his infractions as ones in need of punishment rather than grace extended from our own brokenness.

21.

For the Law was given through Moses; grace and truth **were realized** *through Jesus Christ* John 1:17

Hebrew Manifestations

Were Realized – Let's examine the Hebraic character of John's syntax. A footnote to the NASB translation tells us that the original Greek text literally means, "came into being" (*egeneto*). But this is a Greek construction that does not reflect the underlying Hebrew thought. Our English translation does even less justice to the Hebrew perspective. Since John deliberately uses the Genesis motif in his introduction, we can be fairly sure that he wants us to read this Greek as if it reflects Hebrew thinking, so that means we have to take a second look at the way Hebrew uses the verb "to be."

Now this is a bit complicated, but well worth the effort to explore. In Greek (especially) as in English, "being" is viewed as a static state – a state of rest – so that the characteristic described by the verb "to be" is separate from the actual subject but attached to it. For example, we say, "That car is red." We mean that there is a car and the color red happens to be attached to this particular car. We can imagine the car without the color – and we often do, unless of course, it's a Ferrari and then it *must* be red. In other words, we use the verb as a connector, bringing two different independent things together. But this is not the way Hebrew works. In fact, Hebrew often doesn't even employ the word "is" in its sentences. Why not? Because in Hebrew the subject actually *is* the attributes that describe it. Without being "red," it wouldn't be this car. The description inheres in the subject. For example, God's word cannot be conceived as anything other than true and just. It is not as if truth and justice are appended to God's word, rather truth and justice are exactly the same as God's word.

Now let's consider this Greek verb from a Hebrew perspective. Greek syntax demands the use of *egeneto* but in Hebrew this verb is unnecessary. Why? Because grace and truth didn't come into being through Yeshua. Grace and truth are what Yeshua is. To speak of grace and truth in the same sentence with Yeshua is to utter a tautology. The expressions are exactly equivalent. In other words, it is not possible to think of Yeshua without thinking of grace and truth.

Of course, the same thing applies to the first part of John's statement. To think of Moses is to think of the Law. They are not two separate subjects connected by a verb. Moses *is* the Law and the Law *is* Moses (see this use by James in Acts 15:21). So far so good.

Now let's look at the way a Hebrew thinker would combine Moses and Yeshua. The same rules apply. The Hebrew perspective suggests that the Moses-Law inheres in the Christ-grace-truth. One clause is the equivalent of the other. These two clauses are typical of Hebrew thought. The first statement is duplicated in the second in a way that the second elucidates the first. This occurs frequently in Proverbs and Psalms. It is a pattern of Hebrew thinking. I say something one way, then I say the same thing again another way, and I connect the two with an *implied* copula.

We have learned several things (besides this interesting technical bit about Hebrew). First, we learn not to *assume* that our way of reading the text is the only proper way. We have discovered that deep paradigms, even about the use of the verb "to be," affect our understanding of the text. Second, we learn that Hebrew thought infuses what we would call attributes or descriptions directly into the subject. Hebrew sees tautologies where we see contingent descriptions. This is particularly important when we read the New Testament passages about the nature and character of God, faith, forgiveness and sanctification. Finally, we learn that Hebrew thinking is radically different than our Greek-based conception of the world, and this provokes us to extreme caution when it comes to theological proclamations. We will have to walk in the rabbi's shoes for a long time before we really have something to say.

22.

Consider *my affliction and my travail; and forgive all my sins.* Psalm 25:18

Derailed

Consider - David isn't like me. At least he's not like me in his wholehearted cry to the Lord. We may share other things. His faults maybe my faults, but God Himself recognized that David continued in faithful *direction* even if he was derailed once in awhile. I am more like the description of the spiritually impoverished man in Abraham Heschel's words, "We do not refuse to pray. We merely feel that our tongue is tied, our mind inert, our inner vision dim, when we are about to enter the door that leads to prayer. We do not refuse to pray; we abstain from it. We ring the hollow bell of selfishness, rather than absorb the stillness that surrounds the world,"[9]

I want to pray. I want to listen to the voice of my God. I desperately need His comforting reassurance, the symphony of His care. At times my concerns for those I love overcome my trepidation, my unworthiness, and I

---

[9] Abraham Heschel, *Spiritual Audacity and Moral Grandeur*, p. 340.

stammer affirmation of His sovereignty. I know He cares. I know He even cares about me, but I feel His silence as if a vise closed around my body. Why? God has not abandoned me. I have failed Him. When I am derailed by circumstance, emotion or temptation, I miss the mark of His blessing. I find myself on a spur, switched to another direction. I cease to pray because I know that I am not on the main line and I don't know what to do about it. How often I need to remember Brother Lawrence's straightforward approach to sin. Repent, accept the unwavering grace of the Lord, trust His word of faithful comfort, *and get back on the track.*

David is able to ask God to "consider" his affliction and travail. This is a noble word from a broken heart. *Ra'ah* (to see) is metaphorical for looking into the heart of a matter. No one hiding from the Lord would ever ask to be considered. Adam did not want the Lord to consider him. He wanted to cover his shame (which was not nakedness, by the way) and hide. I am much more like Adam than David. But David is a son of Abraham, and so am I. There is hope for me too. Even when I hide, God asks, in surprise, why I am not standing by His side. He expects me to be there. That is my destiny. He is always surprised when I do not fulfill the purpose for which I was born. His surprise is my shame. I don't want to be like this – afraid to pray. I want conversation with Him. I want to be known, but because I know my own faults and failures so well, I simply can't imagine that there is a God who could love me in spite of them. And the cancer in my imagination, that tumor of disbelief, really shouts out how little I actually trust Him. He promises to forgive me when I come in contrite humiliation. It is only my distorted sense of rebellion and unworthiness that prevents His promise from affecting my life. It isn't that I want to pray but am unable. It is that I refuse to pray because I am unwilling. I am unwilling to admit that my failure is not grounds for His rejection, that there is no inverted pride in spiritual distance and that He loves me when I do not love Him or me.

"Consider." Lord, look at me. Yes, I know you will often find things I detest, things I do not want to see, things I pretend are not me. But look anyway. And peel away the layers of my resistance. Remove the scales so that what I know may become what I see too. Let me see me as you see me. Consider my afflictions. They start here, in me.

23.

Hear, Israel, YHWH is our God, YHWH is one. Deuteronomy 6:4

The Shema (1)

Hear – The Hebrew verb *shama* means both "to hear" and "to obey, respond." Moses does not call the people to listen to his words. He calls the people to *do* what the words say. In Hebrew, I do not hear *unless I respond*. The same double sense of this word is applied to God when the Psalmist cries out for God to *hear* his plea. Of course God hears, but it is of no value unless God responds. To hear is to do something about it. To hear is to act upon the words spoken.

Since Hebrew is a dynamic, active language, this is exactly what we would expect. Torah study isn't about recitation or regurgitation. It's about transformation. If my life isn't changing because of these words, then I haven't learned anything. I haven't heard. It is completely inadequate to store away information, even theological information, in my cognitive vault. Action is the only measure of successful listening.

Only a moment's reflection verifies that this is what we really want with our own words. What is the point of speaking, speaking, speaking if no one acts upon our proclamation.   Do we really think our children are listening to us when their behavior ignores our admonitions?   Does our boss believe we have incorporated his direction if we don't make any changes in our actions? Do you think God is interested only in a checklist of correct information? Of course not! If we expect more than intellectual assent, don't you think He does too? The problem was never about hearing. It was about *responding*.

This raises a more difficult issue. Now that we know God expects us to *act* on His words, the next question is "What

does He say?" Heschel is absolutely right. Belief is not about deriving divine principles or producing heavenly abstractions. To believe (a verb) is to *remember*. It is to remember what God did and what He *demands*. If my life is determined by my response, I must know what God is asking of me. The most important question in all of my life is this: "What does God demand of me?" If I can't answer that question, I am not able to hear for hearing is the response *required* by the question. That's why the Shema is *not* Deuteronomy 6:4. Deuteronomy 6:4 is the *introduction* to the demand. It is the call to respond, but it is not the content of what I am to hear. *Shema yisrael, YHWH Eloheinu, YHWH ehad* is not what I must do. It is the framework that surrounds what I must do. Deuteronomy 6:4 establishes the reason why I must hear and obey. There is a God. His name is YHWH. He is the *only* God. And the fact that He is God is the reason why I *must* respond to His demands.

It is useless to read His words without committing myself to do what they require. It is worse than useless. It is blasphemy, disobedience and sin. It is pointless to call myself a follower and ignore the behavioral changes He demands. It is worse than pointless. It is self-defeating. So, begin with the invitation to His demands, but do not stop there. Don't open the envelope and leave the letter inside. It's time to take up what follows.

24.

*And you shall **love** YHWH your God with all your heart, and with all your soul, and with all your might.* Deuteronomy 6:5

The Shema (2)

Love – The first action of the Shema is to listen-respond. The second is to love. The second verb (*ahav*) begins the series of demands. YHWH demands that we love Him. The scope of that love is explained in the demand it places on our hearts, our souls and our strength, although we will soon discover that these English words don't quite capture what the Hebrew implies.

The first thing to notice is this: God *commands* us to love Him. This is not how we think of love. It would be nonsense in our culture to tell someone that she *must* love another. She would object. "OK, you can demand that I respect this man or that I be nice to him, but you can't demand that I *love* him. That's like telling me to love a job I hate. You can command my behavior, but you can't force me to *feel* a certain way. Feelings aren't subject to rational decisions." But there it is in Hebrew –

veahavta et YHWH eloheikha. The Shema *demands* that I love God.

This can only mean one thing. Love is not how we *feel.* Love is what we *do*, how we respond. It doesn't matter how we feel. It only matters how we act. God will never demand something of us that we cannot accomplish. He knows us. He knows that feelings are fickle (the Greeks were right about this one). But He also knows that actions do not require feelings. Feelings follow actions. So, act first and wait for the feelings to catch up. Actually, act first, second, third, fourth and so on – and eventually the feelings will arrive. To hear is to respond with action. To love is to act according the God's directions.

It's easy to nod approvingly as we read these words. Yes, of course loving God means acting according to His instructions. Sure, we understand that feelings follow. We are confident that God will provide the theology of
emotion once we take up the theology of action. But before we become self-righteous in our new-found insight, let's consider the larger implications of this definition of love. Loving God is not different from loving a spouse, a friend, a companion or an enemy. Love is defined by what I *do*, not how I feel. This is so counter-cultural that it is worth elaborating. We do not *fall* in love according to the Bible. We *act* with love. We are not passive recipients of an emotional onslaught. We *do* what love demands – and wait for the rest. Loving God by keeping His instructions for life is only the preparation for loving others in the same active way.

Paul provides us a summary of love's active ingredients. Each characteristic is an action, not a feeling. Be patient. Be kind. Do not be jealous. Don't boast. Do not be arrogant. Don't act inappropriately. Don't seek your own agenda. Don't be provoked. Forgive. Rejoice in righteous behavior. Be joyful over the truth. Be content. Be reliable. Hope. Persevere. Of course, this list depends on the *Hebrew* thought behind the words. But you get the idea. Love is not being swept away. It is not falling head over heels. It is not heart flutters or passionate longing. It is doing what is demanded even when you don't feel like it.

With this definition in mind, it's fairly easy to determine if you love someone. Do these actions apply to your relationship? Would an outside observer describe your behavior toward the other person with Paul's categories? Two decades ago I sat across a restaurant table from a friend, complaining bitterly about the state of my marriage. My friend looked me in the eyes and asked, "Do you love her?" Of course, I said. Then I got hit with the two-by-four. "I don't know how you can say that when I see how you act." Wham! The truth was I didn't *love* my wife in spite of my words. My actions cost me a skin-tearing, soul-ripping divorce. A *most* painful lesson brought about by my own selfish desires. Never again. Love is a verb. Don't forget it.

25.

*And you shall love YHWH **your God** with all your heart, and with all your soul, and with all your might.* Deuteronomy 6:5

The Shema (3)

Your God – Not just any god. Your God. *eloheikha*. How did that happen? Well, it had nothing to do with our decision. "You will be my people and I will be your God."

It was His choice. He established the relationship, not us. We belong to Him because we have been chosen, grafted in, adopted by Him. Of course, there is a reason for this – but it is His reason, His purpose, not ours. Once we were chosen, we were obligated. "You will be *my* people," doesn't mean that we can determine how we will belong to this nation. He determines how we will belong because He constituted us as His people. Once we were lost. Now we are found. We are found *within* the congregation of Israel. We are commanded to love this particular God (who happens to be the only God in spite of other claims of divinity). The reason we are to love Him is because we belong to Him – and He belongs to us.

Heschel makes an interesting observation. "In this world God is not God unless we are His witnesses."[10] God is not restoring the world to its perfect original condition without us. He is in cooperation with us. We are partners with Him. We have been invited to join the work party, to complete with Him the master plan of the redemption of everything. He is *our* God because we are wedded to His work and His character. Under these circumstances, the command to love Him is entirely reasonable and acceptable. How could it be otherwise? Under these circumstances, to act on His behalf in the work of restoration is to love Him. Only those who put hand to the plow demonstrate that He is their God. They love Him with every furrow, with every drop of sweat, with every callus, with every aching muscle. There is work to do – His work – and loving Him is feeling the blade slicing through the good earth.

"Ultimately religion is not based on our awareness of God but on God's interest in us."[11] He declares us His people

---

[10] Abraham Heschel, *Spiritual Audacity and Moral Grandeur*, p. 163.
[11] *Ibid.*, p. xxii.

just as His Son declares us His friends.[12]   Both have obligations. Both are Hebrew tautologies. Your God = His people. To be known = friends. People and friends = obligation to respond.

How will the world know that He is our God?   Not because we proclaim that we believe He exists.   The divine principle of first cause is not *our* God. He is the God of the philosophers. The heavenly overseer of higher ethics is not *our* God. *Our* God is the God of Torah and if we are to be His witnesses (and He is to be *our* God), then we will live according to His demands – and not anything else.

Is He *your* God?

26.

*And you shall love YHWH your God with **all** your heart, and with all your soul, and with all your might.* Deuteronomy 6:5

The Shema (4)

All – "You're so intense." I've often heard this back-handed compliment. Maybe it's true. When you get me wound up about Hebrew thought, it might take a long time for me to release the tension in the spring. The conversation will be laced with scribbles on a page, excited inflections and driving arguments. I'm definitely not passive about this stuff. Apparently God is too.

Kol-levavka – with *all* your heart – intensifies the demand.   Love God, but do not love Him partially, incompletely, imperfectly. Suddenly this seems

---

[12] John 15:15

impossible. Who among us has not wavered in our affection for God? Who has not failed to remain steadfast and true? Who has not doubted, stumbled or idolized what does not revere Him? Love Him? Yes! But with *all* my heart? How? There is hardly a single feeling in my life that doesn't contain a hint of diversion or a twinge of conflict. It seems as if there isn't a single event that doesn't get a second-thought, a hesitation. Life is joy shaken and stirred with sorrow and questions.

But God doesn't demand what we can't deliver. So if He asks for *all*, He knows that we can deliver *all*. It might be hard, but it is not impossible. And if that is the case, then we better be very clear about the meaning of *kol* (all). "Everything, the whole of something, entire" is applied according to context, but the pictograph helps us see the underlying thread. An open palm (*Kaf*) and a cattle prod (*Lamed*) paint the picture of "open authority," or "allow control." How are these pictures related to "all"? Turn your thinking upside-down. Our view of "all" is usually couched in possession. When we think of "all," we think of acquiring everything. Getting it all. That's the name of the game. But the biblical view of "all" is giving everything, emptying the storage chest, distributing the treasure. We need to stand on our heads if we are going to display "all" in Hebrew (and, by the way, when you stand on your head, what's in your pockets all falls out!). To love God with *all* my heart is to *empty* myself of normal agendas, personal plans and individual objectives. God fills empty containers.

The heart is the center of my will, my emotions, my actions and my cognition in Hebrew thought. There is no battle between the body, the mind and the spirit. *All* are combined in one indissoluble embodiment called *me*. God wants it all emptied for Him. What I decide, how I feel, what I do and how I think are to be consumed with His perspective. Heschel says that this is "sharing life with God." He's right. Life, in all the ways it comes, is to be saturated with His point of view. "Take every thought captive," says Sha'ul. He might as well be commenting on Moses who is speaking for God. Fulfilling the command to love is divine Texas Hold'em. "I'm all in." I've emptied my reserve. I'm going for broke (and I'll have to become broke to get there). Maybe we ought to call it "Texas no-Hold'em."

Are you in? Are you empty?

27.

*And you shall love YHWH your God with all your **heart**, and with all your **soul**, and with all your **might**.* Deuteronomy 6:5

The Shema (5)

Heart/ Soul/ Might – If we are commanded to love God with *all* (*kol*) we've got, obviously that command affects the entire body of behaviors. Rather than allow us to fumble around trying to decide exactly what is included in the "all," God's Word provides three general categories. Each category helps us focus on the wider implications of *kol*. Unfortunately, in a Greek-based culture, we tend to think of these categories as *separate* boxes. This division of Man into separate parts often allows us to imagine that we can be "all in" in one area and have less commitment in another. But Hebrew never views Man as the combination of separate pieces. Man is a completely unified, embodied, homogenized whole. Using the three words "heart," "soul," and "might," doesn't mean we can divide the Hebrew Man. It only means that Hebrew asks us to pay particular attention to what it means to love God in these three ways.

So what are the three ways? The first is "heart," (*lev*), the way of our choices, our emotions, our actions-decisions, and our thinking. You could conclude that this covers it all. How we decide, what we decide, what we do as a result of what we decide, how we feel about what we do and what we think about all of that is "heart." To love God with all your heart is to apply God's point of view and character to our ways in the world. Make Him count in every thought, word and deed.

So what's left? Hebrew suggests that there is a second area of application – the "soul." Of course, our Greek understanding of soul follows Plato. In his view, the soul is a separate, divine spark imprisoned in a moral, fleshly body. The objective of Greek-based religion is to free the soul from the corruptible body and allow it to ascend to heaven. If this sounds a little like our theology of "saving souls" and "insuring you'll get to heaven," don't be too surprised. Most of the early Christian theologians introduced this Platonic interpretation as a replacement of the Hebrew unified view. The "mind-body-soul" view of Man comes directly from Greek philosophy, not Scripture.

"Soul" is the Hebrew word *nephesh*. It is better translated "person." It's everything that makes me who I am. But isn't that what "heart" just described? Not quite. "Heart" focuses on the individual "me." It is about *my* thoughts, words and deeds. But who I am as a person is also defined by my *relationship to others*. *Nephesh* isn't my internal, hidden, spiritual "soul." It is the whole person, defined by his relationship to his Creator and to creation.

Since we know that being human is a verb, a process of becoming through a dialog with the Creator and service to the creation, we know that who I am is defined by my connections to God and to His world. I am to love God through all these connections. By the way, there is considerable overlap between *lev* and *nephesh*, so I can never divide the two in Hebrew.

Finally, there is *me'od* (translated "might"). Unfortunately, the translations like "might" or "strength" aren't quite correct. The word isn't a noun. It is either an adverb or an adjective that is sometimes used like a noun. But what it really means is "great," or "very," or "exceedingly." It is the *what-ness* of life, all the stuff we have on loan to do His bidding. This is the great abundance of what is put into our hands for His use. We are to love Him with all our on-loan provisions.

Combining these three areas of focused attention demonstrates that God commands love as the active behavior of treating everything as He would. His thought must become our thoughts. His deeds our deeds. His care of creation our care. His expressions of emotions ours as well. Love is what we do in all that we do. The standard is the behavior of God. "Be holy for I am holy." That pretty much sums it up, doesn't it?

28.

*And He said to him, "You shall love the Lord your God with all your heart, and with all your soul, and with all your **mind**." Matthew 22:37*

The Shema (New Testament version)

Mind – If you remember (and I hope you do), the word in

the Hebrew passage is not "mind." It is *me'od* – greatness, very, much, exceedingly. Somehow the Matthew version of Yeshua's quotation from Deuteronomy 6:5 shifts *me'od* to the Greek word *dianoia* and the Greek *dianoia* seems to have very little to do with an adverb about lots of stuff. What are we to make of this? Did Yeshua forget what the Hebrew text says?

Forgetting the Shema is like forgetting your name. Unless Yeshua had a total collapse of mental faculties, it is simply impossible that He would have used some other word except *me'od*. Therefore, the problem has to be in the *translation* from Hebrew to Greek, not in the actual words Yeshua spoke. We can see more evidence of a translation problem when we look at this same event recorded in Mark and Luke. Mark's version is "with all your mind and with all your strength." Apparently, the translator of Mark realized that *me'od* had a connection to "strength" so he added this, but he still left in the surprising Greek word *dianoia*. Luke keeps both of Mark's phrases, but reverses their order ("with all your strength, and with all your mind"). How are we to understand this linguistic sleight-of-hand?

It's very clear that Yeshua recited the Deuteronomy passage as it is written in Hebrew. It's also very clear that the Greek gospels have a great deal of trouble trying to capture the Hebrew meaning of *me'od*. All three authors use *dianoia*, but two of them realize there is more to this Hebrew word than mental activity, so they attempt to include some idea of strength in the context. If any passages demonstrate that the Gospels are *translations* of Hebrew into Greek, this is one of those. It's apparent that the various authors stumble around trying to capture a word that has no direct Greek equivalent.

Why did they choose *dianoia*? First, we should contrast *dianoia* with *nous*. *Dianoia* is the mind *at work*. It includes thinking, feeling and understanding, but it is the *active function* of the mind, not simply the mental storage compartment. At least this approaches a Hebrew point of view. Whatever the translators thought, they knew that the Hebrew expression was about action and purpose, not a state of being. But why use *any* expression that seems to divide man into component parts? The answer requires a deeper reflection on translation issues. If I attempt to capture a foreign concept in another language, I am often stuck with thought forms that don't quite fit. I have two choices. I can choose the closest compatible expression or I can try to make up a new one. Paul often chooses the latter. Matthew, Mark and Luke seem to have chosen the former. *Dianoia* is as close as they could get to *me'od*, but at least Mark and Luke realized that *me'od* needed the additional support of *ischus* (strength – mental, moral and physical).

What we have in the Gospels is a translation of concept, not a transfer of exact words. You might think of the Gospels as a paraphrase of Yeshua's actual words. We get the point, but the actual words He used are hidden behind the translation. One thing we know *for sure*: Yeshua did not consider loving God as a *mental* state of being. It was *not* about a storehouse of correct theological information or a treasury of the right propositions. Loving God is about *actions*, even if sometimes the best way to describe them requires us to use marginal concepts like *dianoia*.

What's the lesson? First, translations make a big difference. Be careful *how* you read. Second, never let the current culture dictate what the text means. Look to the original audience for understanding. And finally, remember that loving God is not what you *think*. It's what you *do* with the mind awake to Him.

29.

And these words that I am commanding you today **shall be** *on your heart.* Deuteronomy 6:6

The Shema (6)

Shall Be – It looks like a command, doesn't it? When we read this verse, we think of the enormous task of putting these words, all of them, into our memory banks. Seems impossible, doesn't it? In a culture that has universally substituted the written word for the spoken and memorized word, we rely on texts, not voice. We *see*; we do not *hear*. It is so much easier to Google the idea than it is to commit words to memory. In the process, our ability to recall what we need to know in a moment is seriously diminished. We are like travelers who rely on GPS systems but we've lost the signal. Now what?

All is not lost (but it is certainly more difficult). The *first* word in this verse is the verb *hayah* – to be, to become, to be manifest. This is the same construction that we find in "The Word of the Lord came to Hosea." God's message was manifest in Hosea. It became in Him. Perhaps Moses is saying that these commandments given this day will become manifest in your heart; they will become part of your very being in the world. Perhaps this is not a homework assignment followed by a memorization test. Perhaps it is a statement that *doing them* will result in *knowing them*. Repetition produces memory. In this case, repetition produces a change in heart, an

264

incorporation of God's instructions into the very fabric of how we live. The words given this day will initiate the process of becoming God-instructed people. Just keep doing them.

Jeremiah hints that at some time in the future continual repetition as a means of remembering will no longer be necessary. In the renewed covenant, we will follow God's instructions because *He* will write them on our hearts instead of on tablets of stone. It's nice to have tablets of stone, but in order to convert words inscribed on stone into actual behavior, I have to practice over and over. If those words are part of my very being, my character, my heart, then practice ends.

Yeshua also hints at a connection to the Helper. He will come to bring to remembrance all the words. With His help, these words will be manifest in us. How will we know? Because we will find ourselves doing what God commands.

Does this mean we can sit back and relax? Does this mean that we wait for God to bring it to mind? Hardly. "Work out your rescue with fear and trembling," says Sha'ul. Moses would remind us to speak about these words in every transitioning action during the day. If God's Word is to be your guide, you will have to *work it in*. The process of theological education is *doing*, then knowing. A Boy Scout doesn't need a map. He can read the signs of the heavens. But believe me, it takes practice.

Time to discard your spiritual GPS. Learn the signs by practicing the instructions until you know them like the back of your hand.

30.

*And you shall **teach** them **diligently** to your sons, and shall
speak of them as you sit in your house, and as you walk in
the way, and as you are lying down, and as you are rising
up.* Deuteronomy 6:7

The Shema (7)

Teach Diligently – The intensive form of the Hebrew
verb *shanan* means "to teach incisively." These words are
intended to cut deeply into the hearts of our children.
They are to be inscribed into their hearts (remember that
means will, emotion, cognition and action) just as an
engraver would inscribe words of love on a golden ring.
If we knew the origin of the Hebrew verb *shanan*, we
would
see just how "pointed" this is to be, for the literal
meaning of *shanan* is "to sharpen with a whet stone." It is
commonly used of sharpening the points of arrows in
preparation for battle. When you teach your children the
Word of YHWH, you will probably draw some blood. You
will puncture some defenses. You will cut into resistance.
If you don't, you did nothing to sharpen your sons and
daughters.

The pictograph of *Shin-Nun-Nun* is "double life teeth," in
other words, "what consumes or destroys applied twice."
Iron sharpens iron. Iron twice. Well, life sharpens life,
especially when a life of Torah observance (the parents)
is diligently applied to the life of the children.   The
purpose of such sharpening is to grind off the rough
edges so that the arrow point has the most effective
result.   In life, this means that no activity escapes
smoothing. Sit, walk, lie down, rise up – all transitional
actions during the periods of the day are to be whet

stones in the hands of parents for the education of children.

Sounds great until we reflect on our position as Torah-observant instructors. Then we realize that we aren't communicating information. We are communicating consumption and destruction. I don't teach my children how to get up, sit, lie down or walk. I teach them how *I sit, walk, lie down and rise up according to God's Word.* I can't give them user manuals or encyclopedias. I have to *show* them how I live. They have to *copy me!* I am the whet stone. I have to grind away some of my life in order to sharpen theirs. It takes *friction* to change behavior. It doesn't happen by *reading* about it. You've got to grind a little to make a point.

In a world where information transfer is the equivalent of teaching, we are more likely to desire our children to pass the exam, to regurgitate useless facts and opinions, to adopt problem-solving techniques that have little or nothing to do with life's real issues. We want them to have A's in remembering what the world wants to cram into their available mental capacity. But we certainly don't want them to *copy* us. We already know how lost we are, what failures haunt us, what pains we carry inside. We don't want any of that for our sons and daughters. We want them to be successful. So, we don't apply the whet stone. We don't let our lives grind them into a finely honed weapon for God. We don't want friction. As a result, we get rookies who are easily overwhelmed in battle.

To teach diligently is to *press the point*, to grind when it hurts both parent and child, to scrape off some of my life for the sake of my children's life. How will my actions help sharpen them if my actions have not yet been ground to a fine arrow tip?

31.

*And you shall bind them for a **sign** on your hand; and they shall be for frontlets between your eyes.* Deuteronomy 6:8

The Shema (8)

Sign – What do Exodus 4:8, Jeremiah 32:20, I Samuel 2:34 and Isaiah 20:3 have in common with binding *tefillin* on the arm and the head? Maybe we should start with the question: What are *tefillin*? The use of *tefillin* is considered by orthodox Jews to be one of the most important *mitzvot* (obligations) of Torah. *Tefillin* are two small leather boxes attached to leather straps. Each box contains four sections of Scripture (The Shema of Deuteronomy 6:4-9, the Vehayah of Deuteronomy 11:13-21, the Kadesh of Exodus 13:1-10 and the Vehayah of Exodus 13:11-16). These four sections of Scripture are crucial in identifying the people God chose and the obligations they accepted. These boxes are bound to the arm and the head. You can see what this looks like here.

What does a small leather box have to do with these other Scripture references? If you look them up, you won't find anything about boxes. But you will find the Hebrew word *'ot*, the word for "sign." What you need to know is that *'ot* is most often the word for God's awe-inspiring events and miracles; *signs* of His sovereignty over all men and their history. So, *tefillin* might be boxes but their *purpose* is to act as reminders of who God is, seen in His mighty acts of power. That little box suspended from the arm and tied to the head is designed to never let us forget what God did to rescue us and make us His own people.

Christians have universally substituted other icons for *tefillin*. These are usually symbols of the cross, the nails or some saint. I don't believe I have ever seen a Christian with *tefillin* bound to his arm. And while it is true that a cross hung around the neck reminds us of the death of our Messiah, don't you find it a bit curious that there is never any mention at all in Scripture (even in the New Testament) about a sign of the cross. Since we know that Paul was a practicing Torah-observant Jew, we know that he bound *tefillin* to his arm and his head. But he didn't wear a cross on a silver chain. In fact, the only place in the entire Bible where some kind of symbolic emblem is part of the instructions of living is here, with *tefillin*. There must be a very good reason why God wants us to remember His mighty deeds. Perhaps Heschel is right: "To believe is to remember."

We should also notice that there are no artistic representations of God in Judaism. There are reminders of His acts, but there are no paintings, icons, drawings or any other physical representations of Him. Have you ever wondered why? Our contemporary Christian world is not only filled with alternative signs, it is also saturated with iconic and artistic representations. Michelangelo even painted God on the ceiling. What happened in the transition from the Jewish Messianic assemblies of the first century to the church of the third century that allowed an artistic expression that never occurred in the previous sixteen hundred years? And why are we so accustomed to these expressions today that we don't even reflect on their total absence in Scripture? Do you suppose that we have stopped remembering? Do you suppose that we have substituted imagery for the living God?

"The primary function of symbols is to express what we

think; the primary function of the *mitzvot* is to express what God thinks. Religious symbolism is a quest for God, Jewish observance is a response to God."[13]

32.

*All things are **lawful** for me, but not all things are profitable. All things are lawful for me, but I will not be mastered by anything.* 1 Corinthians 6:12

Missing Punctuation

Lawful – Brian Rosner makes an off-hand remark about this passage that deserves considerably more attention. He says, "Apparently some Corinthians were eating in pagan temples and using the prostitutes on offer on such occasions and defending both behaviors with the slogan, 'all things are lawful for me'."[14] Rosner is the senior lecturer in New Testament at Moore Theological College. He is a well-respected scholar. What he says here is startling. This remark catches us off-guard because it alters completely the context of Paul's statement. What it suggests is that Paul really needed to add some quotation marks. Of course, those aren't available in Greek so sometimes, but not always, Paul indicates that he is citing a straw man or his opponents or someone else. But on some occasions Paul doesn't bother to tell us who is speaking. Since he is writing to people who would *know* what was said, he simply repeats the comment. These occasions are the most perplexing. That's when we have to rely on the context.

We know that this occurs because we find the same

---

[13] Abraham Heschel, *Spiritual Audacity and Moral Grandeur*, p. 92.
[14] Brian Rosner, *Greed as Idolatry*, p. 114.

citation without quotation marks in Galatians when the text concerning the silence of women says, "as the law says." But, of course, the law doesn't say this. It can't be found *anywhere* in Hebrew Scriptures. So, obviously, Paul is not telling us that this is what he thinks. He is citing his detractors. We're just missing the quotation marks.

Rosner's point is that Paul's context here is all about members of the assembly who are still incorporating common pagan practices into their lives. Paul has just referred to these pagan practices, among which were temple prostitution and pagan festivals (which were usually an excuse for orgies). What Rosner suggests is that this famous phrase, "All things are lawful for me," is *not* Paul's words but rather the words of those he is debating.

Oh, my! Take a deep breath. Recall the agonizing theological machinations we all went through while we tried to explain these words within the context of a Torah-observant morality, or even within the higher ethical expectations of Christian holiness. Remember how difficult it was to walk the razor's edge between moral imperatives and ethical choice. Imagine how that would have changed if we just added the quotation marks.

Rosner's comment makes a lot of sense. Paul is Torah-observant. He says so. Torah observance does *not* make all things lawful. In fact, there are a lot of things that are expressly forbidden. Changing the translation to "all things possible" doesn't help much. While the Greek verb, *exesti*, can be translated "what is possible," the implication is morally or legally possible or permitted.

But clearly not all things are permitted, morally possible or endorsed by the Torah. The only way we can make sense of this statement *as Paul's own words* is to claim that Paul adopted a view of grace that set aside *all* the requirements of the Torah and therefore, the Torah no longer instructed him. But this is impossible. Paul never set aside the Torah. It was his guide to every facet of life. As Heschel would say, "A Jew without Torah is obsolete." And Paul was certainly a Jew.

This means that the words, "all things are permitted, lawful, possible" makes no sense whatsoever as Paul's view of the world. These are words that describe that man who wishes an excuse for his behavior.

All we needed were the quotation marks.

Do you feel better now?

33.

*They have grown fat and sleek. They know no bounds in deeds of wickedness; they judge not with justice the cause of the fatherless, that they may prosper; they **do not defend** the rights of the poor.* Jeremiah 5:27-28

Government For The People

Do Not Defend – Is Jeremiah speaking about us? Have we grown fat and sleek at the expense of overlooking wickedness and refusing to defend the rights of the poor? You might say, "No. I'm not like that. I'm struggling too. I'm not rich. I'm just one of the ordinary people." But Jeremiah's accusation still stings. The richest 250 people in the world have more wealth than the poorest 2.5 *billion* people in the world. Does that seem right to you?

Does your lifestyle support this enormous disparity? Eighty-nine percent of all pornographic websites are produced in the United States. Forty-nine percent of men do not believe that an online affair is adultery. And forty percent of all pregnancies in America end in abortion (50 million children have been murdered so far). Are these not terrifying evils? Who has benefitted from such atrocities? Did you know that Comcast made $50 million on in-home pornographic television last year?

The Hebrew verbal root translated "do not defend" is *shaphat*. It is a much bigger umbrella than simply legal or moral defense. *Shaphat* is about *government*! In Hebrew thought, *shaphat* covers the executive, legislative and judicial aspects of governing. Everything from creating laws to rulings in the court are covered. Consider the application. Jeremiah holds the entire *government* responsible, particularly the leaders and the powerful.
Anyone who contributes to the exploitation of the poor stands in opposition to God. No wonder my accountant friend Micah is concerned about even being a part of the United States economy.

Now notice one other important element. We have often mentioned that no follower of YHWH has any inalienable rights. Life itself is a gift. It does not come with a bill of rights. We do not *deserve* housing, jobs, justice, education, fair treatment, free speech or anything else simply because we are alive. The fact that we enjoy some of these gifts is entirely due to God's grace and human alignment with His mercy. But there are some who do have rights – God-given rights. Jeremiah is not alone among the prophets to mention them. Those who have *rights* granted by God are the *ebonim* (singular *ebyon*), people who are in want or need of material goods. There are four Hebrew words translated "poor." *Dal* is a person at the bottom of the social ladder ("the poor will always be with you"). *Rash* is a person who is weak or destitute. *Anaw* are the oppressed. *Ebyon* emphasizes the lack of material goods. In a culture where possessions were the basis of power, these people are exploited because they have no resources to resist the powerful. They are the powerless. It is the *king's* job to stand up for them. God grants them *rights*!

You and I probably have no claim on the rights God grants. Most likely, we are not among the *ebonim*. We are much more often associated with the fat and the sleek. But when we ignore those rights granted by God we incur terrible consequences. And any government that exploits the ones God protects will surely be punished.

I wonder what God hears from the blood of 50 million powerless infants. I wonder how He feels about the cry of those who are victims of greed. I wonder how His heart is turned when He witnesses the millions who live in squalor because the rich world cares more about the newest iPhone. If the bloods (yes, it is plural) of Abel cry out from the earth, and God brings swift judgment, how much more does our world deserve His wrath?

Is there time to turn the tide? Perhaps not. James Black's work suggests we have passed the point of recovery. But there is time today to recover our personal alignment. We can stop our own endorsement of the disparity. We can do justice today. That might be all we can do but God will use it for His good.

34.

*So then, the Law is holy, and the commandment is holy and righteous and **good**.* Romans 7:12

Law And Order

Good – What is good? Well, there's the good news. What's good about that? It's the announcement that we can have peace with God. That's pretty good. In the scheme of things, peace with God counts a lot. What else is good? God tells us in Jeremiah that caring for the sick, the homeless, the orphans and the widows is good. Why? Probably because *He* cares for them and if we involve ourselves in compassion for these little ones, we are likely to meet God doing the same thing. Being in His presence is good. Then there's Sha'ul's remark that the Law is good. Unfortunately, many Christians have been taught that the Law isn't good. They have succumbed to the theology
that the Law has been replaced with grace because it was inadequate. How tragic! This misunderstanding is based on a distorted paradigm about the role of law. Let's take a deeper look.

Heschel helps us see the paradigm structure. "It is not law and order itself, but the living God Who created the universe and established its law and order, that stands supreme in biblical thought. This differs radically from the concept of law as supreme, a concept found, for example, in the Dharma of Mahayana Buddhism. Before the Torah, the covenant was. In contrast to our civilization, the Hebrews lived in a world of the covenant rather than in a world of contracts. The idea of contract was unknown to them. The God of Israel 'cares as little for contract and the cash nexus as He cares for mere slavish obedience and obsequiousness. His chosen sphere is that of covenant.' His relationship to His partner is one of benevolence and affection. The indispensible and living instrument holding the community of God and Israel together is the law."[15]

Since our culture is so seeped in the concept of the supremacy of Law, we might have to read Heschel's comment again. The Hebrew concept of the "law" is not about rules and regulations. It is about the links within the community that demonstrate benevolence and affection. In other words, the Torah is the love manual of the community. It teaches YHWH's children how to love each other. How will we know that we are His disciples? By the love we show for each other. And what is that love? It is the exercise of *mitzvot*. Moshe Kapinski told me that Torah offered 613 opportunities to love God, but Abraham Heschel tells me that those 613 ways are also the loving fabric of the community. Faith in action. Practice of perfection. Not rules. Relationships.

Why does Torah contain an ethical hierarchy? Why are some Torah commandments more important, more necessary, than others. Because Torah is an expression of benevolence and affection. Helping another person is more important than maintaining a worship ritual if, and only if, the two options come into conflict. Healing trumps ritual. Devotion trumps dedication.

Time to reassess our paradigm. How often have we thought of Torah as prescribed behaviors instead of love connections? How much will have to be reordered once we see the world as a place where God teaches us to love Him through the ways we love each other? What will

---

[15] Abraham Heschel, *The Prophets*, Vol. 2, p. 10.

happen to our neatly packaged existence once we recognize that "law" is a synonym for "love"? Grace and law were never disconnected. That is why Sha'ul can say, "The law is holy, righteous and good." No kidding!

35.

*These are the **generations** of the heavens and the earth when they were created, in the day that YHWH Elohim made the earth and heaven.* Genesis 2:4

Spelling Bee

Generations – Rabbi Robert Gorelik makes an observation about the Hebrew word translated "generations" in his lectures on the genealogy of Yeshua. It is worth remembering. The Hebrew word *toledot* is spelled four different ways in Scripture. In this verse in Genesis, it is spelled Tau-Vav-Lamed-Daleth-Vav-Tau (where the two instances of the consonant Vav act as the vowel "o"). This *full* spelling of the word occurs in only one other verse in Scripture, in Ruth 4:18. All the other occurrences of *toledot* (and there are over 100 of them) are "misspelled." The other occurrences are missing either the first or the second Vav. Is this just a mistake?

Hardly! Hebrew Scripture contains quite a few oddities like enlarged letters, words with missing letters, a word with "broken" letter, extra small letters and stretched letters. Of course, none of these are apparent in translation. In fact, they can hardly be seen in typeset editions. But they are meticulously copied in hand-written Torah scrolls because the rabbis do not believe any of these oddities are accidents. They all have deeper meanings. Let's consider the "misspelling" of *toledot*.

277

The rabbis taught that the full spelling of T-V-L-D-V-T in Genesis 2:4 indicates that this account of the generations of the world occurred *before* sin entered the world, before death and the angel of death existed in the world. In other worlds, the *full* spelling of *toledot* was appropriate here because the world was not yet corrupted. But a few verses later, when Genesis recounts the generations of Adam, *toledot* is spelled without the initial Vav. It's the same word, but just like the generations of Adam, it has been corrupted. The spelling matches the status of the generations it recalls. This corruption is true in every other occurrence of *toledot* – except one.

That single exception is Ruth 4:18. In this verse, and only in this verse, the word *toledot* is found in its full spelling. The obvious question is "Why here?" Bob Gorelik points out that in this single instance, the recounting of the generations is the critical link between Boaz and David; a link that is part of the genealogy of the Messiah. Jewish rabbis explain that the full spelling of *toledot* in this verse is based on the fact that Ruth and Boaz are progenitors of the Messiah in the line of David and the Messiah will *restore* God's original creation and remove death from the earth. The Messiah will remove the corruption brought about by sin. When he comes to sweep away sin, *toledot* will be fully spelled out again.

So, you're saying, "Wow. That's so interesting. But does it really matter to *me*?" Maybe the spelling of *toledot* doesn't matter in your routine today, but the subtle intricacy of Scripture does matter a great deal. This is one more incredible demonstration of the amazing planning of God. This is one more bit of evidence that He cares about *all* the details, right down to the spelling. This matters to me today because it tells me that I serve a God who can be completely trusted in the smallest detail.

36.

*For he who in this way serves Christ is acceptable to God and **approved** by men.* Romans 14:18

The Real McCoy

Approved – Who is acceptable to God and approved by men? To answer this question, we need to look at the Greek word *dokimos*. It means, "to be certified as completely real." It is not about tolerance. It is about perfect conformity to an accepted standard. To be approved is to be recognized as the real McCoy. Paul writes to fellow believers. He instructs them to live in such a way that they will be acceptable to God *and* found to be the real deal by men. But his instructions don't

make any sense at all if he thinks that the approval needs to come from *fellow believers*. If I am in the house of the Lord, I am already approved by my brothers and sisters and I am certainly acceptable to God. In order for Paul's exhortation to make sense, we must recognize that the approval must come from *outside* the circle of believers. In other words, we must live in such a way that those who would be critics are forced to admit we are the genuine article. Our lives must give no offense to those who are looking for an excuse to reject our beliefs. Paul isn't talking about gaining the approval of fellow believers. He is talking about gaining the approval of those who *don't believe*. In the context of first century Rome, Paul is talking about his fellow Jews who have not accepted Yeshua as the Messiah.

But we don't live in the Rome in the first century. What

does this mean for us? The first thing to notice is that Paul is teaching about *service to the Messiah*, the Christ. This isn't *optional*! We are responsible for the salvation of others. That doesn't mean we "save" them. But it does mean that we are required to live in such a way that they will not view us as hypocrites. If we wish to serve Yeshua, we must meet the standard set by God and men. That standard is Torah (Paul would never have meant anything else). That's why Paul can say, "Against these things there is no law." We are not to live with such inconsiderate arrogance that we use our "freedom" to damage the witness of our claims to serve the living God. We *could* claim our salvation sets us free (whatever that means), but if we are going to emulate the Master, our freedom will be relinquished in an act of selfless humility (just as Yeshua Himself gave up His freedom to become a slave – Philippians 2). Do you want the mind of Christ? Then act like He acted. Give up your "rights" and take on a life that will magnify Him. Live with such purity that men have no choice but to approve you and the God you serve.

Within the household of God, all are equal. All are redeemed sinners, unworthy recipients of God's grace. All are called to humble obedience. All are adopted children of the King. But that also means that all are expected to shine in ways that attract others to the King. There is no room for displays of superiority. The goal is to attract through humility.

So tell me, are you living in such a way that those who do not believe are drawn to YHWH because you are the real deal?

37.

*"I will give them one heart and **one way of life**, to reverence me at all times, for their own good and the good of their children after them."* Jeremiah 32:39

A Sign Of The Covenant

One Way Of Life – The old beliefs are die hard. Tradition is difficult to revise. Comfortable conclusions resist correction. But a love of the truth will lead us to constantly reconsider what remains questionable. As contemporary believers, we might need to review our thinking about the "new" covenant, but Jeremiah certainly doesn't need to. He has it straight from the mouth of God. He uses a word that cements the permanence of the covenant in as strong a way as possible.

The Hebrew phrase *lev ehad vederek ehad* (one heart and one way) makes it clear that YHWH describes a unity in commitment (heart) and a unity in behavior (way). The word *ehad* is found in the Shema. It is a particularly critical word in Judaism, marking YHWH as the *only* true God, the one and *only* divine being. Since this passage is in the same context as Jeremiah's revelation about the "new" covenant, it seems obvious that the "new" covenant is intended to be the *only* way of life for all of God's people. Describing the one way of life with the same strength as the declaration of monotheism emphasizes the centrality of this covenant. There is no substitution and there are no alternatives. There is *one* and *only one* way of life that teaches men to show reverence and awe (*yare*) for YHWH and is also for their own good (*tov*).

How is it that we missed this? Maybe our lack of understanding of the "Old" Testament caused us to overlook the core beliefs of the New Testament Jewish background. We acknowledge that circumcision was a sign of the covenant. God declared it so. But did we fail to see that the covenant from Sinai was also a sign – a sign that we are God's people under His authority directed by His instructions?

"One way of life" is a pretty startling pronouncement in our world. We are cultural and ethical polytheists. We have succumbed to the epistemological bankruptcy of the West, arriving at the place where everyman's inner life is his own creation, where truth is what works for me. It is virtually impossible to argue the idea of *one* way of life today. Even within the 28,000 denominations of the "unity" of Christianity, there is no consensus about how to live. Peter Leithart is correct when he says that Christianity (not Christians) is institutionalized worldliness. Christianity mimics the organization, ethics and epistemology of the world. It's up to the Christians to change that – to live according to God's instructions as the *one way of life.*

The real question is this: Why don't we? Most responses are about inconvenience than about truth. We have accommodated to the culture. It's hard to break the patterns. It's difficult to explain to our neighbors. We are in captivity in Babylon. It might be useful to read God's instructions to His people when they went into Babylon 2500 years ago. God's advice worked then. I don't see any reason why it wouldn't work now.

38.

*"Yet these things you have **concealed** in Your heart; I know that this is within You."* Job 10:13

The Hidden God

Concealed – Job's complaint is our complaint. In the time of his crisis, he cries out to God. "I loathe my life. You made me, Lord. You know everything about me. You understand me right to the core. And You can do with me as You wish, for You are my creator. But, Lord, why? Why do you churn me like butter? Why do you pour me out like spilt milk? I know that You are loving and kind and full of grace. I know this! But yet, these things seem hidden from me."

The Hebrew word *tsafan* is used fro concealing something, like hiding the baby Moses from Pharaoh. It has both positive (God treasures His people) and negative (the wicked lie in wait) applications. Perhaps most intriguing are the occasions when this word is used to describe God's hidden and secret actions and habitation (see Ezekiel 7:22). The consonants *Tsade-Pey-Nun* paint the picture, "a desire or need to open or speak life." God conceals what must be revealed if we are to have life. Does that mean He is an ogre, maliciously withholding something essential for living? May it never be! What it means is that God understands the mystery of existence and we recognize that He alone plumbs the depth of this mystery. What it means is that everything is *not* reducible to an known set of universal laws. Behind it all is mystery. To stand in the presence of God is to face the unknowable, not just the unknown. The result should be awe.

But we live in a world dominated by the paradigm of the supremacy of reason. We think everything can be explained, including God. That's why we expend centuries of effort writing systematic theologies. We attempt to reduce the *experience of the mystery* to a set of explainable categories. We have a well-thought-out God; not a God of unique and hidden splendor. In our culture, truth is timeless and detached. It consists of uniform laws the govern all repeatable events. Truth is discovered by uncovering these eternal, comprehensive rules of operation. And whatever cannot be explained according to the timeless laws of the cosmos is really not real at all.

The biblical view is radically different. "Here truth is not timeless and detached from the world but a way of living and involved in all the acts of God and man. The word of God is not an object of contemplation. The word of God must *become* history" (emphasis added).[16] Contemplate this insight. Biblical revelation, God's disclosure of His point-of-view about us, is tied directly to unrepeatable, unique historical events. It comes from outside the schemata of general laws. It has no precedent and no subsequent parallel. If we are to understand, we must realize that God's word is, in itself, an incarnation. It is God becoming history – our history. The hidden mystery of God splits our *chronos*, repeatable experience and leaves us with a slice of the divine, exploded in an event in life here and now. The hidden quality of God is discovered in His desire to open a window into heaven. It could not be more momentous.

Is that what you realize when you read His word? Do you find yourself captured by a mystery? Are you consumed by the event of His disclosure, stunned by His presence? Do you read the words trembling that God allows you to peek behind the curtain, even if only for a split second? Are you in awe? Or do you read in order to categorize, systematize and universalize?

---

[16] Abraham Heschel, *God In Search Of Man*, pp. 196-197

Index of Scriptural References

Old Testament

New Testament

Matthew 28:19	60
Matthew 28:19	62
Matthew 28:19	64
Luke 19:41	31
Luke 21:2	216
John 1:17	246
John 3:16	27
John 17:3	29
John 17:3	182
John 17:15	38
Acts 2:5	89
Acts 16:31	66
Romans 2:13	236
Romans 3:28	81
Romans 3:31	83
Romans 5:21	230
Romans 7:12	275
Romans 14:18	279
Romans 16:5	7
Romans 16:5	9
Romans 16:5	11
Romans 16:25	138
1 Corinthians 1:2	85
1 Corinthians 2:4	87
1 Corinthians 6:12	270
2 Corinthians 3:2	79
2 Corinthinas 12:9	135
2 Corinthinas 13:7	98
Ephesians 2:12	15
Ephesians 2:14-15	205
Ephesians 6:18	122
Philippians 3:6	220
Colossians 2:14	212
1 Thessalonians 5:17	131
Titus 3:9	207
Hebrews 11:21	121
James 1:3-4	142
James 2:8-9	167

Other Works

Made in the USA
Charleston, SC
24 September 2016